Issues in Corrections

Issues in Corrections

Research, Policy, and Future Prospects

Edited by
Carly Hilinski-Rosick
John P. Walsh

LEXINGTON BOOKS
Lanham • Boulder • New York • London

Published by Lexington Books
An imprint of The Rowman & Littlefield Publishing Group, Inc.
4501 Forbes Boulevard, Suite 200, Lanham, Maryland 20706
www.rowman.com

Unit A, Whitacre Mews, 26-34 Stannary Street, London SE11 4AB

British Library Cataloguing in Publication Information Available

Library of Congress Cataloging-in-Publication Data Available

Library of Congress Control Number: 2016955619
ISBN 9781498541213 (cloth : alk. paper)
ISBN 9781498541237 (pbk.: alk. paper)
ISBN 9781498541220 (electronic)

Printed in the United States of America

Contents

Part I

Institutional Corrections

Chapter One

Introduction

Corrections Today

Carly M. Hilinski-Rosick and John P. Walsh

Until the nineteenth century, corrections in the United States did not do much to reform or rehabilitate criminals. Rather, those who were convicted of a crime were held in detention facilities while awaiting punishment, which most often involved some type of public, corporal punishment, or in other cases, execution. Punishments were public, brutal, and allowed no opportunities for criminals to change their behavior. The Enlightenment brought about a shift in punishment philosophy, however, and placed an emphasis on fairness, individual rights, and humane punishments. The penitentiary emerged out of the Enlightenment period, and was the first type of correctional facility in the United States to focus on changing offenders so that they could return to society as productive citizens. The main focus was on repentance and reflection; offenders were supposed to spend their time thinking about their wrongdoing and atoning for their actions through religious influences (the Bible was the only reading material permitted in Eastern State Penitentiary in Pennsylvania, for example). The creation of the first penitentiaries in Pennsylvania and New York began a century-long experiment in "what works" in corrections.

Eventually, the penitentiary gave way to the reformatory, which was created when the penitentiary system was deemed a failure. The reformatory purported to reform criminals using hard labor and allow them to develop skills that they could use on the outside (in reality, the hard labor was more of a profit-making venture for corrections officials than the development of useful skills for inmates). The reformatory focused more on vocational and educational skills rather than the heavy religious focus of the penitentiary. The reformatory also used an indeterminate sentencing structure, where inmates could earn their release based on successful reformation and good behavior. Eventually, the idea that inmates could earn release through reform gave way to the medical model of corrections in the 1920s and 1930s, which treated criminality as a disease. If we could determine the cause of the disease, we could treat it, and then inmates would, presumably, be "cured" of their criminal behavior. During this time, penitentiaries and reformatories, as well as new correctional facilities being built, began to be known as "correctional institutions" that were focused on correcting behavior. Despite this move to treat the causes of crime, many of these facilities attempted to correct behavior in name only. There were many struggles between prison administrators, security staff, and the treatment staff. Prison administrators and corrections officers were often most concerned with the safety and security of the institution, while treatment staff wanted the flexibility to provide the best treatment possible. The struggles between the two groups never truly were resolved during this time period, however, and the focus on rehabilitation began to decline. It has been argued that the 1974 report from Robert Martinson and his colleagues that proclaimed "nothing works" in corrections treatment was one of the deciding factors in the end of the treatment and rehabilitation era of corrections.

The 1960s also was a period of change for corrections systems and has been known as the "inmates' rights era." During this time, as the courts began to expand due process rights outside of prison walls, inmates also gained more rights. The 1960s and, to a lesser extent, 1970s saw the lower courts and US Supreme Court take on many cases brought by inmates who alleged that their rights were being violated. During this time, the courts were much more likely to side with inmates, expanding and reifying the rights of inmates when their conditions of confinement were questioned. The only other area the federal courts have intervened more than in the area of corrections is within the area of public school segregation. Expanded inmate rights included, but are not limited to, an expanded ability for inmates to practice their religion while incarcerated, required access to adequate law libraries or legal assistance, and also the right to access health care. This expansion of rights, however, began to decline in the 1970s and into the 1980s as the overall punishment philosophy in the United States shifted to a more punitive, tough on crime approach and the Supreme Court experienced a conservative shift in leadership.

Since the 1970s, the corrections system has experienced exponential growth. Over the past four decades, the number of inmates held in US prisons and jails has quadrupled (Carson, 2015). Beginning in the 1970s, the crime rate in the United States began to increase. This increase can be attributed largely to the war on drugs and shifting punishment philosophies in the United States. Sentencing policies that emerged from the war on drugs and as a result of the shift in philosophies generally produced harsher sentences that sent more offenders to prison for longer periods of time than ever before, many times for offenses that were considered misdemeanors in the past. This incarceration boom has resulted in a correctional population that tops 2 million people (Carson, 2015). The incarceration rate in the United States is higher than in any other country in the world. According to Mauer (as cited in Schlosser, 1998, para. 4), "We have embarked on a great social experiment. No other society in human history has ever imprisoned so many of its own citizens for the purpose of crime control."

PRISON-INDUSTRIAL COMPLEX

The so-called prison-industrial complex arose out of this push to be tougher on crime. The prison-industrial complex can be traced back almost four decades, with the call for tough on crime policies in the 1970s resulting in a dramatic increase in prison construction. Perhaps the location where the prison-industrial complex really began was in the state of New York, where the Rockefeller Drug Laws, arguably the strictest drug laws in the country, were passed in the 1970s. As a result of these new laws and the ensuing increase in inmates in New York, more prisons needed to be built. During the 11 years that Mario Cuomo was governor of New York, 29 new prisons were built; 28 of them were located in rural counties in upstate New York. The belief at this time was that prisons could provide a strong economic benefit to struggling communities, and towns in upstate New York. Soon these financially struggling communities and their political representatives began competing for new prisons (Schlosser, 1998).

The prison-industrial complex does not only apply to prison construction, however. More recent trends in corrections have involved privatization of prison services, such as health care and food services, and entire prisons. As will be discussed in chapter 3, the privatization movement has gained momentum as states look to quell their ever-growing corrections budgets. Privatization, whether it is of an entire facility or of a service provided within the facility, is argued to save money and provide a better quality service. The alleged cost savings of privatization experienced by the states and the federal government means a profitable business for private prison companies and shareholders. Seeking more cost-effective ways to operate prisons and jails at both the state and federal level was deemed necessary, as the move toward a more punitive punishment philosophy that focused on incarceration was a very expensive policy shift.

Many states are spending into the billions on corrections while their funding for higher education is significantly less. According to the US Department of Education (2016), spending on corrections has increased more than three times faster than on education. Eighteen states currently spend more on corrections than higher education (Ingraham, 2016). An examination of the relationship between education and crime, however, reveals a number of issues with these funding discrepancies. Most notably, those who are incarcerated generally have lower educational attainment. Two-thirds of prison inmates have not completed high school (Harlow, 2003). Further, young black males who are between the ages of 20 and 24 and do not have a high school diploma are more likely to be incarcerated than employed (Neal & Rick, 2014). The school-to-prison pipeline underscores this issue.

The school-to-prison pipeline is a trend in the US that funnels students out of schools and into the juvenile justice and adult criminal justice system for things that are often minor infractions, but are not tolerated in schools with zero tolerance policies (ACLU, n.d.). These students often have histories of abuse, learning disabilities, are overwhelmingly poor, and would benefit from additional educational and counseling services, not the justice system (ACLU, n.d.). More funding for education could reduce the prison population and correctional expenditures; research has suggested that a 10% increase in graduation rates could result in a 9% reduction in arrest rates (Lochner & Moretti, 2004). Investment in education that is directed toward high-risk areas could achieve reductions in crime and arrest rates while avoiding the heavy social costs of mass incarceration (Belfield, Nores, Barnett, & Schweinhart, 2006; Heckman, Moon, Pinto, Savelyev, & Yavitz, 2010; Reynolds, Temple, Robertson, & Mann, 2001).

Another significant impact of the incarceration boom is on the communities where large numbers of inmates are from. Low income communities with high minority populations often have disproportionately more residents in prison and jail, with the majority of these individuals being male. Removing such a large number of males from the communities impacts the economy of that area as well as the family structure, as many of those who are incarcerated leave behind children who must be raised by single mothers and without a father-figure in their life.

The mass incarceration of minority men from a small number of neighborhoods create what have been called "million dollar blocks." A million dollar block is one where so many residents of one single city block are incarcerated that it costs over one million dollars to incarcerate residents from that block alone (Kurgan & Cadora, n.d.). These blocks can be found predominantly in low-income neighborhoods in most major cities across the United States, indicating that the vast majority of inmates come from and return to the same small geographic area. This means that the community must function without these individuals while they are incarcerated; these men are often the primary or only breadwinner in their households and often have dependent children. Once they are returned to the neighborhood, the struggles continue, with high crime areas now flush with parolees trying to find jobs and remain crime while attempting to successfully complete their parole terms.

The impact of incarceration extends beyond state and federal budgets and local communities and families. There also are significant impacts on the individual inmate, both while he or she is incarcerated, and when he or she is released, as more than 90% of inmates will eventually be returned to society (Hughes & Wilson, 2016). As a result of the increase in the prison population, many states are operating well over the capacity of their prison systems. Some are, or have been, under court order to reduce their prison populations. Prison overcrowding has many negative consequences on inmates, such as putting them at a higher risk for victimization and infectious disease, contributing to declines in their mental health, and contributing to prison misconduct.

JUSTICE REINVESTMENT AND EVIDENCE-BASED CORRECTIONS

More recently, the shift from "nothing works" to "what works?" has been happening. This shift has been slow, but has picked up momentum in recent years as lawmakers and the public begin to question the costs of corrections, who is in prison, and what we are doing to rehabilitate offenders while they are incarcerated. One way that the United States is trying to reverse the effects of mass incarceration is the "Justice Reinvestment Initiative" (JRI). The goal of the JRI is to use data to improve public safety, examine criminal justice system spending, manage and allocate offenders under criminal justice supervision in a more cost-effective manner, and reinvest those savings into crime prevention strategies and programs to hold offenders accountable and strengthen neighborhoods (Bureau of Justice Assistance, n.d.).

One of the main areas of focus of the JRI are data-driven policies and programs. The JRI provides technical and financial assistance to states to collect and analyze data to determine what impacts criminal justice populations and costs, to identify and implement changes to make the criminal justice system more efficient, and to measure the impact of these changes. These goals are the basis for evidence-based corrections, which call for rigorous scientific testing to determine what programs work, which are promising, and which do not work. Programs that work or are promising should be implemented, while programs that do not work should be discontinued.

Many studies have identified the principles of effective corrections programs, including targeting criminogenic needs, taking a multimodal approach, including aftercare, structures follow-ups, continue of care and relapse prevention, and ensuring integrity in program implementation and delivery, among others (Andrews, 2000). Using these principles of effective correctional programs, correctional institutions and agencies that administer community corrections are able to offer treatment programs and programming in prisons that will help to ensure the success of offenders once they return to the community or ensure their continued success if they are already under community supervision. Chapters 8, 9, and 10 will explore psychological treatment, substance abuse treatment, and educational and vocational programming in more depth.

Throughout the reading of this text it is important to continually reflect upon the rationale for punishment. In other words, why are we doing what we are doing? When we refer to the "we" in what we are doing we are not only referring to correctional administrators and criminal justice officials but also to the elected and appointed officials who legislate and set policy, as well as each and every one of us who partake willingly or unwillingly in the process of democracy. We are all responsible for how we punish the citizens within our communities. In general the five rationales for punishment are retribution, deterrence, incapacitation, rehabilitation, and restoration. Each of these rationales exists within the modern correctional landscape. Yet, as illustrated at the beginning of this introduction and overview of the historical timeline of corrections in the United States, there is a consistent unevenness as to which of these rationales is most prevalent in any given time period. Beginning in the 1970s, with the advent of the crime control era, we witnessed a shift that has become heavily reliant on the rationales of retribution and incapacitation. This is the correctional legacy which we are currently enmeshed. Much of this shift is rooted in citizen fear of crime and victimization in some cases real and many times socially constructed or imagined. In general crime, specifically violent crime, has been on the decline since the 1990s.

This volume provides an in depth analysis of some of the major issues affecting inmates, correctional administrators, corrections officers, and treatment providers within our nation's jails and prisons. These issues are not always mutually exclusive of one another and many times leave us with more questions than answers. Each of the authors chosen for this volume have spent decades exploring, analyzing, and researching the particular topics they present. Each chapter is organized to provide an overview of the nature of the issue, trends and current research on the topic, policies, and challenges for the future. At the end of each chapter the authors have provided discussion questions for the reader to either reflect upon individually or hopefully to springboard into wider conversations concerning the use of punishment and incarceration.

Part I of this volume provides an overview and analysis of the current US prison system, US jail systems, and gender within the incarcerated setting. John P. Walsh and Sarah Light (chapter 2) analyze the nature of US jails as a separate and understudied area within criminal justice research. Differences and similarities between jails and prisons are discussed, as well as the role litigation and local politics has played in shaping local level incarceration. Carly M. Hilinski-Rosick (chapter 3) delves into current trends and research regarding physical and sexual misconduct and violence, special populations in the incarcerated setting, and prison healthcare. Included in her discussion are current policy issues related to recidivism, reducing inmate populations, increasing efficiency, and the private prison industry. Carrie L. Buist and Emily Lenning (chapter 4) examine the role of gender within the incarcerated setting with special attention toward the particular challenges and policy considerations for cisgender, as well as transgender, inmates in the era of mass incarceration.

Within part II, issues of inmate and institutional safety and well-being are discussed with an analysis of inmate classification, prison gangs or security threat groups, and the use of segregation and solitary confinement. Mari B. Pierce (chapter 5) explores the challenges, trends, and policies regarding institutional classification within the incarcerated setting. An overview of the Federal Bureau of Prisons and the Texas Department of Corrections classification approaches provide a glimpse into the value of classification in regard to institutional safety and service and the difficulty in this relatively new and changing landscape within overburdened correctional settings. Beverly R. Crank and Catherine D. Marcum (chapter 6) investigate the current state of prison gangs or security threat groups and the administrative policy decisions that are associated with this inmate subpopulation. Strategies for controlling these groups, challenges regarding institutional misconduct, and programmatic issues are discussed. Jody Sundt (chapter 7) provides an analysis and investigation into the use of solitary confinement and restrictive housing including disciplinary segregation, protective custody, and administrative segregation. The rise of these administrative tools, the effects of this type of punishment, its relationship to institutional safety, inmate health, mental illness, and current litigation are discussed.

Part III delves squarely into rehabilitative programming within prisons and jails. Psychological programming, substance abuse programming, as well as educational and vocational programs are discussed at length. Emily Lasko and Chad Posick (chapter 8) discuss the relatively new and ever developing psychological programs that are being offered to inmates during their incarceration. An overview of what works, what doesn't work, and what is promising across program types and therapies is discussed. Special attention is provided to discussing incarcerated women, juveniles, and suicide prevention. David Olson (chapter 9) provides an in-depth analysis of substance abuse programming within prisons and jails. Included is a discussion of the nature of substance abuse treatment, the institutional trends associated with treatment, and the underlying tension with providing the most valid treatment within facilities that struggle with safety, security, and ever burgeoning populations of substance abusers. Daniel R. Lee (chapter 10) explores correctional education and uses criminological theories to highlight the importance of education and its effect on recidivism. He includes a discussion of the need for increased methodological rigor in evaluations of correctional education programs and also focuses on the bright future that correctional education has, as we are seeing a shift toward reentry and reintegration programs in general and a focus on education specifically.

As you begin delving into the chapters, keep an open mind about the state of corrections in the United States. Reserve judgment until you complete all of the chapters and reflect on the questions posed by the authors. In the concluding chapter, we will ask you to reflect on where you fall along the continuum of pessimism or optimism based on what you have gleaned from the chapters. We hope that the differing viewpoints and the variety of authors will provide you with a well-rounded picture of the current state of our corrections system and allow you to think critically about corrections policies and the future of corrections in the United States.

REFERENCES

Andrews, D. A. (2000). The principles of effective correctional programs. In L. L. Motiuk & R. C. Serin (Eds.), *Compendium 2000 on effective correctional programming*. Ottawa, Canada: Correctional Service of Canada: Ministry of Supply and Services.

Belfield, C. R., Nores, M., Barnett, S., & Schweinhart, L. (2006). The High/Scope Perry Preschool Program: Cost benefit analysis using age 40 follow up data. *Journal of Human Resources, 41,* 162–190.

Bureau of Justice Assistance (n.d.). *What is JRI?* Washington, DC: Office of Justice Programs.

Carson, E. A. (2015). *Prisoners in 2014*. Washington, DC: Bureau of Justice Statistics.

Harlow, C. W. (2003). *Education and correctional populations*. Washington, DC: Bureau of Justice Statistics.

Heckman, J. J., Moon, S. H., Pinto, R., Savelyev, P. A., & Yavitz, A. (2010). The rate of return to the High Scope Perry Preschool Program. *Journal of Public Economics, 94,* 114–128.

Hughes, T., & Wilson, D.J. (2016). *Reentry trends in the U.S.* Washington, DC: Bureau of Justice Statistics.

Ingraham, C. (2016, July 7). The states that spend more money on prisoners than college students. *The Washington Post.* Retrieved from https://www.washingtonpost.com/news/wonk/wp/2016/07/07/the-states-that-spend-more-money-on-prisoners-than-college-students/.

Kurgan, L., & Cadora, E. (n.d.). *Million dollar blocks.* Retrieved from http://spatialinformationdesignlab.org/projects/million-dollar-blocks.

Lochner, L., & Moretti, E. (2004). The effect of education on crime: Evidence from prison inmates, arrest, and self-reports. *American Economic Review, 94*(1), 155–89.

Martinson, R. (1974). What works? Questions and answers about prison reform. *The Public Interest, 35,* 22–45.

Neal, D., & Rick, A. (2014). The prison boom and the lack of black progress after Smith and Welch. Working paper 20283. *National Bureau of Economic Research.* Retrieved from http://www.nber.org/papers/w20283.

Reynolds, A. J., Temple, J. A., Robertson, D. L., & Mann, E. A. (2001). Long-term effects of an early childhood intervention on educational achievement and juvenile arrest. *Journal of the American Medical Association, 285,* 2339–2346.

Schlosser, E. (1998, December). The prison-industrial complex. *The Atlantic.*

US Department of Education (2016). State and local expenditures on corrections and education. Retrieved from http://www2.ed.gov/rschstat/eval/other/expenditures-corrections-education/ brief.pdf.

Chapter Two

Jails

John P. Walsh and Sarah Light

In general, local jails have received little attention within the criminal justice research literature as compared to the research focusing on prisons. In recent years the literature focusing on mass incarceration and post-prison release mechanisms have dominated the field of corrections. Yet, jail systems within the United States process and hold hundreds of thousands of citizens each and every day. Jails are the entry point into the correctional system. It is safe to say that almost every individual who has been sentenced to prison has spent time within a local jail facility. In addition, many individuals who are never sentenced to prison also have spent time within local jail facilities. The underwhelming amount of research dedicated to local jail facilities is many times a product of the extreme variation in size and scope of jail facilities and their populations. Social science research seeks to generalize across time and space. In other words, the value of research findings are judged based upon whether the inferences found in one setting are applicable to other settings. As local jails vary greatly across region and community, generalizations become quite challenging. In addition, similar to the incarceration setting of the prison, jails are difficult to access for social scientists. Local criminal justice officials are oftentimes reluctant to allow external evaluations and research of these closed societies.

This chapter provides an overview of the historical underpinnings of local incarceration within the United States. Included within this chapter is an overview of the magnitude of local level incarceration, the demographic make-up of current jail inmate populations, and existing trends in jail research. The chapter pays special attention to particular population trends, the differences between jails and prisons, and administrative changes and challenges spurred by litigation. The chapter concludes with a discussion of local incarceration and its relationship with criminal justice systems and local politics, as well as the future direction of the local jail in relation to recent challenges to mass incarceration.

NATURE OF THE ISSUE

Jails in the United States emanate from early England. English settlers imported many traditions and institutions to the American colonies. Criminal justice traditions and institutions were no exception. Today's county sheriff, the executive branch administrators of the vast majority of local jails within the United States, descend from the *shire reeve* who collected taxes, enforced order, and operated the local *gaol* or jail (Rothman, 1971). Initially instituted to detain accused individuals awaiting trial, the jail was also used as a local institution to house short term convicted offenders, vagrants, prostitutes, and the mentally ill. As the penitentiary system changed and expanded through the 1800s and into the 1900s, reform movements in juvenile justice and state mental hospitals removed many delinquents and many mentally ill adults from the nation's jails. The development and expansion of probation and the expansion of state penitentiary systems rooted in the classification of prisoners based on gender, seriousness of crime, criminal history, etc. removed others. Yet, jails continue to retain local control over the majority of accused and convicted misdemeanant adults.

It is important to keep in mind that jails are the entryway to the correctional system. Almost every individual who is incarcerated within the prison system was first incarcerated in a local jail. In addition, jails are local entities, usually at the county level, varying in size, population, and amenities. Due to these differences, comparison and generalization across local jails is challenging for researchers, policy-makers, and social scientists. Administratively, jails are controlled by locally elected county sheriffs. Jail budgets are predominantly controlled by locally elected county board members while local police, prosecutors, and judiciary make the discretionary decisions as to who will be sequestered in jail. Overall, jails are a local affair shaped by the discretion of locally elected officials.[1]

Who Is in Jail?

Prior to 1978 the number of people passing through the nation's jail systems was not subject to a clear objective analysis. Due to the local nature of jail administration, clear baselines, annual and daily counts, and basic demographics of the jail inmate were not uniformly gathered. Beginning in 1978, the Bureau of the Census in conjunction with the Bureau of Justice Statistics conducted a nationwide census of jails. The National Census of Jails has been conducted every five years since 1978 with supplemental annual survey data supplied by the top one-third largest population jails.

Nationally, jails admitted roughly 11.4 million people between June 30, 2013 and June 30, 2014 (Minton & Zeng, 2015). Since 2000, the jail inmate population has increased 1% each year and at mid-year 2014, the population of jails nationally was 744,600. Yet, the jail incarceration rate has decreased from a high of 259 per 100,000 in 2007 to 234 per 100,000 at midyear 2014 (Minton & Zeng, 2015). There are over 2,800 jails within the United States (Golinelli & Minton, 2014). These numbers exemplify the overall magnitude of the population within city and county jail facilities.

What does the population that resides in jail facilities look like? Jails accommodate a diverse group of individuals that are experiencing varying levels of the criminal justice system. Portions of the population of inmates in jail facilities are serving their sentences for misdemeanors with a sentence length of a year or less. However, nearly 40% of felony defendants are sentenced to jail (Cohen & Kyckelhahn, 2010). In addition, the amalgam of offenders and defendants include approximately 40% of individuals in pre-trial status who have yet to be convicted and who are awaiting hearings and trials, convicted felons awaiting sentencing to state prison, probation and parole violators awaiting hearings, transfers from state prisons, as well as the mentally ill and homeless.

The demographics of individuals in jail facilities are over-represented by young men of minority status. African Americans represent about 34% of the jail population, Hispanics represent 16%, and whites make up 47% (Minton, Ginder, Brumbaugh, Smiley-McDonald, & Rohlof, 2015). It is important to note that the term over-representation is not a comparison between differing racial group percentages within the incarcerated setting but instead a comparison between the percentage of a racial group incarcerated and the percentage of that same racial group within the US population. Therefore, while African American men make up 34% of the nation's jail population, the overall population of African Americans in the US population is less than 13% (Rastogi, Johnson, Hoeffel, & Drewery, 2011). Males make up approximately 86% of the national jail population. The admission of females, however, continues to increase, currently making up approximately 14% of the jail population (Minton et al., 2015). Beginning in 2010, the number of males incarcerated in jails declined by 4.2% while the number of women incarcerated has increased by almost 11% (Golinelli & Minton, 2014). Jail populations are also young with 28% of the population being between the ages of 18 and 24 and 60% of this population under the age of 34 (Golinelli & Milton, 2014). Finally, in addition to young men disproportionally of minority status, jail populations are in general undereducated. Almost one-third of jail inmates lack a high school degree (Golinelli & Milton, 2014).

Jail Differences and Cultural Adaptation

The difference between jails and prisons is rooted in administrative and demographic factors. As mentioned previously, in general jails are locally controlled entities with leadership, funding, and general administrative decision making emanating from local political actors. Alternatively, state prison systems are controlled by state level executive leadership and state legislative funding. Demographically, jail inmates range from misdemeanants to felons to individuals who are deemed as public nuisance problems such as the homeless and/or the mentally ill who lack alternative social support networks. State and federal prison systems incarcerate convicted felons.

Differences across jails also exist. As noted earlier, there are over 2,800 jails across cities and counties within the United States. Populations within these facilities vary by region. Jail rates (the proportion of a state's population in jail) are traditionally higher in western and southern states. A mega-jail system such as Rikers Island in New York City, the Los Angeles County Jail system, and the Cook County Department of Corrections in Chicago house anywhere between 10,000 and more than 14,000 inmates at any given time. These jail population numbers rival entire state prison populations in smaller populous states such Iowa and Minnesota (Walsh, 2013). Yet, nearly 40% of all jails hold fewer than 50 inmates (Stephan & Walsh, 2011).

There are also similarities between jails and prisons. Obviously, the removal of a citizen's liberty through incarceration is the main similarity between these different institutions. In addition, the social reality of incarceration and the adaption processes experienced by incarcerated populations in jails and prisons have been found to have similarities. There has been a plethora of literature spanning decades regarding the culture of prisonization and inmate adaptation within prison systems (Hassine, 2009; Irwin & Cressey, 1962; Rose & Clear, 1998; Schmid & Jones, 1993; Stowell & Byrne, 2008; Sykes, 1958; Toch, 1977). John Irwin's (1985) *The Jail: Managing the Underclass in America* provided a critical analysis of the political rationale for jails, as well as an outline of the inmate adaptation process within the jail setting. From an inmate adaptation perspective, Irwin argued that the socialization process that occurs upon jail confinement has the capacity to alter an individual's life trajectory. The disintegration of conventional ties to society, the disorientation of the jail environment, and the degradation of control by the criminal justice system all serve to prepare the jail inmate for indoctrination into the rabble class (Irwin, 1985). Politically, Irwin argued that jails are merely warehouses for societies' rabble class. In other words, jails are used to sequester public order violators and those perceived offensive or threatening to the rest of society. Attributes such as threatening and offensive behaviors coupled with poverty, low educational attainment, unemployment, and minority status define the rabble class.

Backstrand, Gibbons, and Jones (1992), argued that Irwin's rabble class hypothesis was an overstatement. In their research across six jail units on the west coast they found a large number of pretrial and convicted time servers in jail had been charged with serious felonies. While Irwin's rabble hypothesis may very well be an overstatement of the charges for which individuals are confined, the profile of jail inmates continues to be poor, young, black, Hispanic, uneducated, and unemployed persons with drug abuse problems (Welch, 1997). The socialization process outlined by Irwin continues to resonate in many of today's jails. Inmates entering and confined within jail systems are straddling the deprivations associated with confinement and proximity to the communities where they reside (Klofas, 1990). Unlike prison systems, jails offer far less programming opportunities for inmates. Due to the transient nature of the jail client (i.e., a short length-of-stay based on posting bond, transfer, dismissal of charges, etc.) there is a consistent turnover of inmates. Programming opportunities such as vocational training, education programs, and drug rehabilitation take time to succeed. As such, many jail administrators do not see the financial value of investing in rehabilitative programming. The socialization process occurring within these impoverished facilities further socializes inmates into the margins of society. The pseudo-isolation of sporadic jail incarcerations reinforces differing subcultural values and adaptation processes than the prison environment (Garafolo & Clark, 1985; Irwin, 1985; Klofas, 1990; Rottman & Kimberly, 1985; Walsh, 2013).

Jail Conditions and Litigation

Overcrowding is at the core of many of the problems that jail facilities face. High admission rates and long pretrial waits, coupled with a lack of resources allocated to jails contribute to the extremely poor conditions and treatment of the individuals being held. In extremely crowded jurisdictions such as Cook County in Chicago, neglected facilities and large populations lead to unfit living conditions in the jail's facilities (Walsh, 2013). Cook County's inability to maintain an adequate number of beds for the increasing number of inmates led to inmates regularly sleeping on the floors of the jail facility between 1993 and 2003. In addition, neglected facilities in Cook County created unsafe living environments as ceilings began to crumble and heating and cooling units failed. Rats and other pests infested cells, creating an unclean and unhealthy living environment for inmates. In some divisions of the jail facility, sewage and sanitation systems had completely failed (Walsh, 2013). These extreme conditions all contributed to consistent judicial intervention that required Cook County officials to remedy the poor conditions of the jail facilities.

Crowded conditions and subsequent unhealthy living environments within impoverished jail facilities have been associated with numerous jails historically and today. Crowding is generally measured by the rated capacity of a facility by state and local rating officials. Rated capacity is defined by the highest number of prisoners or inmate beds a facility can hold while providing a proper amount of service and management (Bleich, 1989; Golinelli & Minton, 2014; Stojkovic & Klofas, 1997). In general, 80% capacity is the benchmark for identifying a facility as overcrowded (Klofas, Stojkovic, & Kalinich, 1992). The first decline in rated capacity, since the Annual Survey of Jails was initially conducted in 1982, occurred between 2012 and 2013. Yet nationally, the rated capacity during this period of decline was 84% on an average day and 91% on their most crowded day in June 2013 (Golinelli & Minton, 2014). In essence, on average our nation's jails have been continually overcrowded. Finally, and an important point to keep in mind is our earlier discussion of the difficulty in generalizing across the vast number of jails nationwide. While the average rated capacity indicates consistent crowding problems this statistic is overrepresented by mega-jails and large jurisdiction jails. As Golinelli and Minton (2014) point out, jail facilities with an average of 1,000 or more inmates held 48% of the inmate population at midyear 2013 yet only accounted for six% of the nation's jails. Mega-jails such New York City's Rikers Island, and the L.A. County Jail have inmate populations in excess of 10,000 individuals.

Historically, inmates who filed formal complaints regarding the poor conditions of incarceration found little help from the judicial branch. Feeley and Rubin (2000) define the time period from 1776 to the late 20th century as the "hands off" approach to judicial intervention. During this period, complaints regarding the conditions of confinement from inmates found little help in the rulings of the Supreme Court. This is exemplified by Supreme Court cases such as *Atterbury v. Ragen* (1956), which asserted that prisoners had no grounds under the Civil Rights Act to challenge physical abuse by employees acting within the context of their job. This case echoed the tone of the courts in response to inmate rights for most of the 19th and 20th centuries.

Beginning in the 1960s, however, judicial intervention began to lead the way in correctional reform, prisoner rights, and criminal justice reform in general. Cases such as *Atterbury v. Ragen* (1956) and others that limited prisoner's rights severely were overturned in court opinions. For example, *Monroe v. Pape* (1961) redefined the role of a police officer as acting on behalf of the state, thereby restoring prisoner's rights to file complaints under the civil rights act. In *Cooper v. Pate* (1964), the Supreme Court ruled that prisoners have the standing to sue in federal court under the Civil Rights Act of 1871. Historically, the judiciary has maintained its role as an interpreter of the constitution, however, the role of the judicial branch during this reformative period is unique in the force and influence that the courts used to achieve change in correctional facilities.

Judicial intervention between 1960 and 1965 began to simultaneously change the court's role within the context of correctional reform. Between 1965 and the mid 1980s, courts took a much more active approach to reform in prisons across the country that were considered in violation of constitutional rights. During this time period, the court upheld inmate's religious rights, first amendment rights in regards to prisoner's mail, abolished segregation within facilities, and strictly regulated prison management codes (Feeley & Rubin, 2000). Overcrowding was a large contributor to many of the violations found by the courts in correctional facilities. Courts became more active regulators of prisons and local jail facilities by forcing changes through consent decrees and supervisory boards that closely watched progress in individual facilities. The extent to which the judiciary shaped and molded corrections during this time is comparable only to their involvement in dismantling segregation within public schools (Feeley & Hanson, 1990).

Beginning in the mid-1980s, judicial intervention began to pull back and take a more passive tone toward inmate complaints. As Feeley and Rubin (2000) suggest, "Many judges found the worst of violations within correctional facilities resolved, resulting in a shift toward administrative efforts" (pp. 46–47). Courts began to loosen their grip over the management of correctional facilities, giving more flexibility to administrations to resolve violations. This marked the end of large reforms in prisoner rights and correctional management. Specific cases such as *Rhodes v. Chapman* (1981) concluded that double-celling of prisoners did not violate the Eighth Amendment and that harsh conditions are part of a criminal offender's penalty. In *Rufo v. Inmates of Suffolk County Jail* (1992), the court ruled that a flexible standard of review should apply to government requests to modify consent decrees (Fieweger, 1993).

Coupled with judicial retreat, the legislative branch of the federal government codified within the Violent Crime Control and Enforcement Act of 1994 that an individual prisoner must prove that crowding constitutes cruel and unusual punishment. The Prison Reform Litigation Act (1996) applied barriers to all condition and confinement claims by prisoners and the Antiterrorism and Effective Death Penalty Act (1996) limited the ability of prisoners to file writs of habeus corpus. Overall, through the crime control era of the 1980s and 1990s, judicial and legislative action reduced the rights of prisoners in regard to claims revolving around conditions of confinement and overcrowding.

TRENDS AND CURRENT RESEARCH

The crime control era beginning in the 1970s through the early and mid-2000s ushered in an unprecedented number of citizens into our prisons and jails in the United States. Mass incarceration in the United States is often discussed in reference to its impact on federal and state prisons (Mauer, 2006; Western, 2006). However, just as significant is the impact that local jails have experienced as a result of the overwhelming number of citizens being processed through the criminal justice system. Overcrowding in jail facilities has resulted in poor environmental and health conditions for inmates. Arguably, all of the individuals in state prisons have spent a portion of time in jail cells, suggesting that attention should be paid to these local facilities as well. In addition, because jails are an entry point for many offenders of the criminal justice system, they house a diverse population of individuals that vary in the magnitude of their offenses. Also, jails are additionally expected to meet the needs of public health, as well as the needs of the mentally ill. The unique characteristics of jails have resulted in specific trends within local jail facilities that differ and overlap with state and federal prison inmates.

Pretrial Detention

95% of the increase in jail populations is contributable to inmates within jail facilities who are still awaiting trial (Minton et al., 2015). Nationally, over 400,000 individuals in the jail population are unconvicted and awaiting trial (Minton et al., 2015). Due to tight budgets at the local level, a lack of staffing in courts, and poor pretrial release procedures, trials and court schedules become backed up forcing individuals who have not been convicted of a crime to sit and wait in jail cells (Lurigio, 2016; Subramanian, 2015). This extended wait to receive justice is a growing issue within jails as it contests the Sixth Amendment constitutional right to a speedy trial. Length of stay (LOS) for pretrial defendants and subsequent overcrowded jail facilities has fueled jail building expansion in the late 20th century and more recently supervised alternative release mechanisms for those awaiting trial (Walsh, 2013). Yet in large urban jurisdictions the LOS between arrest and disposition is on average six months (Cohen & Kyckelhahn, 2010). Alternatively, small jail jurisdictions (jails holding fewer than 50 inmates) experience the highest turnover rate. High turnover rates are defined as a larger number of admissions and release relative to the jails average daily population (Minton & Zeng, 2015). In other words, about 40% of new jail admissions are entering large jail systems and those individuals on average have a longer LOS than their counterparts within small jail systems (Minton & Zeng, 2015).

Female Inmates

In recent years, jails have increasingly detained female inmates. While the population of male jail inmates decreased by 3.2% between mid-year 2010 and 2014 the female jail population increased 18.1% (Minton & Zeng, 2015). While there continues to be many more men detained in jails (over 635,000 in 2014) than women, the increase in the number of women being detained continues to grow. In 2014, over 109,000 women were detained in local jails (Minton & Zeng, 2015). Researchers have found that incarcerated women have particular treatment needs that differ from many of their male counterparts; specifically, comorbidity issues surrounding experiences of interpersonal violence and mental health (Belknap, Lynch, & Dehart, 2016). Scott, Lurigio, Dennis, and Funk (2016) found that female inmates in the Cook County Jail in Chicago experienced on average 6.1 types of trauma in their lifetimes. Trauma incidents included exposure to economic pressure, witnessing violence, as well as rape, battery, and armed robbery victimization. Trauma incidents are positively correlated with post-traumatic stress disorder, depression, and substance abuse problems (Dehart, 2008; Lynch, Fritch, & Heath, 2012). Frequent jail incarcerations and the inevitable break from the community, family, and children magnify these traumas. While recent research examining adverse life events leading to comorbidity issues, offending and incarceration for women and girls have expanded under the development of pathways theory further treatment and programs within local jail facilities is needed (Belknap & Holsinger, 2006; Green, Miranda, Daroowalla, & Siddique, 2005; Ritchie, 1996).

Special Populations

Special populations within jail facilities raise unique administrative concerns that traditionally would not seem to fall under the realm of criminal justice services. Yet, because there is an overrepresentation of the poor in jails, the populations that pass through jail facilities are often underserved and undiagnosed for medical, mental health, and addiction issues. In accordance with the Supreme Court ruling *Estelle v. Gamble* (1976), and as a general public health and institutional health concern, jails have taken on the role of public health provider by screening for a large range of medical health, mental health, and addiction conditions. In their analysis of jails, Dumont, Gjelsvik, Redmond, and Rich (2013), found that 80% of male offenders surveyed reported being screened for medical or mental problems. Yet, variation across jurisdiction in the extent and focus of screening does exist (Dumont et al., 2013). Walsh's (2013) analysis of the Cook County Jail in Chicago revealed that populations in need of expanded physical health, mental health, and drug addiction services became a major point of contestation and subsequent fiscal investment within the Cook County Department of Corrections federal consent decree regarding overcrowded conditions. The Vera Institute (2015) argued that large urban jail systems have become the new asylums for the mentally ill. The Los Angeles County Jail, Rikers Island in New York

City, and the Cook County Jail are many times referred to as the three the largest mental health hospitals in the United States (Elsner, 2006; Vera Institute, 2011; Walsh, 2013).

In recent years, the emphasis on these special populations, particularly mentally ill inmates, has refocused administrative and research initiatives within large urban jail systems. Practitioners and academics alike have argued for increased screening for short-stay jail inmates, reducing barriers between public health and criminal justice professionals, increasing inmate linkage to community-based treatment programs, and the expansion of jail based crises intervention teams (Dumont et al., 2013; Kerle, 2016; Lurigio, 2012). In 2015, Cook County Sheriff Thomas Dart named Dr. Nneka Jones, a clinical psychologist, as the Executive Director of the Cook County Department of Corrections (Williams, 2015).

Family and Community Relationships

In addition to pretrial detainees and special populations, researchers have increasingly focused on the relationship between family members and those who are incarcerated in jails and prisons. Initially, this research was predominantly focused on the effects of children and communities with incarcerated parents in prison systems (Comfort, 2008; Hagan & Dinovitzer, 1999; Western & Wildeman, 2009). In general this research drew attention toward the role parental incarceration played in contributing disparities in childhood development within poor communities of color. More recent examinations have explored the effects incarceration has on the children, families, and relationships of those incarcerated in jail settings (Apel, 2016; Comfort, 2016; Wildeman, Turney, & Yi, 2016). Wildeman's et al. (2016) analysis found similarities between spillover effects of familial consequences across facility types (i.e., federal prison, state prison, and jail). Apel's (2016) research concluded that incarceration in jails and prisons is highly disruptive to existing cohabitation and marriage, as well as for long-term marriage prospects. Comfort (2016) found that brief jail stays, and community supervision create specific hardships for family members that are distinct from hardships that are created from longer term prison stays. In essence, all of this research is drawing attention toward the secondary and tertiary effects that incarceration in prison and jail creates not only for those being held but for their children, families, and communities. Considering that incarcerated populations are drawn at a disproportionate rate from poor communities of color, these outcomes have long lasting impacts on individual and community trajectories beyond the individual offender or defendant.

Jail Administration

As discussed earlier in this chapter, of the more than 2,800 jails in the United States the vast majority are at the county level and administered by elected sheriffs. In addition the population capacity within these jails differs greatly. Jail administration varies greatly depending upon their elected officials, budgets, size, population, and geographic location. As such, many smaller jails suffer from budgetary shortfalls that effect daily operation, services, and medical care. One recent trend that has attempted to address this issue is the regional jail system. Regional jail systems combine jail administration across multiple counties or jurisdictions. The rationale behind regional jail systems is that smaller county level jails can share resources and budgetary costs. Yet, while regional jails offer an opportunity for smaller jail systems to provide better service at less cost they have not been adopted widely within the United States. Local jail systems large and small have historically been connected to local politics and patronage (Walsh, 2013). The development of regional jail systems would threaten the status quo of autonomy, local level politics, and patronage jobs that county level political forces across the United States have traditionally controlled.

During the crime control era beginning in the 1970s and through the 1990s brick and mortar expansion of prisons throughout the United States took on unprecedented growth. During this period new jail facilities and expanded jail facilities through new building projects also flourished. Much of this building emphasis was based on civil litigation regarding the conditions of confinement within old county level jails (Feeley & Rubin, 2000; Walsh, 2013; Welsh, 1995). Within newer jail construction, architectural design moved toward what is known as the new-generation jail. New-generation jails employ a podular design that provides a localized interaction space for a smaller amount of inmates. The design promotes personal space, common living areas, and closer proximity to programs and direct supervision with correctional staff (Applegate, 2011). In addition, podular unit design provides economic benefits to overall jail budgeting as units can be temporarily closed down for construction upgrades or non-use. Fixed position furniture design, direct supervision by correctional officers, and the smaller populations within podular units has also been found to increase inmate safety (Tataro, 2002). Most problematic in the shift toward the new-generation jail is convincing local taxpayers and their elected county officials to invest in upgraded facilities that provide qualitative enhancements to those incarcerated in jail. In general, the public and politicians are reluctant to spend tax money on those who are incarcerated.

Reluctance to invest in local incarceration is not specific to inmates and building upgrades. Local correctional officers (i.e., custodial employees) are among the lowest paid positions within the criminal justice system (Bureau of Labor Statistics, 2015). Low pay and poor working conditions contribute to high levels of employee burnout and high levels of staff turnover (Lambert, 2001). In addition to severing employment ties entirely, Walsh's (2013) analysis of Cook County Jail highlighted large numbers of correctional staff regularly on medical leave. This in turn created a shortage of supervision and increased cross-watching whereby correctional officers were tasked with supervising multiple tiers of inmates. The cyclical nature of the administrative problem contributed further to poor working conditions and inmate safety issues.

Historically, administrative changes within local jail facilities which have positively changed conditions of confinement and safety for inmates, improved workplace conditions for jail employees, and in general created a better environment for jail facility management have resulted from litigation. Jail employees and their supervisors can be held legally liable for their actions. Under 42 U.S.C. Section 1983, inmates deprived of their civil rights can sue jail officials to halt the violation and collect damages. Actual litigation and the threat of litigation have forced many local counties to invest tax dollars into local level incarceration that they would not have done otherwise (Feeley & Rubin, 2000; Walsh, 2013; Welsh, 1995). While the extent and outcome of this investment has varied widely across jurisdiction, not only by region but by specific county, the judicial branch of government has continually served as a check and balance on the most egregious executive level jail administration problems. In addition, the adoption of jail standards has served to provide proactive criteria to guide the day to day operations of jail administrators (American Correctional Association, n.d.). Unfortunately, many of these guidelines are voluntary and the courts are required to continually intervene in many jurisdictions.

Pretrial Release

Overcrowding continues to be a predominant underlying problem in jail facilities. The strain of large numbers of inmates has created poor living conditions within facilities. Yet, reform aimed to remedy problems with overcrowding has been historically slow and often merely symbolic. As judicial litigation has forced the hand of some local criminal justice actors to respond, alternatives to incarceration have been adopted across many jurisdictions. In addition to traditional bail release, front end approaches that include expedited processing, citation, and summons to appear in court for minor crimes have been adopted in some jurisdictions (Baumer, 2007; Baumer & Adams, 2006). In addition, pretrial release for individuals who cannot make bail ranges from release on recognizance (ROR) programs to intermediate sanction style diversion programs such as electronic monitoring and day reporting. The latter programs rooted in intermediate sanctions rely on higher levels of surveillance by criminal justice officials than release on recognizance. Overall, local jurisdictions experiencing overcrowding and subsequent litigation regarding the conditions of confinement as a result of overcrowding have found themselves expanding their surveillance and control of lower-level pretrial criminal defendants beyond the incarcerated setting of the jail and into the community.

Pretrial diversion programs have been found to be more cost efficient than jail incarceration and also allow defendants to retain ties to their communities (Walsh, 2013). Yet, many citizens who may be eligible for release under these programs are deemed ineligible due to judicial and executive level risk assessments that include prior criminal history and failure to appear, current offense charges, as well as the conclusion that a defendant has weak ties to the community. Criminal justice officials' fear of pretrial defendants absconding and/or committing further crimes while on release in the community curtail the opportunity for release for many who are incarcerated. Cohen and Kyckelhahn (2010) found that approximately 18% of those released are rearrested prior to their original trial data. Pretrial release has also been found to vary by race. Demuth and Steffensmeier's (2004) analysis of pretrial detention across 75 US counties found that African Americans and Hispanics were more likely than whites to be detained in jail prior to trial. Even as pretrial release programs have expanded, public concern over individuals who may be dangerous if released created political pressure which led to preventative detention policies. Initiated during the crime control era, authorized under the 1984 Comprehensive Crime Control Act, and reified by the courts in *Schall v. Martin* (1984) and *United States v. Salerno* (1987) preventative detention provides the judiciary with a discretionary option to hold those deemed dangerous without bail.

POLICIES

A combination of judicial intervention based on overcrowding, conditions of confinement, and the exponential increase in incarcerated populations spurred by the crime control era and the war on drugs beginning in the 1970s has continued to shape local level incarceration policy for the past 40 to 50 years. More recent policy changes have been spurred by increasing special populations of mentally ill defendants and offenders and an increase in the female incarcerated population within jail facilities. Yet, local level incarceration policies vary across region and institution based upon local level politics, the nature of local criminal justice systems and their local subsystems of police, courts, and corrections. These subsystems operate together as either loosely or tightly coupled, depending on the sociopolitical atmosphere where they exist. Loosely coupled subsystems can independently operate to manage the impact of policy change in other subsystems (Hagan, 1989). For example, the courts have the ability to independently manage new policies in law enforcement, such as a crackdown on a particular low-level crime, by not proceeding with the prosecution of defendants. Local jails can address over-crowded conditions spurred by high bail amounts and increases in incarceration by expanding release on recognizance programs (Walsh, 2013). The use of discretionary decisions by differing actors and organizations within each subsystem can shape policy outcomes within other subsystems.

When crisis occurs in the sociopolitical atmosphere (real or socially con-structed), these subsystems can tightly couple, giving them the ability to operate fluidly and process offenders at efficient and rapid speeds (Hagan, 1989). When tightly coupled, these subsystems have the ability to achieve agreed upon goals swiftly. Yet, tight coupling has led to issues with over-crowding in both prison and jail facilities. The "get tough on crime" and "war on drugs" policies of the crime control era are examples of tight coupling of subsystems that led to an overwhelming increase of inmate populations. Al-ternatively, Welsh (1995) argued that tightly coupled subsystems in smaller counties in California were the most successful at addressing overcrowding in jail facilities in the 1990s. Welsh and his colleagues argued that smaller counties were less resistant and promoted a higher level of inter-agency cooperation across subsystems when addressing court ordered jail reform (Welsh & Pontell, 1991; Welsh, 1995).

California's Public Safety Realignment in response to the landmark deci-sion *Brown v. Plata* (2011) and in a broader sense the downsizing prisons movement spurred by the fiscal constraints of the great recession of the late 2000s have shifted alternatives to incarceration and the questioning of state based mass incarceration onto the active public policy agenda (Gottschalk, 2009; Henrichson and Delaney, 2012; Simon, 2010). Specifically, Califor-nia's Public Safety Realignment is an attempt to reduce the state's prison population by shifting responsibility of non-serious felonies to the local con-trol of counties through a combination of eliminating state prison sentences as a punishment option for specific crimes and transferring non-serious felo-ny state inmates to county facilities (Simon, 2016). Integral to the California realignment shift is the development of interagency cooperation and partner-ship. These judicially initiated changes through the *Brown v. Plata* (2011) decision forced legislative reform at the state level which may or may not have positive outcomes for local level jails, jail policy, and their clients. Simon (2016) argues that the local level incarceration and subsequent over-sight may have positive implications for not only the scale of incarceration but for service to clientele. Yet, a positive impact associated with local incar-ceration policy by emboldening the power of local level criminal justice actors is contingent upon the current and future interorganizational practices of those particular counties and their subsequent policy decisions within loosely and/or tightly coupled criminal justice sub-systems.

ISSUES AND CHALLENGES

There clearly is not one specific set of issues and challenges facing local jails across the United States. Just as it is difficult to generalize across jails that differ by region and size it is also difficult to generalize across the issues and challenges of those institutions. Yet, a commonality across the vast number of these institutions can be found within the clientele they serve and the dearth of services for these clients within many jail facilities. As noted earlier jails differ from prisons in the diversity of their inmates. Jail populations contain an amalgamation of low-level felons and misdemeanants who are disproportionately of minority status, poor, and undereducated. In addition, many suffer from mental illness and addiction issues. Within the impoverished jail facility there is a dearth of services to address mental illness and substance dependency. Due to shorter lengths of stay and in the case of smaller jail jurisdictions the "economy of scale" for needed services many jails offer limited programming for mental health and addiction. Of particular challenge is the recent growth of female jail inmates. While this sub-population within jail facilities has continued to grow, the majority of inmates continue to be men. As such when budgetary decisions are made to increase services within facilities male inmates continually receive expanded services and new programming before their female counterparts. In addition many of these citizens, regardless of gender, find themselves returning to the jail setting on a continual basis for short stays and upon return to their neighborhoods must redevelop or resurrect broken and strained family and community relationships. The continual disruption cycle and lack of services that many individuals frequenting our nation's jails experience is an issue and a challenge for local communities to address.

In addition to the challenges experienced by short stay inmates cycling in and out of jail systems are the general conditions of many of our jails for individuals who are also spending significant amounts of time incarcerated. Those awaiting trial on serious felony charges, parole violators awaiting hearings, and convicted individuals awaiting transfer to state facilities are also residing in these impoverished facilities. Change and reform can be difficult to achieve for jail facilities and administrations. Needed changes to jails, such as beds for all inmates, resource allocation, and staffing expansion even when change is demanded through judicial intervention, such as consent decrees, is slow and often times symbolic (Walsh, 2013; Guetzkow & Schoon, 2015).

Historically, the consequences of reformative litigation have not proven to reduce the number of inmates or the number of citizens under any type formal control of the criminal justice system. In an analysis of prison reform litigation spanning from 1971 through 1996 Guetzkow and Schoon (2015), found that prison overcrowding litigation for US prisons had no significant impact on the reduction of prison overcrowding. However, litigation did significantly increase spending on prison capacity and prison construction (Guetzkow & Schoon, 2015). As Guetzkow and Schoon (2015) suggest, this disconnect between the original goal of the reform (reduction in facility overcrowding) and the resulting consequence of the litigation stems from what is referred to as the "endogeneity of law." Originally developed to explain organization's responses to anti-discrimination legislation, this perspective argues that the response that an organization has to new laws can shape the meaning of the law and what counts as compliance to that law (Edelman, Uggen, & Erlanger, 1999). Overcrowding litigation within jails has experienced this reshaping of the definitions of compliance as administrations and bureaucracies attempted to achieve compliance while also not disturbing already present policies (Walsh, 2013).

FUTURE PROSPECTS

Within the United States, the national experiment of mass incarceration of the past 40 years is being challenged. As penal policy at the state level changes so will the policies of local level incarceration. California's Public Safety Realignment has reduced the prison population in the Golden State by 17% without an increase in violent crime (Sundt, Salisbury, & Harmon, 2016). The legislative and policy shift to a higher reliance on local jails and jail programming will obviously provide new challenges to jail administrators especially in those jurisdictions which have relied most heavily on state prisons. The MacArthur Foundation Justice and Safety Challenge (2016) has recently funded technical assistance projects across numerous jail sites nationwide in an effort to address the immense number of individuals processed through our jail systems. Developing interorganizational partnerships at the local, state, and national level with government officials and policy experts to address local correctional challenges as outlined in this chapter has the capacity to provide long term best practices that are scalable to particular jurisdictions.

The adoption of public health perspectives that serve substance abuse and mental health concerns of jail inmates is essential in the future administration of jail facilities. In addition, and as Maruna (2016) points out, the cyclical short stays of the jail inmate as an artifact of the conservative neoclassical deterrence modeling of the 1980s and 1990s is in need of change. Consistent and cyclical short jailings do not help but may in fact hinder individuals and the communities from where they are drawn. Alternatives to jail that take into consideration the complex nature of crime causation are needed at the community level.

Justice reinvestment or reallocating existing criminal justice funding into the specific communities that are most affected by local incarceration and crime control is a promising idea toward realigning local corrections toward what is "just" (Clear, 2007). A localized approach to reclaiming responsibility for informal social control that promotes and invests in community development and services outside of the incarcerated setting of state and local prisons and jails, justice reinvestment has gained traction in recent years. Yet as Monterio and Frost (2015) point out, community-based justice reinvestment has not been fully realized even with the backing and promotion of the US Department of Justice. Local criminal justice and political entities have reinvested criminal justice funding but with further reinvestment into expanded forms of social control in the community such as probation and intermediate sanction style programming. The capacity for local correctional net-widening under a mantra of justice reinvestment is plausible. Reforming local level criminal justice and correctional perspectives will undoubtedly be challenged by the endogenity of law discussed earlier in this chapter.[2]

DISCUSSION QUESTIONS

1. How do local jails differ from prisons?
2. Who is in jail and what are the particular challenges posed by these jail populations?
3. How has jail litigation and judiciary decision making shaped the administration of local level jail facilities?
4. What are the challenges for jail administrators in providing services for jail inmates? How do local politics and criminal justice subsystems influence these challenges?
5. How do local jails affect their communities? What do you see as the major challenges for communities as they attempt collaborate with local jail facilities?

NOTES

1. The states of Alaska, Connecticut, Delaware, Hawaii, Rhode Island, and Vermont have integrated jail-prison systems.
2. For a nuanced discussion of the processes of local level incarceration reform and its relation to progressive politics and governance see Judah Schept's *Progressive Punishment: Job Loss, Jail Growth, and the Neoliberal Logic of Carceral Expansion*, New York University Press (2015).

REFERENCES

American Correctional Association (n.d.) Standards and accreditation. Retrieved fromhttp://
   www.aca.org/ACA_Prod_IMIS/ACA_Member/Standards___Accreditation/ACAMember/
   Standards_and_Accreditation/SAC.aspx?hkey=7f4cf7bf-2b27–4a6b-b12436e5bd90b93d.
Antiterrorism and Death Penalty Act of 1996, Pub. L. No. 104–132, § 6, 110 Stat. 1214 (1996).
Apel, R. (2016). The effects of jail and prison confinement on cohabitation and marriage.
   Annals of the Academy of Political and Social Science, 665, 103–126.
Appelgate, B. (2011). Jails and pretrial release. In M. Tonry (Ed.), *The Oxford handbook of
   crime and criminal justice* (795–824). New York: Oxford University Press.
Backstrand, J., Gibbons, D., & Jones, J. (1992). Who is in jail? An examination of the rabble
   hypothesis. *Crime and Delinquency, 38* (2), 219–229.
Baumer, T. (2007). Reducing lock-up crowding with expedited initial processing of minorof-
   fenders. *Journal of Criminal Justice, 35,* 273–281.
Baumer, T., & Adams, K. (2006). Controlling a jail population by partially closing the front
   door: An evaluation of "summons in lieu of arrest" policy. *The Prison Journal, 86* (3),
   386–402.
Belknap, J., & Holsinger, K. (2006). The gendered nature of risk factors for delinquency.
   Feminist Criminology, 1, 48–71.
Belknap, J., Lynch, S., & Dehart, D. (2016). Jail staff members' views on jailed women's
   mental health, trauma, offending, rehabilitation, and reentry. *The Prison Journal, 96* (1),
   79–101.
Bleich, J. (1989). The politics of prison crowding. *California Law Review, 77,* 1125–1180.
Bureau of Labor Statistics (May, 2015). Occupational employment and wages, May 2015:
   33–3012 correctional officers and jailers. United States Department of Labor. http://
   www.bls.gov/oes/current/oes333012.htm.
Civil Rights Act of 1871, Pub. L. No. 42–22, § 31, 17 Stat. 13 (1871).
Clear, T. (2007). *Imprisoning communities: How mass incarceration makes disadvantaged
   neighborhoods worse.* New York: Oxford University Press.
Cohen, T., & Kyckelhahn, T. (2010). Felony defendants in large urban counties. NCJ 228944,
   Washington DC: US Department of Justice, Office of Justice Programs, Bureau of Justice
   Statistics.
Comfort, M. (2008). *Doing time together: Love and family in the shadow of prison.* Chicago
   IL: University of Chicago Press.
Comfort, M. (2016). A twenty-hour-a-day job: The impact of frequent low-level criminal
   justice involvement on family life. *Annals of the Academy of Political and Social Science,*
   665, 63–79.
Dehart, D. (2008). Pathways to prison: Impact of victimization in the lives of incarcerated
   women. *Violence Against Women, 14,* 1362–1381.
Demuth, S., & Steffensmeier, D. (2004). The impact of gender and race-ethnicity in the pre-
   trial release process. *Social Problems, 51,* 222–242.
Dumont, D. M., Gjelsvik, A., Redmond, N., & Rich, J. D. (2013). Jails as public health
   partners: Incarceration and disparities among medically underserved men. *International
   Journal of Men's Health, 12*(3), 213–227.
Edelman, L., Uggen, C., & Erlanger, H. (1999). The endogeneity of legal regulation: Grievance
   procedures as rationale myth. *American Journal of Sociology, 105,* 406–454.
Elsner, A. (2006). *Gates of injustice: The crises in America's prisons.* Upper Saddle River, NJ:
   Prentice Hall.
Feeley, M., & Rubin, E. (2000) *Judicial policymaking and the modern state: How the court's
   reformed America's prisons.* Cambridge, MA: Cambridge University Press.
Feeley, M., & Hanson, R. (1990) The impact of judicial intervention on prisons and jails: A
   framework for analysis and review of the literature. In J. Dilulio (Ed.), *Courts, corrections
   and the constitution* (pp. 12–46). New York: Oxford University Press.
Fieweger, M. (1993). Consent decrees in prison and jail reform: Relaxed standard of review for
   government motions to modify consent decrees. *The Journal of Criminal Law and Criminology,* 83 (4), 1024–1054.

Garafolo, J., & Clark, R. (1985). The inmate subculture in jails. *Criminal Justice and Behavior,* 12, 415–434.

Golinelli, D., & Minton, T. (2014). Jail inmates at midyear 2014. NCJ245350, Washington, DC: US Department of Justice, Office of Justice Programs, Bureau of Justice Statistics.

Gottschalk. M. (2009). Money and mass incarceration: The bad, the mad, and penal reform. *Criminology and Public Policy*, 8 (1), 97–109.

Green, B., Miranda, J. Daroolwalla, A, & Siddique, J. (2005). Trauma exposure, mental health functioning, and program needs of women in jail. *Crime & Delinquency, 51,* 133–151.

Guetzkow, J., & Schoon, E. (2015). If you build it, they will fill it: The consequences of prison overcrowding litigation. *Law & Society Review*, 49 (2), 401–432.

Hagan, J. (1989). Why is there so little criminal justice theory? Neglected macro- and micro-links between organization and power. *Journal of Research in Crime and Delinquency*, 26 (2), 116–135.

Hagan, J., & Dinovitzer, R. (1999). Children of the prison generation: Collateral consequences of imprisonment for children and communities. *Crime and Justice, 26,* 121–162.

Hassine, V. (2009). *Life without parole: Living in prison today.* New York: Oxford University Press.

Henrichson, C., & Delaney, R. (2012). The price of prisons: What incarceration costs taxpayers. New York: Vera Institute of Justice.

Irwin, J. (1985). *The jail: Managing the underclass in American Society.* Berkeley CA: University of California Press.

Irwin, J. & Cressey, D. (1962). Thieves, convicts and inmate culture. *Social Problems,* 10, 142–155.

Kerle, K. (2016). The mentally ill and crises intervention teams: Reflections on jails and the U.S. mental health challenge. *The Prison Journal*, 96 (1), 153–161.

Klofas, J. (1990). The jail and the community. *Justice Quarterly*, 7 (1), 295–317.

Klofas, J., Stojkovic, S., & Kalinich, D. (1992). The meaning of correctional crowding: Steps toward an index of severity. *Crime and Delinquency*, 38 (2), 171–188.

Lambert, E. (2001). To stay or quit: A review of the literature on correctional staff turnover. *American Journal of Criminal Justice*, 26 (1), 62–76.

Lurigio, A. J. (2012). MCJA keynote address: Responding to the needs of people with mental illness in the criminal justice system: An area ripe for research and community partnerships. *Journal of Crime and Justice*, 35 (1), 1–12.

Lurigio, A. J. (2016). Jails in the United States: The "old-new" frontier in American corrections. *The Prison Journal, 96*(1), 3–9.

Lynch, S., Fritch, A., & Heath, N. (2012). Looking beneath the surface: The nature of incarcerated women's experiences of interpersonal violence, mental health, and treatment needs. *Feminist Criminology, 7,* 381–400.

MacArthur Foundation (2016). Safety and justice challenge. Retrieved from http://www.safetyandjusticechallenge.org/challenge-network/.

Maruna, S. (2016). Time to get rid of the skid bids? What good are short stays of incarceration? *The Annals of the American Academy of Political and Social Science*, 665, 98–102.

Mauer, M. (2006). *Race to incarcerate.* New York: New Press.

Minton, T. D., & Zeng, Z. (2015). Jail inmates at midyear 2014. NCJ 248629, Washington, DC: US Department of Justice, Office of Justice Programs, Bureau of Justice Statistics.

Minton, T. D., Ginder, S., Brumbaugh, S. M., Smiley-McDonald, H., & Rohlof, H. (2015). Census of Jails: Population Changes, 1999–2013. Bulletin. NCJ 248627, Washington, DC: U.S. Department of Justice, Office of Justice Programs, Bureau of Justice Statistics.

Monteiro, C., & Frost, N. (2015). Altering trajectories through community-based justicereinvestment. *Criminology and Public Policy*, 14–3, 455–463.

Office of Justice Programs (Department of Justice). (2011). Prison inmates at midyear 2009: Statistical tables : Bureau of Justice Statistics Bulletin; 2011 ASI 6066–25.210;NCJ 230113.

Prison Reform Litigation Act of 1996, Pub. L. No. 104–134, § 1, 110 Stat. 1321 (1997).

Rastogi, S., Johnson, T., Hoeffell, E., Drewery, M. (2011). The black population 2010: 2010 census briefs. C2010BR-06, Washington, DC: US Department of Commerce, Economics and Statistics Administration, US Census Bureau.

Ritchie, B. (1996). *Compelled to crime: The gender entrapment of battered Black women.* New York: Routledge.

Rose, D., & Clear, T. (1998). Incarceration, social capital and crime: Implications for social disorganization theory. *Criminology, 36,* 441–480.

Rothman, D. (1971). *The discovery of the asylum: Social order and disorder in the new republic.* Boston, MA: Little Brown.

Rottman, D., & Kimberly, J. (1985). The social context of jails. In R. Carter, D. Glaser, & L. Wilkins, (Eds.), *Correctional institutions,* 3rd ed. (pp. 125–139). New York: Harper Row.

Scott, C., Lurigio, A., Dennis, M., & Funk, R. (2016). Trauma and morbidities among female detainees in a large urban jail. *The Prison Journal,* 96 (1), 102–125.

Schept, J. (2015). *Progressive punishment: Job loss, jail growth and the neoliberal logic of carceral expansion.* New York: New York University Press.

Schmid, T. & Jones, R. (1993). Prison adaptation strategies for first-time, short-term inmates. *Journal of Contemporary Ethnography,* 21, 439–463.

Simon, J. (2010). Clearing the "troubled assets" of America's punishment bubble. *Deadalus,* 139 (3), 91–101.

Simon, J. (2016). The new goal: Seeing incarceration like a city. *Annals of the American Academy of Political and Social Science,* 665, 280–301.

Stephan, J., & Walsh, G. (2011). Census of jail facilities, 2006. NCJ230188, Washington, DC: US Department of Justice, Office of Justice Programs, Bureau of Justice Statistics.

Stojkovic, S., & Klofas, J. (1997). Crowding and correctional change. In T. Alleman & R. Gido (Eds.), *Turnstile justice: issues in American corrections* (pp. 90–109). Upper Saddle River, NJ: Prentice Hall.

Stowell, J., & Byrne, J. (2008). Does what happens in prison stay in prison? Examining the reciprocal relationship between community and prison culture. In J. Byrne, D. Hummer, & F. Taxman (Eds.), *The culture of prison violence* (pp. 27–39). Boston: Pearson Publishing.

Subramanian, R. (2015) Incarceration's front door: The misuse of jail in America. New York: Vera Institute of Justice.

Sundt, J., Salisbury, E., & Harmon, M. (2016). Is downsizing prisons dangerous? The effect of California's realignment act on public safety. *Criminology and Public Policy,* 15 (2), 315–341.

Sykes, G. (1958). *The society of captives: A study of maximum security prison.* Princeton, NJ: Princeton University Press.

Tataro, C. (2002). The impact of density on jail violence. *Journal of Criminal Justice, 30,* 499–510.

Toch, H. (1977). *Living in prison; The ecology of survival.* New York: Free Press.

Violent Crime Control and Law Enforcement Act of 1994, Pub. L. No. 103–322, § 3, 108 Stat, 1796 (1994).

Vera Institute of Justice (2011). *Los Angeles county jail overcrowding reduction project: Final report: revised.* New York: Author.

Walsh, J. P. (2013). *The culture of urban control: Jail overcrowding in the crime control era.* Lanham: Lexington Books.

Welch, M. (1997). Jail overcrowding: Social sanitation and warehousing of the urban underclass. In P. Cromwell & R. Dunham (Eds.), *Crime and justice in America: Present realities and future prospects* (pp. 89–120). Upper Saddle River NJ: Prentice-Hall.

Welsh, W. (1995). *Counties in court: Jail overcrowding and court ordered reform.* Philadelphia: Temple University Press.

Welsh, W., & Pontell, H. (1991). Counties in court: Interorganizational adaptation to jail litigation in California. *Law and Society Review,* 24 (1), 73–101.

Western, B. (2006). *Punishment and inequality in America.* New York: Russell Sage.

Western, B., & Wildeman, C. (2009). The black family and mass incarceration. *Annals of the Academy of Political and Social Science, 621,* 221–242.

Wildeman, C., Turney, K., & Yi, Y. (2016). Paternal incarceration and family functioning: variation across federal, state, and local facilities. *Annals of the Academy of Political and Social Science,* 665, 80–97.

Williams, T. (2015, July 30). A psychologist as warden? Jail and mental illness intersect in Chicago. *New York Times.* Retrieved from http://www.nytimes.com.

CASES CITED

Atterbury v. Ragen, 237 F. 2d 953 (7th Cir. 1956).
Brown v. Plata, 563 U.S. 131 (2011).
Cooper v. Pate, 378 U.S. 546 (1964).
Estelle v. Gamble, 429, U.S. 97 (1976).
Monroe v. Pape, 365 U.S. 167 (1961).
Rhodes v. Chapman, 452 U.S. 337 (1981).
Rufo v. Inmates of Suffolk County Jail, 502 U.S. 367 (1992).
Schall v. Martin, 467 U.S. 253 (1984).
United States v. Salerno, 481 U.S. 739 (1987).

Chapter Three

Prisons

Carly M. Hilinski-Rosick

The earliest prisons in the United States can be traced back to the 1800s. Prior to this, most punishment involved corporal punishment and few offenders were incarcerated; jails were mostly used for those who were awaiting trial or who were unable to pay their debts. There was little effort to reform criminals and the common belief was that crime was part of human nature and could not be changed. During the late 1700s, a shift in punishment philosophy occurred, both in Europe and the United States. Much of this shift can be attributed to Cesare Beccaria and the classical school of criminology, which questioned the long-held belief that crime was due to being depraved or caused by evil spirits. Beccaria and the classical theorists argued that crime was the result of free will and rational choice, and, given the proper amount of punishment, could be deterred. Beccaria also called for criminal justice system reforms, such as a focus on individual rights, elimination of corporal and capital punishment, more transparency and fairness in court proceedings, and more proportionality of punishments. These reforms were incorporated into the Bill of Rights in the United States and also influenced reformers in Europe as well.

One impact of these reforms was on the use of prisons as a form of punishment. One of the impacts of the classical school was the emergence of the penitentiary, which was first built in the United States in the early 1800s. The penitentiary was designed to allow inmates to repent for their actions, think about their wrongdoing, and come out of prison a better person. Since the first penitentiaries were built nearly 200 years ago, the US prison system has undergone a number of different changes and evolutions. The current state of the US prison system is rather tenuous. Prisons are overcrowded, extremely costly, rife with allegations of abuse and misconduct, plagued by the introduction of contraband, and, in general, ineffective.

Since the 1970s, the correctional population in the United States has grown four-fold. In 2014, over 1.5 million inmates were in state and federal prisons in the United States (Kaeble, Glaze, Tsoutis, & Minton, 2016). Although this number has been decreasing over the past five years, it is still four times as high as it was in 1970. The largest corrections systems in the country are in California, Florida, Texas, Pennsylvania, and Georgia (Kaeble et al., 2016). There are currently over 1.5 million people incarcerated in prisons in the United States, which is a rate of about 612 inmates per 100,000 people, the highest incarceration rate in the world (Carson, 2015).

Many different reasons have been offered to explain this unprecedented growth. Arrest rates have increased since the 1970s, making it more likely that you will be arrested if you commit a crime. Further, offenders who are arrested also are more likely to receive a prison sentence than in previous decades. Recidivism rates also have increased, with offenders who are on parole returning to prison more often for new crimes or technical violations; about 66% of those released from prison will be rearrested within three years and about 33% of those released from prison will be reincarcerated within three years (Durose, Cooper, & Snyder, 2014).

Overall, sentencing policies in the United States have become tougher. The 1980s and 1990s saw the creation of mandatory minimum sentences, three strikes sentencing provisions, and in general, longer sentences and a higher likelihood of a prison sentence than ever before, particularly for drug crimes. Many of these tough sentencing policies have been geared toward drug crimes. Dating back to the 1980s, the war on drugs has focused on eradicating drugs from our streets; unfortunately, the only area where the war on drugs has been effective is in filling prisons with drug offenders. In 1980, only about 6% of the prison population were convicted of a drug offense (Carson, 2015). By 2013, this number doubled, with more than 15% of offenders incarcerated for drug offenses. This number is even higher in the federal prison system, with half of all federal inmates incarcerated for drug offenses (Carson, 2015). Mandatory minimum sentences for drug offenders make it very difficult for judges to have any discretion when handing down sentences and limit their ability to alter sentence length for many drug offenders.

Prison overcrowding has been a problem for several decades. Dating back to the 1970s when punishment philosophies began to shift towards a more punitive focus, prisons were operating at or above capacity (Pitts, Griffin, & Johnson, 2014). Attempts to relieve prison overcrowding have included building new facilities, early release of offenders, greater use of community sanctions and diversion programs, and transferring inmates to other facilities (Pitts et al., 2014). However, even as inmates are being released, many states are closing prisons to reduce costs, thus increasing the number of inmates in other facilities (Pitts et al., 2014). Many different states have been under court orders at one point, directed to reduce the number of inmates in their prison system. In 2011, California was court-ordered to reduce their prison population by 30,000 and to place a cap on new prison admissions in order to comply with the order in the future. At the time of the court order, the California Department of Corrections and Rehabilitation was at nearly 200% capacity (MacDonald, 2013). Reducing the prison population by 30,000 still only took the CDCR to 137% capacity, 37% over the number of inmates that the system and prisons were designed serve (MacDonald, 2013).

These massive prison populations come at a high cost, as well. Estimates suggest that the US corrections budget exceeds $30 billion (Henrichson & Delaney, 2012). On average, each state spends approximately $32,000 per year, per inmate. The range of annual expenditures per inmate ranges from a low of $14,603 in Kentucky to a high of $60,076 in New York (Henrichson & Delaney, 2012). In many states, the high cost of corrections comes at the expense of higher education; many states, including California and Michigan, spend more money on corrections than higher education. Strategies to reduce the correctional budget vary, and include options to reduce costs while also maintaining safety, such as recidivism reduction strategies, sentencing policies to reduce the inmate population, and ways to increase the efficiency of the prison facilities (Henrichson & Delaney, 2012). These strategies, along with a number of different issues facing prisons, will be discussed in this chapter. In addition to overcrowding and budget constraints, some of the other current issues facing prisons include physical and sexual violence, committed by both inmates and corrections staff, inmate misconduct, controlling the introduction of contraband into the facility, addressing the unique needs of special population groups within the inmate population, inmate health care, and privatization.

TRENDS AND CURRENT RESEARCH

Physical and Sexual Violence and Misconduct

One of the most significant adverse effects of prison overcrowding is violence, both physical and sexual. The Bureau of Justice Statistics has indicated that the rate of inmate-on-inmate violence is 28 assaults per 1,000 inmates (Stephan & Karberg, 2003). However, statistics measuring the amount of physical assault happening inside prisons are difficult to obtain; inmate assault is often highly underreported, so gathering reliable and complete estimates on the amount of physical and sexual assault happening within a prison can be problematic. In addition to the physical impacts of victimization, inmates who are assaulted in prison are more likely to be depressed and experience symptoms associated with posttraumatic stress disorder (PTSD), which has been shown to be related to inmate misconduct (Hochstetler, Murphy, & Simons, 2004).

Recent years have seen increased efforts in learning more about rape and sexual assault within prisons. In 2003, the Prison Rape Elimination Act (PREA) was signed into law. PREA requires information to be gathered on the prevalence of prison rape across the United States. Additionally, PREA established grants for combatting prison rape as well as resources for the creation of policies for states to address the problem. The most recently available PREA data indicates that 2% of prison inmates in the United States- reported that they had been involved in a nonconsensual sexual encounter with another inmate, 2.4% reported that they had been victimized by a staff member, and 0.4% reported being victimized by both another inmate and a prison staff member (Beck, Berzofsky, Caspar, & Krebs, 2013). Victims of prison rape and sexual assault tend to be those who are first-time offenders, incarcerated for nonviolent crimes, those who have committed a crime against a minor, those who are physically weak and effeminate, those who are not affiliated with a gang, and those who are believed to have snitched on another inmate (English & Heil, 2005).

In addition to physical and sexual assault, inmates are engaged in other forms of misconduct as well, ranging from minor rule infractions, like disobeying direct orders or refusing to leave their cell, to more serious infractions, like escaping or attempting to escape. Several explanations have been offered for inmate misconduct. Two of the most widely discussed and accepted explanations are the deprivation/pains of imprisonment model and the importation model. The deprivation model attributes inmate misconduct to the "pains of imprisonment" or things that an inmate is deprived of while he or she is incarcerated. Sykes (1958) identified the deprivation of liberty, autonomy, security, goods and services, and heterosexual relationships as the pains of imprisonment. Conversely, the importation theory argues that the values and norms that are found within the prison are similar to those in the outside world, and are imported into the prison with the inmates. Irwin and Cressey (1962) argue that inmates are predisposed to violence and misconduct, both on the outside and within the correctional institution.

Contraband

Contraband within prisons is not a new problem; however, as society changes, the contraband brought into prison facilities (as well as the mechanisms used to smuggle the items in) changes as well. Contraband could be anything from drugs to weapons to cell phones. In 2014, two inmates escaped from a prison in upstate New York, using tools that were smuggled into the prison by a prison teacher. The teacher hid the tools in various homemade food items that she brought in and then passed on to the inmates.

She was able to circumvent the metal detectors that all employees were to go through in order to bring the tools into the facility. The inmates used the tools to cut through a series of pipes and ultimately escape from the prison. This incident, and the ensuing manhunt, put a spotlight on the prison, their security practices, and the problem of contraband within prisons. For months, the media focused on uncovering how the teacher was able to get these items into the facility, how the inmates were able to slowly cut through the pipes, and then ultimately escape successfully. This incident highlighted the difficulties in controlling the introduction of contraband into prison facilities, as prison employees, the ones expected to stem the flow of contraband, may be the source.

Drugs in prisons also are a significant problem. Drugs can be introduced into the prison environment by visitors, corrupt staff members, or even through more creative means, such as using a paintball gun or throwing a football, filled with drugs and drug paraphernalia, over a prison fence. Drones also have been recently used to smuggle drugs and other contraband items into prisons.

Many states have implemented a variety of different mechanisms to combat contraband. Florida, for example, uses drug-detecting dog teams, metal detector searches of staff and visitors at all prisons, and even conducts random pat-down searches of staff. Random and for-cause drug tests are also done in many prisons. During fiscal year 2014–2015, the Florida Department of Corrections conducted nearly 57,500 random drug tests and over 1,800 for-cause drug tests (based on reasonable suspicion of involvement with drugs or alcohol) (Florida Department of Corrections, n.d.). Of these drug tests, less than 1% of the random tests were positive and over 50% of the for-cause tests were positive. Inmates who tested positive were most likely to test positive for cannabis for both random and for-cause tests (Florida Department of Corrections, n.d.).

Cell phones are viewed as a convenience to most people. However, within prisons, cell phones are a threat to the safety and security of the institution. The issue of cell phones in prison gained nationwide media attention in 2010 when a group of inmates in Georgia used cell phones to coordinate a strike among inmates at several Georgia prisons. The strike included work stoppages as inmates protested prison conditions, the quality of meals, and the lack of pay for working prison jobs. They used cell phones to create e-mail and text lists to communicate with other inmates, update social media on the progress of the strike, and to conduct interviews with members of the media.

As phones have gotten thinner and smaller, they are easier and easier to hide. In California, for example, nearly 1000 cell phones were found in an 18-month period, from July 2014 to December 2015 (California Department of Corrections and Rehabilitation, 2015). This number seems small compared to the over 1,100 cell phones found among Federal Bureau of Prisons facilities in the first four months of 2011. Similar to other types of contraband, cell phone interdiction efforts include random cell searches, requiring visitors and inmates to go through metal detectors and pat downs, and using dogs trained to sniff out cell phones. Other efforts include electronic cell phone detection systems. These systems can be either wireless or hardwired and indicate when a cell phone is being used within a facility (Burke & Owen, 2010).

Other efforts that have been suggested to combat the cell phone problem is the use of signal jammers. These jammers block cell phone signals, rendering them useless. Resistance to this strategy comes from cell phone companies, who argue that this is illegal, and those questioning the safety of the institution if no one inside (including corrections officers or other prison administrators) is able to use a cell phone. If cell phone jammers are used, emergency calls may not be made from the prison on cell phones and they could also disrupt communications of emergency responders (Federal Communications Commission, n.d.). One solution that has been offered by the Federal Communications Commission (FCC) is called "inmate call capture." Inmate call capture is a system that captures all outgoing cell phone calls and if the phone making the call has a number that is on an approved list, the call can go through. If the number is not on an approved list, the call does not go through. This allows 911 emergency calls to go through and also allows corrections officers and other prison administrators to use cell phones within the prison without issue. The inmate call capture system was tested at a prison in Mississippi and in one month, over 215,000 unauthorized calls to and from inmates were intercepted (FCC, n.d.). Additionally, this type of system is much more affordable than the cell phone jammers. As cell phones and technology are not going away any time soon, cell phones in prison will continue to be a problem that prison administrators must constantly address.

Special Populations

There are a number of different special populations within the prison system that pose unique issues to prison administration. Most notably, the mentally ill, elderly inmates, inmates with special needs and disabilities, and female inmates have specific characteristics and needs that require special accommodations. In more recent years, transgender inmates have required prison administrators to attempt to create policies and procedures to best serve this population as well. Special populations are discussed throughout this book; this section will focus specifically on elderly inmates, inmates with disabilities and special needs, and inmates who are military veterans.

Elderly Inmates

As the prison population as a whole has increased, the elderly inmate population has followed suit. Due to longer sentences, decreased use of discretionary parole, declining parole approval rates, and an increase in the number of elderly people in the general population, the elderly prison population has increased over 750% since the 1970s (Carson, 2015). In the late 1970s, there were fewer than 7,000 elderly inmates in the United States. By the year 2000, there were more than 50,000 elderly inmates, and this number continues to grow (Carson, 2015). Some estimates suggest that by the years 2030, one-third of all US inmates will be considered elderly (Enders, Paterniti, & Meyers, 2005).

Elderly inmates, in general, have a physiological age that is 10 to 11.5 years older than their nonincarcerated counterparts (Rikard & Rosenberg, 2007). Inmates often have long histories of drug and alcohol abuse, do not seek preventative medical care, and do not have a healthy diet; as a result, have a higher physiological age than their actual chronological ages (Fellner, 2012). Because of years of neglecting their medical well-being and using drugs and alcohol, many elderly inmates have more medical problems and need additional health care beyond basic preventative care. This health care comes at higher cost; Fellner (2012) reports that medical care for elderly inmates costs three to eight times more than health care for inmates who are young and healthy. In total, Smyer and Burbank (2009) estimate that it costs approximately $70,000 per year to house an elderly inmate in prison.

Dementia is one of the more common diseases affecting the elderly inmate population. Wilson and Barboza (2010) argue that dementia may be two to three times more common among inmates and often impacts the ability of elderly inmates to adjust to prison life. Dementia also impacts their ability to understand and follow orders given by correctional officers, which is often mistaken for intentional defiance rather than as a result of their illness (Wilson & Barboza, 2010). First-time elderly inmates have been found to have a particularly difficult time adjusting to prison life. Crawley and Sparks (2006) found that elderly inmates who were sentenced to prison for the first time had significant rates of anxiety and depression.

As sentences have gotten longer, more inmates are, as Smyer and Burbank (2009) have called it, "aging in place" (p. 35). As inmates are aging within the prison, prison officials must determine how to address their issues while minimizing costs. One way to do this is a strong proactive health program that focuses on things like healthy aging, diet and exercise, understanding and managing symptoms of diseases, and frequent cancer screenings (Smyer & Burbank, 2009). Additional strategies to help inmates age in place include focusing on stress management and the development of healthy coping mechanisms to respond effectively to stressful prison situations, such as feeling unsafe, physical abuse, and depression. Further, it is also necessary to assess where elderly inmates are housed within the prison. Putting elderly inmates in the general population can be problematic, as most prisons were designed for younger, noisier, and active inmates and do not meet the needs of elderly inmates (Aday, 2003). To address these issues, some states are building special care units for elderly inmates. These range from secure nursing homes to special units in existing buildings that are designed for elderly inmates with mobility issues.

Inmates with Disabilities

Like elderly inmates, inmates with disabilities and special needs are often vulnerable when housed with the general population of a prison. Disability type could be related to hearing, vision, cognitive, ambulatory, self-care, or independent learning (Bronson, Maruschak, & Berzofsky, 2015). Bronson et al. report that between 2011 and 2012, about 33% of state and federal inmates reported having at least one disability. Across gender, about 40% of female inmates and 31% of male inmates reported that they had a disability. Inmates also are more likely than individuals in the general population to have at least one disability and about 20% of prison inmates self-disclosed a cognitive disability, which was the most common disability type. Further, female inmates also were more likely than male inmates to report a cognitive disability (Bronson et al., 2015).

Having a disability in prison has many adverse consequences for inmates. When compared to inmates who do not have a disability, inmates with a disability were nearly four times more likely to experience serious psychological distress. Additionally, inmates with a disability were more likely to have a co-occurring chronic condition, such as an infectious disease and obesity. Despite the prevalence of inmates with disabilities and rights provided by the Americans with Disabilities Act (ADA), many inmates allege that their rights are being violated and they are not receiving reasonable accommodations for their disabilities.

A lawsuit filed against the Alabama Department of Corrections (ADOC), for example, alleges that inmates with physical disabilities are housed in units that cannot safely accommodate them, that they are routinely denied services and devices, such as sign language interpreters and wheelchairs, and that they are housed in higher security level facilities only because of their disability, not for any security or classification reasons (Southern Poverty Law Center, 2016). Inmates in other states have made similar claims of negligence and lack of accommodations and still others have alleged that they are denied access to educational, vocational, and rehabilitation programs, all because of their disabilities.

Inmates Who Are Veterans

Military veterans have always been present in the prison population. In the late 1970s, veterans made up nearly one-fourth of the prison population (Bronson, Carson, Noonan, & Berzofsky, 2015). From 1980 to 2008, the number of veterans who were incarcerated increased, in conjunction with the increase in the general prison population, but the number of incarcerated veterans has decreased since 2008 (Bronson et al., 2015a). Current estimates suggest that about 8% of inmates are veterans (Bronson et al., 2015b). Vietnam veterans are the largest group of incarcerated veterans, in both state and federal prisons. Inmates who are veterans also are more likely to be sex offenders or violent offenders, and are more likely than non-veteran inmates to have victimized women and minors (Noonan & Mumola, 2007). Despite this decrease, military veterans in prisons, like military veterans in the community, have different experiences and characteristics that may impact their time in prison.

Much like other special groups within the prison population, those who are military veterans have unique issues that need to be addressed. Veterans returning from combat can suffer from things such as physical injuries, psychological trauma, including PTSD, depression, and drug and alcohol abuse. Given the proliferation of PTSD among inmate veterans, corrections officers could benefit from additional training that focuses on PTSD and how it is manifested in the correctional environment. The National Institute of Mental Health (n.d.) has identified indicators of PTSD as things like tension, agitation, and hypervigilance, sleep disturbances, flashbacks, mood swings and depression, panic attacks, and emotional detachment. If corrections officers are trained to recognize and respond to these signs of PTSD in an effective manner, they could avoid interpreting their behavior as an act of misconduct, thus avoiding unnecessary punishment.

To provide a supportive environment for veterans, some states, like Virginia, have created special housing units solely for military veterans. The housing units resemble military barracks and each inmate has a role within the dorm. It is quiet and orderly and any conflicts are dealt with by the group through an intervention. PTSD therapy groups are available and inmates identify a high level of trust within the dorm. Much of the anecdotal evidence from Virginia, and other states who have implemented similar programs, has found that inmate veterans who are housed away from the general prison population are more successful, participate in more programming, and commit fewer rule infractions while they are incarcerated.

Prison Health Care

One of the common shared characteristics among the many special groups within the prison population is the need for additional, or special, health care services. As established in the Supreme Court cases of *Estelle v. Gamble* (1976), inmates have a right to health care while they are incarcerated. The quality of the care that must be provided, however, is not as clear. Health care is one of the areas where prisons spend the most money, with some estimates suggesting that, on average, states are spending about $5,800 a year on inmate health care (Kyckelhahan, 2012). As a group, inmates generally have significant health problems. Many are due to high-risk behaviors that inmates engage in before they are incarcerated, including promiscuity, drug use, including sharing needles, and alcohol use and abuse.

Other needs for health care often mimic the needs of the general population; however, inmates overwhelmingly lived in poverty before being incarcerated. This often means that they did not seek preventative medical care or did not seek medical care for any health issues they encountered; further, living in poverty also often results in an inadequate diet, contributing to their overall lack of a healthy lifestyle. Female inmates often have more serious health issues than male inmates and also have higher rates of mental health issues; female inmates also are more likely than male inmates to report a medical issue while incarcerated (Maruschak, 2015).

Despite the host of medical problems that inmates present, prison health care is far from top-notch. In general, prisons have a full-time staff of nurses and some part-time physicians or physician assistants. Much of the prison health care is handled by nurses and inmates see doctors when necessary. Any major medical emergencies are typically handled outside of the prison at a local hospital. Despite the range of medical services offered in prisons, many prison administrators resist providing medical services until it is absolutely necessary, due to the cost of medical care.

To reduce costs, many prison administrators are exploring ways to continue to provide adequate medical care at an affordable cost. One strategy is the use of telemedicine. Telemedicine uses interactive audiovisual media to allow health care professionals to provide consultations to inmates remotely. This is especially useful for inmates who need to see a specialist. Allowing the inmate to interact with the medical professional remotely reduces security risks, because inmates do not have to be transported anywhere (Ollove, 2016). Telemedicine has been lauded by some as a way to reduce costs for prisons while still allowing inmates to receive medical care, particularly care by specialists, who do not practice within the prison. However, others have criticized its use, arguing that it is used too frequently and inappropriately, mainly to cover what would be considered inadequate health care within the prison; critics also argue that telemedicine doctors do not have the full medical history of a patient when interacting with them remotely, which could potentially compromise their care (Ollove, 2016).

Many prisons also require a copay if an inmate wants to seek medical attention, similar to the copays paid outside of prison walls. This helps offset some of the cost of providing inmate health care and also may act to deter inmates from overusing the medical services. It may, however, also deter inmates from seeking medical care when they really need it. Another strategy used to reduce costs is privatization of prison health care services. A number of states have fully privatized their correctional health care, and pay a private company to provide all aspects of the inmate care. Corrections administrators favor using private companies to provide medical, dental, and pharmaceutical services to inmates because it is less expensive than employing the medical professionals as state workers. By using a private company, the state does not have to pay benefits and pension costs for the workers.

Despite the cost savings that privatized correctional health care may provide, they have recently come under fire in several states. Critics argue that the lower cost comes with a decline in the quality of care. Audits completed in a number of states have found that staffing is inadequate, HIPAA rules are being violated, medical records are lost or incomplete, and equipment is broken or outdated. Some argue that the incentive to cut costs has become too great. Private companies are less concerned with the quality of care and more concerned with being able to sign and retain contracts with state corrections departments.

POLICIES

When discussing prisons, two things are very clear: prisons are extremely costly to operate and their effectiveness is questionable. With prison budgets reaching into the billions and recidivism rates over 50%, lawmakers and the general public have started to question the way the criminal justice system, particularly corrections, has been operating. In 2008, when the housing market crashed and states experienced severe budget crises, lawmakers finally began to realize that prisons were not working and were a huge drain on states' economies. The ensuing recession provided strong motivation for states to begin looking at how corrections was operating, whether it was effective, and how to reduce the cost of corrections while still maintaining public safety. Strategies that emerged include programs to focus on reentry and reintegration, in an effort to reduce recidivism, ways to reduce the inmate population, also known as backdoor strategies, and solutions to increase efficiency and reduce spending within the prison.

Reducing Recidivism

Each year, approximately 35% of new prison admissions are parole violators (two-thirds of this group are technical violators) (Pew Center on the States, 2011). Success rates vary state to state; in California, for example, less than one quarter of parolees succeed. These inmates are returned to prison for new crimes or for violations of their parole conditions. One way to reduce prison populations is to stem the flow of parole violators back to prison and help parolees succeed in the community. Given the expense of incarcerating an inmate for one year, attempting to keep those inmates from coming back would be a worthwhile endeavor. However, despite the high recidivism rates, many states are still failing to provide parolees with the tools that they need to be successful once they are released from prison.

Three main things necessary for successful reentry include controlling substance abuse, getting a job, and developing a support group of family and friends (Clear, Reisig, Petrosino, & Cole, 2017). However, achieving success at these three things does not guarantee that a parolee will ultimately be successful at staying out of prison, however. Many do not have adequate coping mechanisms to address the many problem situations they may encounter. Further, they may often react in ways that worsen the problem rather than to solve it (Zamble & Quinsey, 1997).

One tool used to help ensure that parolees can be successful are reentry courts. Reentry courts were introduced in the 1990s as a way to provide close supervision and assistance to parolees during the reintegration process, similar to the goals of drug and sobriety courts. In reentry courts, the judges who originally sentenced an offender maintain contact and oversight with the offender while he or she is on parole. Regular court appearances, combined with supervision by the parole officer, allow the court to assess the parolee's progress and his or her needs. The goals of reentry courts are, in general, to help offenders find employment, housing, become or remain drug-free, and take on familial and personal responsibility; reentry courts usually follow parolees through the first six months of their release (Hamilton, 2010). One important element of reentry courts, similar to drug courts, is the use of praise and incentives to reward success within the program. When a parolee completes the program successfully, he or she is recognized at a graduation ceremony, often attended by family members and other important individuals in the parolees' life.

Evaluations of the effectiveness of reentry courts have found that participants in reentry courts are rearrested and reconvicted less often than those on traditional parole. Reentry court participants are also out of prison for a longer amount of time before they reoffend, when compared to offenders on traditional parole (Hamilton, 2010). Parolees who are the most successful in completing reentry courts and remaining crime free are those who have not been on parole before, are married or living with a significant other, and have higher educational attainment (Hamilton, 2010). Overall, reentry courts appear to be a promising tool in helping parolees achieve success when they are returned to the community.

Reducing the Inmate Population

As discussed previously in this chapter, many prisons are overcrowded, with 19 states and the federal government operating at 100% capacity or more (Carson, 2015). The extreme overcrowding in some states has resulted in the federal government ordering that states reduce their prison populations (like in California) and also has prompted some governors and state legislatures to take it upon themselves to enact policies that will aid in reducing the prison population. These prison population reduction strategies are often called backdoor strategies. To reduce the prison population, many states have allowed offenders to earn early parole (typically reserved for nonviolent offenders, and in many cases, drug offenders).

Three states that experienced great success in reducing their prison populations are New York, New Jersey, and California. Between 1999 and 2012, New York and New Jersey reduced their prison population by 26% and between 2006 and 2012, California reduced its prison population by 23% (Mauer & Ghandnoosh, 2014). During the time of the prison population reduction, each of these states also experienced declines in violent crime that exceeded the declines nationwide. Further, New York and New Jersey experienced reductions in property crime that were greater than the reductions nationwide, and California experienced a reduction in property crime that was slightly higher than the nationwide average (Mauer & Ghandnoosh, 2014). Overall, reducing the prison population by one-fourth had only positive impacts on the crime rates in these three states.

To reduce their prison population, New York used a combination of policy and practice changes that included changes to the notoriously tough Rockefeller Drug Laws, a decline in felony drug arrests, diversion of felony drug offenders to alternative sentencing programs, and the introduction of a "Merit Time Program," which allowed non-violent, non-sexual offenders to earn reductions in their sentences and to become parole-eligible earlier if they completed education and vocational programs, treatment programs, and service programs (Mauer & Ghandnoosh, 2014). New Jersey used a combination of front-end and back-end reforms to reduce their prison population. One way of doing this was to revamp the parole process, which resulted in a significant increase in parole approval rates. New Jersey also reduced the rate at which technical violators were returned to prison. In addition, like New York, New Jersey also reformed their drug policies, including exempting low-level drug offenders from some laws, such as the "drug free zone law," which was viewed as creating racial disparity among those offenders incarcerated for drug offense.

California's efforts to reduce its prison population can largely be attributed to the need to comply with a court order calling for a reduction in the prison population. To do this, California passed legislation that would allow offenders with non-violent, non-sexual, and non-serious offense to be incarcerated in county jails but no longer in state prison, that would allow released prisoners who were non-violent, non-sexual, or non-serious offenders to be supervised by county probation departments rather than state parole supervision, and would allow individuals who committed technical violations to only be sentenced to jail and not returned to prison. This jail sentence would also be shorter than past sentences for parole revocation. Although this legislation has resulted in an increase in the county jail populations, the overall net effect in California has been a reduction in the incarcerated person population (prison and jail) (CDCR, 2010; Lofstrom & Raphael, 2013; Mauer & Ghandnoosh, 2014; Petersilia & Snyder, 2013). The experiences in New York, New Jersey, and California illustrate the ability of states to reduce their prison populations, in some cases by 25%, without adverse effects on public safety. More states need to take notice of this and begin acting to do the same in order to see an overall consistent and significant reduction in the prison population across the United States.

Increasing Efficiency

One last way that corrections departments are working to try to reduce costs is to increase efficiencies in prison, including videoconferencing for court appearances and visits with family members and friends, and the use of kiosks to check on the status of any pending cases, order items from the prison commissary, and communicate with family members and friends via email.

Many of the efforts of prisons to streamline prison processes involve reducing the resources needed to accomplish daily prison tasks. Visitation between inmates and family and friends requires a great deal of resources. Visitors must be searched before they can come in contact with inmates and inmates must be searched before coming in contact with their visitors, and then most prisons require searches of the inmates (and in many cases, strip searches) when the visit has concluded. In addition, corrections officers must be present to observe the entirety of the visit. Video visitation can take on a number of different forms, including video visits where the visitors are in their homes and use Skype-like programs to visit. Other video visitation may require the visitors to actually go the prison and go to a separate area that is set up with the video technology. The inmate will often be in his or her pod or housing unit, which is equipped with the video visit equipment. On the surface, video visitation sounds like an effective way to cut costs and conserve limited resources. It does not require the invasive searches of visitors and inmates alike. Minimal supervision is required, as there is no physical contact between inmates and visitors. Video visits also may enable visits between inmates and family members who live very far apart; family members may not have the resources to travel to the prison, but the video visits may allow them the opportunity to see their loved ones from the comfort of their own home (Fulcher, 2014).

On the other hand, there are many areas where video visits fall short. Critics of video visitation argue that with few exceptions, the video technology is designed poorly and often does not work well. Further, when video visitation happens from home, the visitors must pay a fee for the visit, which could be up to $1.50 per minute. Those people most likely to use video visitation are often those who are least likely to have the resources to pay for these visits. Although video visits are better than no visits, they do not have the same impact of in-person visits (Rabuy & Wagner, 2015). Eliminating face-to-face visits does not allow inmates to have human contact with their spouses or partners, children, and other loved ones. Video visits also may have detrimental effects on the prison environment, as well, as some facilities have found that inmate violence and misconduct increased after the implementation of video visitation (Renaud, 2014). Visits are a privilege, not a right, and prisons have long used visits as a powerful management tool. The threat of not being permitted to visit with your family is a strong incentive for compliance from inmates. Without the opportunity to visit with loved ones in person, inmates may see little incentive for complying with the rules and regulations of the facility (Renaud, 2014).

Other efforts to increase efficiencies and reduce needed resources in prisons include e-mail systems and information kiosks where inmates can check on the status of pending court cases, order items from the prison commissary, and purchase songs for prison-approved MP3 players. One popular system is the JPay service, which allows family members and friends to send money to prison accounts and allows family and friends to send e-mails and even short video clips to inmates. Inmates are then able to respond to these e-mails and videos. Like video visitation, e-mails are effective at cutting down on resources. By cutting down on the amount of physical mail received at the prison, prisons can reduce the number of person hours necessary to inspect each piece of mail for contraband. E-mail systems are able to quickly scan each e-mail and block any messages that may contain inappropriate content that could jeopardize the safety and security of the prison. Further, inmates also are able to send and receive messages much quicker using email. Messages that could take days or even weeks to be delivered by the post office can be received within 48 hours in some cases. Sending e-mail messages is not free, however, and inmates must pay to send the messages and people on the outside also must pay to send the messages. Proponents of e-mail systems for inmates argue that the cost to send an e-mail is generally less than the cost to send a physical letter.

One final way that prisons are trying to increase efficiency is privatization. Many prisons have outsourced services, like health care, food service, phone calls, video visitation, and money transfers between inmates and their families to private, for-profit companies. These companies argue that they are able to perform these services at a lower cost and higher quality than if the prison itself delivered the service. The outsourcing of prison services can cost inmates and their families more money, as in the case of video visits, e-mails, and phone calls. The Federal Communications Commission (FCC) recently put a cap on how much companies can charge inmates for phone calls and banned any other add-on fees, but prior to this, phone calls in some areas cost up to $14 a minute (Federal Communications Commission, 2016). A federal appeals court has put a hold on these changes, however, after telephone companies and several states filed lawsuits arguing that the FCC had overstepped its authority and disregarded the actual costs of providing phone services to inmates (Gershman, 2016).

Many states are turning to privatized health care for their prison systems to stem the rising costs of health care services. On average, states are spending one-fifth of their correctional budgets on health care for inmates (The Pew Charitable Trusts, 2014). Privatized health care companies replace doctors, nurses, and other medical personnel hired and paid by the state or federal government with workers that they hire and pay. These companies sign contracts with the prison systems and provide all institutional health care services. Two of the biggest companies, Wexford and Corizon, have come under fire it recent years for what has been called inadequate and negligent health care. Since 2012, Corizon has lost contracts with prisons in Minnesota, Maine, Maryland, Tennessee, and Pennsylvania. Most recently, Corizon declined to renew their contract with the Florida Department of Corrections after repeated complaints of rising number of inmate deaths that were not attributed to natural causes, understaffing, inmate maltreatment, and negligence. The future of privatized correctional healthcare remains in limbo as states are consistently discovering issues with the quality of care and health care companies are refusing to renew contracts when asked to make changes to the standards of care.

Privatized food services in prisons have not fared much better. Not only has the quality of the food and preparation been criticized, privatizing food services also takes away prison jobs from corrections officers who specifically work in food services, as well as inmates, who prepare, serve, and clean up the meals. Recent widespread media attention has been focused on the Michigan Department of Corrections (MDOC) and Aramark, a food services company that provides food and beverage services to national parks, colleges and universities, ballparks, hospitals, etc. The MDOC signed a multi-year, $145 million contract with Aramark, but not long into the contract period, Aramark was not holding up its end of the contract (Zullo, 2016).

Investigations into Aramark's work found that there were food shortages, maggots in the food, and that inmates were served food that had been partially eaten by rodents. Investigations also revealed that sharp kitchen tools and tops of metal cans were left unsecured, that Aramark employees were becoming "overfamiliar" with inmates, to the extent that some were having sexual relationships with the inmates, smuggling drugs, and one was convicted of trying to hire an inmate to carry out an assault on another inmate (Egan, 2015). In the wake of all of these issues, the MDOC terminated the contract with Aramark and has hired a new, private company to provide food services. Michigan is not the only state were these problems exist; prisons in Ohio have had similar experiences with Aramark (ACLU, 2014). Overall, efforts to increase efficiencies in prisons have, in most cases, done exactly the opposite. Many of these ventures have turned into expensive failures for states as well as violating basic rights of inmates, such as adequate health care and food.

Private Prisons

The move toward the privatization of prison services stems from the push to privatize corrections all together. Since 1999, the number of inmates held in private facilities has been steadily increasing, reaching a high of nearly 9% of the total US prison population in 2012 (Carson, 2015). In 2014, the most recent year with full data available, there were small decreases in the private prison population (a decrease of 2,100 prisoners). Seven states house nearly 20% of their prison population in private facilities, with some, like New Mexico, housing more than 40% of their inmates in facilities run by private corporations (Carson, 2015).

The privatization movement grew out of the unprecedented growth of the prison population in the United States, stemming from the War on Drugs and the harsh sentencing practices of the late 1970s, 1980s, and early 1990s. The first use of a private prison facility was in Hamilton County, Tennessee in 1983. There, Corrections Corporation of America (CCA) (which is now the largest private prison company in the country) opened the first privately-run prison facility in the United States. Over the next few years, CCA attempted to take over the entire Tennessee prison system, but ultimately failed, after facing strong opposition due to their reputation for going over budget and inmate escapes. They were successful, however, in gaining contracts in additional states, like Texas and Kentucky. Today, CCA and the GEO Group manage over half of all of the private prison contracts in the United States (Mason, 2012).

Proponents of private prisons argue that they can provide a cost-effective alternative for states and the federal government. Studies that have examined the cost effectiveness of private prisons have proved inconclusive. Early studies which purported to show cost savings used problematic methodologies. More recent studies found the same; researchers are unable to provide evidence that private prisons provide a clear advantage or disadvantage to publicly run prisons and that cost savings from private prisons are not guaranteed (Mason, 2012).

One of the main ways that private prisons attempt to control and reduce costs is through their personnel management and practices. Private prisons routinely provide lower salaries, fewer benefits, and opportunities for salary advancement than publicly operated facilities. Private prison employees also receive significantly less training than public prison employees; according to Mason (2012), private prison employees receive an average of 58 hours less training than their publicly run prison counterparts. Employee turnover within private prisons also is much higher than in public facilities. This lack of training and turnover has been argued to contribute to the safety issues often found within private prison facilities (Blakeley & Bumphus, 2004). Research has found that the number of assaults at private prisons may be twice as high as in publicly run facilities (Blakely & Bumphus, 2004; Camp & Gaes, 2001).

In addition to questions about the cost effectiveness, quality of confinement, and safety of private institutions, questions also have been raised about the transparency and accountability of privately run facilities. Opponents to private prisons argue that the need to make a profit may result in subpar services in private prisons. In Idaho, CCA officials were fined after an audit of the CCA-run Idaho Correctional Center found that CCA delayed providing medications, administering vaccinations, and providing mental health care services, and also hired unqualified drug and alcohol counselors (Boone, 2010). Many states have passed laws requiring private prisons to be held to the same standards as publicly run facilities when it comes to public records, but the federal government has not required the same of facilities holding federal prisoners. Members of Congress have tried six times to pass a bill that would require private prisons to be subject to the same public records laws as prisons run by the federal government, but the bill has been repeatedly shot down (2014). Finally, research also has suggested that inmates who served time in private facilities were more likely to recidivate (Spivak & Sharp, 2008) and also have fewer opportunities to participate in work programs, education programs, and counseling (Stephan, 2008). Despite the questions surrounding the cost effectiveness and general effectiveness of private prisons, the number of inmates housed in private facilities has continued to grow, with small declines only being realized in the past few years.

CHALLENGES AND THE FUTURE OF PRISONS

As illustrated throughout this chapter, corrections departments in general, and prisons specifically, are facing an array of challenges to their successful operation. The need to cut budgets has led many states to cut corrections budgets; although it may seem like these budgets are high, when you look at the amount spent per inmate and what they actually get for that spending, cutting corrections budgets is taking resources away from a group of people who already get very little. Although many argue that, as convicted criminals, inmates should get the bare minimum (or in some cases, less than the bare minimum) of services, and should, in no circumstances, be afforded any opportunities not made available to free citizens, what many people fail to realize, or acknowledge, is that over 90% of inmates will be released someday. Inmates who receive no education, no vocational training, no substance abuse treatment, etc. are inmates who are coming back to our cities and towns with no prospects at getting a job and contributing to society. These inmates who have no job prospects became involved in crime quickly and are often quickly arrested and begin the criminal justice system cycle all over again.

The challenge, then, is to use what little resources are available within prisons to try to transform inmates into individuals who can be successful upon release, making valuable contributions to society and remaining crime free. The principles of effective correctional programs have been widely studied and established; however, implementing programs that follow these principles has proven difficult, if not nearly impossible, in a political and social climate that views inmates as a group of individuals who deserves nothing. Until voters and lawmakers accept that we need to be proactive with our efforts to keep inmates from recidivating, and that these efforts should begin while they are still incarcerated, our corrections system will continue to be ineffective and plagued by high recidivism rates. Further, as states are under pressure to reduce their spending on corrections, it is feasible to assume that the private prison will resume growing.

DISCUSSION QUESTIONS

1. Discuss some of the reasons that have been offered to explain the rapid growth in the correctional population since the 1970s.
2. Discuss the current research surrounding physical and sexual violence in prisons. What is the nature and prevalence of this violence?
3. Explain the efforts to reduce the prison population. What measures have states taken to reduce the number of inmates who are incarcerated in their prisons?

4. Discuss the issues associated with private prisons and explain whether you are a proponent or opponent to privately funded prison facilities. Be sure to support your position.
5. Explain what you see as the future of corrections. What do you think our state and federal prisons systems will look like in 10 years?

REFERENCES

Aday, R. H. (2003). *Aging prisoners: Crisis in American corrections*. Westport, CT: Praeger.

American Civil Liberties Union of Ohio. (2014, April 19). *Problems with privatized food service should not surprise Ohio prison officials*. Retrieved from http://www.acluohio.org/archives/press-releases/problems-with-privatized-food-service.

Beck, A. J., Berzofsky, M., Caspar, R., & Krebs, C. (2013). *Sexual victimization in prisons and jails reported by inmates, 2011–12*. Washington, DC: Bureau of Justice Statistics.

Blakely, C. R., & Bumphus, V.W. (2004). Private and public sector prisons—a comparison of selected characteristics. *Federal Probation, 68*, 27–33.

Boone, R. (2010, June 1). Idaho fines private prison for contract violations. *The Boston Globe*. Retrieved from http://archive.boston.com/business/healthcare/articles/2010/06/01/idaho_fines_private_prison_for_contract_violations/.

Bronson, J., Maruschak, L. M., & Berzofsky, M. (2015a). *Disabilities among prison and jail inmates, 2011–12*. Washington, DC: Bureau of Justice Statistics.

Bronson, J., Carson, E. A., Noonan, M., & Berzofsky, M. (2015b). *Veterans in prison and jail, 2011–12*. Washington, DC: Bureau of Justice Statistics.

Burke, T. W., & Owen, S.S. (2010, July). Cell phones as prison contraband. *FBI Law Enforcement Bulletin*.

California Department of Corrections and Rehabilitation (2015). Contraband cell phones in CDCR prisons and conservation camps. Retrieved from http://www.cdcr.ca.gov/Contraband-Cell-Phones/docs/Contraband-Cell-Phone-Fact-Sheet.pdf.

Camp, S. D., & Gaes, G. G. (2001). *Growth and quality of U.S. private prisons: Evidence from a national survey*. Washington, DC: Federal Bureau of Prisons, Office of Research and Evaluation.

Carson, E. A. (2015). *Prisoners in 2014*. Washington, DC: Bureau of Justice Statistics.

CDCR (2010). *CDCR implements public safety reforms to parole supervision, expanded incentive credits for inmates*. Retrieved from http://www.insidecdcr.ca.gov/2010/01/cdcr-implements-public-safety-reforms-to-parole-supervision-expanded-incentive-credits-for-inmates/.

Clear, T. R., Reisig, M. D., Petrosino, C., & Cole, G. F. (2017). *American Corrections, 3rd Edition*. Boston, MA: Cengage Learning.

Crawley, E., & Sparks, R. (2006). Is there life after imprisonment? How elderly men talk about imprisonment and release. *Criminology and Criminal Justice, 6*, 63–82.

Durose, M. R., Cooper, A. D., & Snyder, H. N. (2014). *Recidivism of prisoners released in 30 states in 2005: Patterns from 2005 to 2010*. Washington, DC: Bureau of Justice Statistics.

Egan, P. (2015, December 3). Former Aramark prison worker convicted in "hired hit." *Detroit Free Press*. Retrieved from http://www.freep.com/story/news/local/michigan/2015/12/03/former-aramark-prison-worker-convicted-hired-hit/76748116/.

Enders, S. R., Paterniti, D. A., & Meyers, F. J. (2005). An approach to develop effective health care decision making for women in prison. *Journal of Palliative Medicine, 8*, 432–439.

English, K., & Heil, P. (2005). Prison rape: What we know today. *Corrections Compendium, 30*, 1–5, 42–44.

Federal Communications Commission. (n.d.). *Putting an end to illegal cell phone use in prisons*. Retrieved from https://transition.fcc.gov/pshs/docs/summits/Combating-Contraband-Cell-Phones-in-Prison-Handout-v4.pdf.

Federal Communications Commission. (2016, March 24). *Inmate telephone service*. Retrieved from https://www.fcc.gov/consumers/guides/inmate-telephone-service.

Fellner, J. (2012). *Old behind bars: The aging prison population in the United States.* Human Rights Watch. Retrieved from: https://www.hrw.org/sites/default/files/reports/usprisons0112_brochure_web.pdf.

Florida Department of Corrections (n.d.). *Annual report: Fiscal year 2014–2015.* Retrieved from http://www.dc.state.fl.us/pub/annual/1415/FDC_AR2014-15.pdf.

Fulcher, P. A. (2014). The double edged sword of prison video visitation: Claiming to keep families together while furthering the aims of the prison industrial complex. *Florida A&M University Law Review, 9,* 83–112.

Gershman, J. (2016, March 7). Appeals court puts on hold FCC caps on prison phone-call charges. *The Wall Street Journal.* Retrieved from http://blogs.wsj.com/law/2016/03/07/appeals-court-puts-on-hold-fcc-caps-on-prison-phone-call-charges/.

Glaze, L., Kaeble, D., Minton, T., & Tsoutis, A. (2015). *Correctional populations in the United States, 2014.* Washington, DC: Bureau of Justice Statistics.

Hamilton, Z. (2010). *Do reentry courts reduce recidivism?* New York: Center for Court Innovation.

Henrichson, C., & Delaney, R. (2012). *The price of prisons.* New York: Vera Institute of Justice.

Hochstetler, A., Murphy, D. S., & Simons, R. L. (2004). Damaged goods: Exploring predictors of distress in prison. *Crime & Delinquency, 50,* 436–457.

Irwin, J., and Cressey, D. (1962). Thieves, convicts, and the inmate culture. *Social Problems, 10,* 142–155.

Kaeble, D., Glaze, L., Tsoutis, A., & Minton, T. (2016). *Correctional populations in the United States, 2014.* Washington, DC: Bureau of Justice Statistics.

Kyckelhahan, T. (2012). *State corrections expenditures, FY 1982–2010.* Washington, DC: U.S. Government Printing Office, 7.

Lofstrom, M., & Raphael, S. (2013). *Impact of realignment on county jail populations.* San Francisco, CA: Public Policy Institute of California. Retrieved from http://www.ppic.org/content/pubs/report/R_613MLR.pdf.

MacDonald, M. (2013). Reducing California's overcrowded prison population. *Research Journal of Justice Studies and Forensic Science, 1,* 5–14.

Maruschak, L. M. (2015). *Medical problems of state and federal prisoners and jail inmates, 2011–12.* Washington, DC: Bureau of Justice Statistics.

Mason, C. (2012). *Too good to be true: Private prisons in America.* Retrieved from http://sentencingproject.org/wp-content/uploads/2016/01/Too-Good-to-be-True-Private-Prisons-in-America.pdf.

Mauer, M., & Ghandnoosh, N. (2014). *Fewer prisoners, less crime: A tale of three states.* Washington, DC: The Sentencing Project. Retrieved from http://sentencingproject.org/wp-content/uploads/2015/11/Fewer-Prisoners-Less-Crime-A-Tale-of-Three-States.pdf.

National Institute of Mental Health (n.d.). *Post-traumatic stress disorder.* Retrieved from http://www.nimh.nih.gov/health/topics/post-traumatic-stress-disorder-ptsd/index.shtml.

Noonan, M. E., & Mumola, C. J. (2007). *Veterans in state and federal prison, 2004.* Washington, DC: Bureau of Justice Statistics.

Ollove, M. (2016). *State prisons turn to telemedicine to improve health and save money.* The Pew Charitable Trusts. Retrieved from http://www.pewtrusts.org/en/research-and-analysis/blogs/stateline/2016/01/21/state-prisons-turn-to-telemedicine-to-improve.

Petersilia, J., & Snyder, J. G. (2013). Looking past the hype: 10 questions everyone should ask about California's prison realignment. *California Journal of Politics and Policy, 5,* 266–306.

The Pew Charitable Trusts (2014). *State prison health care spending: An examination.* Retrieved from http://www.pewtrusts.org/~/media/assets/2014/07/stateprisonhealthcarespendingreport.pdf.

Pew Center on the States (2011). *State of recidivism: The revolving door of America's prisons.* Washington, DC: The Pew Charitable Trusts. Retrieved from http://www.pewtrusts.org/en/research-and-analysis/reports/2011/04/12/state-of-recidivism-the-revolving-door-of-americas-prisons.

Pitts, J. M. A., Griffin, O. H., & Johnson, W. W. (2104). Contemporary prison overcrowding: Short-term fixes to a perpetual problem. *Contemporary Justice Review, 17,* 124–139.

Rabuy, B., & Wagner, P. (2015). *Screening out family time: The for-profit video visitation industry in prisons and jails.* Northampton, MA: The Prison Policy Initiative. Retrieved from http://static.prisonpolicy.org/visitation/ScreeningOutFamilyTime_January2015.pdf.

Renaud, J. A. (2014). *Video visitation: How private companies push for visits by video and families pay the price.* Retrieved from http://grassrootsleadership.org/sites/default/files/uploads/Video%20Visitation%20%28web%29.pdf.

Rikard, R. V., & Rosenberg, E. (2007). Aging inmates: A convergence of trends in the American criminal justice system. *Journal of Correctional Health Care, 13,* 150–162.

Smyer, T., & Burbank, P. M. (2009). The U.S. correctional system and the older prisoner. *Journal of Gerontological Nursing, 35,* 32–37.

Southern Poverty Law Center, (2016, March 16). Alabama agrees to improve conditions for inmates with disabilities following SPLC lawsuit. Retrieved from https://www.splcenter.org/news/2016/03/16/alabama-agrees-improve-conditions-inmates-disabilities-following-splc-lawsuit.

Spivak, A. L., & Sharp, S. F. (2008). Inmate recidivism as a measure of private prison performance. *Crime & Delinquency, 54,* 482–508.

Stephan, J. J., & Karberg, J. C. (2003). *Census of state and federal correctional facilities, 2000.* Washington, DC: Bureau of Justice Statistics.

Stephan, J. J. (2008). *Census of state and federal correctional facilities, 2005.* Washington, DC: Bureau of Justice Statistics.

Sykes, G. (1958). *The society of captives.* Princeton, NJ: Princeton University Press.

Thompson, C. (2014, December 18). *Everything you ever wanted to know about private prisons . . . is none of your damn business.* Retrieved from https://www.themarshallproject.org/2014/12/18/everything-you-ever-wanted-to-know-about-private-prisons#.uL6ZUmjJC.

Wilson, J., & Barboza, S. (2010). The looming challenges of dementia in corrections. *Correct Care, 24,* 12–14.

Zamble, E., & Quinsey, V. (1997). *The criminal recidivism process.* Cambridge, England: Cambridge University Press.

Zullo, R. (2016). *Food service privatization in Michigan's Prisons: Observations of corrections officers.* University of Michigan Institute for Research on Labor, Employment, and the Economy. Retrieved from http://irlee.umich.edu/?page=home.

Chapter Four

Gender Issues in Corrections

Carrie L. Buist and Emily Lenning

THE NATURE OF THE ISSUE

This chapter will highlight contemporary correctional issues relating to gender, particularly those issues that impact incarcerated women. Unique to this chapter will be our focus on the experiences of *all* women—both cisgender and transgender—in jails and prisons in the United States. Thus, before we broaden our discussion to the issues facing these women we feel it necessary to define the terms cisgender and transgender, which requires drawing attention to the differences between sex and gender. Quite simply put, sex describes how one is biologically born (i.e., genitalia, DNA) while gender is a social construct that is "characterized by outward presentation of masculinity, femininity, or anything in between" (Buist & Lenning, 2015, p. 4). Women and men whose gender identity is consistent with their biological sex are referred to as cisgender. Women who are biologically born male but whose gender identity, expression, and/or presentation are different than their biological sex are often referred to as transgender or transgender women, MTF (male-to-female), or transwomen. This is also true for biologically born women whose gender identity, expression, and/or presentation are different from their biological sex and are often referred to as transgender men, FTM (female-to-male), or transmen.

So, to be clear, cisgender and transgender women may have been biologically born different, but their gender identity is the same—they both identify as women. For transgender women this is true regardless of whether or not they have undergone sex reassignment. Due to the exorbitant costs associated with full gender transition (e.g., hormones, genital reconstruction, etc., costing in some cases up to $40,000), many transgender women live their entire lives without obtaining complete sex reassignment surgery (Lenning &

Buist, 2013). This is important to note since US jails and prisons typically classify inmates by sex and not gender, and many (if not all) transgender women serving time are housed in male facilities. The rare exception to this are jails that provide segregated wings for transgender inmates (Mathias, 2014). Regardless of whether or not transgender women have been receiving hormone therapy for 25 days or 25 years, and whether or not they have had breast implants, they will be placed in the prison that "matches" their genitals. So, while we discuss the similar and different experiences had by cisgender and transgender inmates throughout this chapter, it must be pointed out that they are having these experiences in two very different institutional contexts.

Transgender women are nearly invisible in the literature about incarcerated women and they are worthy of our attention because of the unique challenges they encounter while incarcerated, including issues regarding classification, housing, and medical care. Not only is our knowledge of the transgender offender and eventual inmate limited in the research literature, but on a societal level as well. This is because much of what the public knows about women—both cisgender and transgender—in prison comes from popular media. For instance, Laverne Cox's portrayal of Sophia Burset on the hit show *Orange is the New Black* is virtually the only point of reference that most people have when it comes to understanding transgender inmates. In fact, if you search the phrase "women in prison" on the popular media website YouTube, what you are most likely to find (mixed in with a documentary or two) are sexploitation films about women in prison. Movies such as *Caged Fury* (1990), *Vendetta* (1986), or the "women in prison triple feature" which includes the films *The Hot Box* (1972), *Escape from Hell* (1980), and *Women in Cell Block 7* (1973) are easy to access. These and other media images of women inmates have been overtly sexualized and in no way speak to the realities of life behind bars. The truth is that women in prison have very real experiences worthy of our attention that lead them to criminal offending, prosecution, and ultimately punishment.

Both cisgender and transgender women have been viewed somewhat as an anomaly, not only regarding incarceration and corrections, but more generally within criminal legal and criminological literature and research. Beginning with cisgender women, indeed, it was not until the late 1960s and 1970s when a women-focused criminology was first developed. Feminist criminology illustrates the experiences that are specific to women and girls and how those experiences may contribute to their criminality and ultimately their punishment, more specifically for some, incarceration. Further contributions to the field of feminist criminology include looking at gender as it relates to both women and men, girls and boys, and how "doing gender" may contribute to offending. As such, boys and men also experience gender and may express that gender through their behavior. This behavior is often couched within hegemonic and hyper-masculinity, which perpetuate the need for boys and men to "prove" their manhood (Connell, 1987; Messerschmidt, 1993). Hegemonic masculinity (culturally enforced male domination over women) is often illustrated through aggression or violence in an effort to assert dominance or control over someone who may be seen by the perpetrator as weaker. This is an important concept to introduce because we argue that it impacts the ways in which women experience violence both outside and inside the correctional setting and in turn how those experiences impact offending, adaptation and rehabilitation.

As we will discuss in more depth later in this chapter, women (both cisgender and transgender) experience higher percentages of abuse and violence in their lives prior to incarceration than do their (cis and trans) male counterparts. In addition to the abuse and violence that women experience at higher percentages than men, there are several other factors that we must take into account that impact women differently, either before, during, or after incarceration. These factors include but are not limited to: drug addiction, mental illness, poverty, pregnancy, mothering, and distance from loved ones. Not only do women have different experiences than men, women's experiences can differ greatly from each other. Intersecting identities like race, social class, and sexual orientation can differentially impact one's experiences and likelihood of interacting with the criminal legal system. Black women, for example, "are three times more likely to be in prison than are white women and twice as likely to be incarcerated as Hispanic women" (Britton, 2011, p. 72).

These aforementioned issues and more highlight the importance of recognizing that the institutional structure within the criminal legal system primarily caters to men. Within corrections, this is no surprise seeing as the vast majority of jail and prison inmates are men, but ignoring the needs of women offenders is not only problematic but can have longstanding implications. Conversely, some correctional strategies address women offenders as if they should be treated the same as men, or what Chesney-Lind (2002) refers to as "vengeful equity." At the structural level, the criminal legal system is designed by men for men and at the institutional level, correctional policies exemplify the influence that patriarchy has within the criminal legal system. Briefly defined, a patriarchy is a societal structure which values men over women, allows for the dominance of men over women, and values masculinity over femininity (see Renzetti, 2013). Additionally, Millet (1970, p. 25) emphasizes patriarchy's influence, noting that "every avenue of power within the society, including the coercive force of the police, is entirely in male hands." If we explore how patriarchy influences the criminal legal system, we can return to the previously introduced concept of hegemonic masculinity and how heteronormativity (favoring heterosexuality on the cultural level) and compulsory heterosexuality (heterosexuality that is assumed, mandated, and reinforced by social institutions) are present within jails and prisons. Bear in mind that prison is a normative system that not only operates based on rules and norms that are implemented through policy directives and carried out by administrators and other officials, but the jail and prison also operate using a normative system that is created and implemented by the inmates. This is true in both women's and men's prisons and the way in which the rules and norms develop and manifest varies, oftentimes based on gender. For instance, 57% of male inmates are incarcerated for a violent offense as opposed to only 34% of women (Carson, 2015; see also The Sentencing Project, 2015). This, obviously, impacts the administrative and inmate cultures that emerge in men's and women's facilities.

In brief, incarcerated women face challenges that differ from men in jails and prisons and those challenges must be recognized before the criminal legal system can develop and implement effective policy. This chapter will explore the research literature that considers factors unique to women in corrections including previous experiences, sexual assault, healthcare, pregnancy and mothering, and pseudo-families. Once we introduce and explore these topics we will offer insight into the issues and challenges facing women behind bars and future prospects regarding the concerns and needs of incarcerated women. But first, we discuss concerning trends in the incarceration of women offenders.

Trends

There is without a doubt an incarceration crisis of epic proportions in the United States. By the end of 2014 over 6.8 million Americans, or 1 in 36 adults, were under some sort of correctional supervision either in their communities or behind bars (Kaeble, Glaze, Tsoutis & Minton, 2015). This, shockingly, was the lowest rate of correctional supervision the US had seen since 1996. Of the 6.8 million Americans under correctional supervision in 2014, approximately 30% were serving time in state or federal prison or local jails; male adults are incarcerated at a rate of 1,169 (per 100,000), while female adults are incarcerated at a rate of 84 (Carson, 2015). While men are more likely to be serving time for violent and public order offenses, women are more likely to serve time for drug and property crimes (The Sentencing Project, 2015).

Though men represent the vast majority of incarcerated individuals, women's incarceration has seen alarming growth—a rate that has surpassed men by around 50% (The Sentencing Project, 2015). Indeed, the total number of women in prison increased by over 700% between 1980 and 2014, from less than 27,000 women to more than 215,000 (The Sentencing Project, 2015). Over half of those women are housed in federal prisons and 59% of them are serving time for drug offenses (Carson, 2015). While most incarcerated women are serving short sentences, nearly half of the women serving time behind bars are serving sentences of longer than one year, a trend currently on the incline (Carson, 2015). No doubt this incline is related to the disastrous sentencing policies that characterize the War on Drugs.

Not all women, of course, are equally represented behind bars. Hispanic women are over 1.2 times more likely to be incarcerated than white women, and African American women are more than twice as likely (The Sentencing Project, 2015). However, it is interesting to note that while the incarceration rate of African American women is on the decline, white women find themselves increasingly likely to be locked up (The Sentencing Project, 2015). Though the exact number of transgender women serving time is unknown, one large study (n = 6,450) of transgender and gender non-conforming individuals found that 16% of respondents reported having spent time in jail or prison (Grant, Mottet, Tanis, Harrison, Herman, & Keisling, 2011). Nearly half (47%) of black respondents in the same study reported serving time behind bars, and transgender women were twice as likely to experience incarceration as transgender men (Grant et al., 2011). Brown (2009) has estimated that there could be as few as two or as many as 400 transgender inmates in any one state prison at any time, and this estimate is not including jails.

Just as concerning as the number of women behind bars is the number of women who are tasked with successfully reentering society. Between 1990 and 2013, during which time the number of incarcerated women more than doubled, nearly 1.4 million women were released from prison (Mancini, Baker, Sainju, Golden, Bedard, & Gertz, 2016). Both the number of women behind bars and the number of women being released raise serious issues for concern, especially since a high percentage of these women have experienced poverty prior to their incarceration. Opportunities for successful reintegration into society, such as reentry programs, or access to jobs and housing are important factors to consider. In the following sections we will highlight the current research on the incarceration of women, focusing primarily on sexual assault, healthcare (with special attention given to how poverty impacts health in general), pregnancy and mothering, and pseudo-families. We will then turn our attention to current correctional policies, and consider the issues and challenges and future prospects that should be of central focus for correctional staff, reform advocates, and criminal legal scholars.

Current Research

Thanks to feminist criminology and, more recently, queer criminology, the issues facing incarcerated women have increasingly become a focus of both criminological research and public discourse. Broadly, queer criminology is "a theoretical and practical approach that seeks to highlight and draw attention to the stigmatization, the criminalization, and in many ways the rejection of the Queer community . . . as both victims and offenders, by academe and the criminal legal system" (Buist & Lenning, 2015, p. 1). Current research on cisgender and transgender women in jails and prisons continues to draw attention to the unique factors that women experience in their lives and while incarcerated. These experiences impact women differently than they do men and it is important to point out these differences, if for nothing else than for policy development and implementation within corrections.

Not only do women experience incarceration differently than men, cisgender women have unique experiences that transgender women do not, such as pregnancy and giving birth while incarcerated. There are, however, more commonalities between cisgender and transgender women than there are differences, such as being abused and at risk of sexual assault, living in poverty prior to incarceration, drug addiction, and access to healthcare before and during incarceration. As you read the forthcoming sections, it is important to keep in mind how many of these issues traverse and are related to one another. It is also important to remember that gender is not the only identity that impacts women's experiences behind bars. All experiences must be understood in the context of the varied intersecting identities that women embody, including but not limited to race, class, and sexual orientation.

First, it is important to realize that the current research on women in jails and prisons often focuses on the impact that their status as women has on their present experiences under correctional supervision. In short, past and current experiences impact current research. As previously mentioned, women face histories of physical and sexual abuse, and health issues that often stem from poverty, such as homelessness and drug addiction. Women also endure mental health problems such as higher percentages of depression and anxiety and for transwomen specifically who experience trauma, which is directly linked to their gender identity. Other healthcare issues that impact women differently than men are pregnancy and mothering and for transwomen who are incarcerated, hormonal therapy or sex reassignment surgery. All of these experiences impact the behaviors that women engage in (including criminal behavior), their likelihood of incarceration, their ability to adapt to life behind bars, and their ability to successfully reintegrate into society after incarceration. The proceeding sections will detail some of the most relevant issues women in jails and prison face: sexual assault, healthcare, pregnancy and mothering, and developing relationships, often called pseudo-families, with other incarcerated women.

Sexual Assault

Over half of incarcerated cisgender women have reported past physical or sexual abuse (Chesney-Lind, 2002; Harlow, 1999; Lynch, DeHart, Belknap,

& Green, 2012; Sentencing Project, 2007). Many young girls who experience abuse and violence in their homes run away and thus experience continued victimization which may contribute to offending (see Chesney-Lind & Shelden, 1998). Research also suggests that women in the criminal legal system report being abused both as girls and women, which is "significant because research on girl's and women's crime often exposes significant links between these traumatic experiences and behavior that later involves the criminal justice system" (Chesney-Lind, 2002, p. 84). Sadly, for some, the abuse continues while incarcerated. According to the 2011–2012 National Inmate Survey, 6.9% of female prison inmates report being sexually assaulted by another inmate, compared to only 1.9% of male inmates, with lesbian, gay and bisexual inmates being at 10 times the risk of their heterosexual counterparts (Beck, Berzofsky, Caspar, & Krebs, 2013). In regards to victimization by correctional staff, men (2.4%) and women (2.3%) report similar experiences, with non-heterosexual inmates being twice as likely to be victimized by correctional staff (Beck et al., 2013).

Transwomen in prison experience disproportionally high percentages of sexual assault with some research indicating that 20% of incarcerated transgender women report being the victim of sexual assault, with black transgender women (38%) being at the greatest risk (Grant et al., 2011). Other research conducted in three California state prisons found that in comparison to a random sample of over 300 cisgender male inmates where 4.4% reported being sexually assaulted, 59% of transgender inmates reported being victims of sexual assault (Jenness, Maxson, Matsuda, & Sumner, 2007).

Like their cisgender counterparts, most rapes against transgender women are reportedly committed by other inmates (Grant et al., 2011) although more current research has found alarmingly high rates of victimization at the hands of correctional staff (see Beck et al., 2013), and we must not forget that incarcerated transgender women who are assaulted by "other inmates" are assaulted by biological men, not other women. This is an important reminder because physical violence remains far less common in women's prisons than in male prisons. In fact, and perhaps not surprisingly, incarcerated men are more likely than women to cope with their issues using violence, because "male inmates subscribe to a normative system that holds that under certain circumstances a prisoner must respond with physical force" (Toch, 1998, p. 168). Toch (1998) uses an example from *Life Without Parole: Living and Dying in Prison Today*, a memoir written by Victor Hassine (2011), who details his experiences as an inmate serving life in prison. Hassine speaks to the necessity of using violence as a means of physical defense, to protect one's belongings, and to essentially show others that you are not weak and that you cannot be taken advantage of. Additionally, Johnson (2002) comments that violence in men's correctional institutions is not unusual in the prison setting and common too are acts of deception. In comparing what he calls the "slum streets" to the prison setting it "would appear to be that lying to and physically harming others are but behavioral cousins on a continuum of adaptive abuse" (Johnson, 2002, p. 91). This so-called "adaptive abuse" speaks to the (informal) normative system in the prison and the importance placed on asserting dominance and control, which in turn speaks to both the power of patriarchy and hegemonic masculinity as discussed earlier.

These issues, while problematic for men in prison, have a major impact on the experiences of transwomen in prison, as they are classified by their biological sex rather than their gender identity and thus are commonly housed in male prisons, making them arguably the most vulnerable population within the prison. Again, as hegemonic masculinity relates specifically to power and control and is closely related to both compulsory heterosexuality and heteronormativity we often see gender identity conflated with sexual orientation as transwomen are mistakenly perceived by other inmates as gay rather than transgender. Being labeled as gay in prison can be viewed as an affront to the hyper-masculine environment of the prison and, as incongruent as it may seem, contribute to the physical and sexual abuse of transwomen in prison. Despite the amount of physical violence transwomen in jails and prison experience including rape, prison officials rarely have policy in place to protect these women, with the exception of using solitary confinement as a means to keep them in protective custody. This is by and large a failure of the correctional branch of the criminal legal system and in direct opposition to policy that has been previously passed with the Prison Rape Elimination Act (PREA) of 2003 which states that prisoners should not be isolated or segregated in order to keep them safe. Some may believe that segregating transgender inmates is the only option currently available in the jail and prison settings, but officials must keep in mind the detrimental impact this segregation plays on all inmates. First, being segregated in prison is considered a punishment for an inmate's behavior and is often used for violent inmates—some consider solitary confinement or segregation to be a prison within a prison. Here, inmates are on lock down for up to 23 hours per day. Further, research has shown that prolonged isolation can have severe psychological effects such as "paranoia, inability to control emotions, increased risk of suicide, and hallucinations" (Buist & Lenning, 2015, p. 97). Certainly, potential effects of segregation can impact all prisoners, but special attention should be paid to segregation of transgender inmates especially if they are being segregated to protect them from being victimized. Also, since transgender inmates already have higher rates of mental health issues, segregating them from the general population and socialization that comes with that could potentially exacerbate those issues.

It is important to also note that past trauma and victimization has long-lasting effects on the survivors of sexual assault and abuse. For instance, women who have experienced this victimization in the past can suffer from post-traumatic stress disorder, or can be re-victimized while incarcerated because of particular policy or procedures such as strip searches (George, 2015). In addition to traumatic events such as sexual assault and abuse, it is important to note the impact of other past experiences that play a role in women's lives that can lead to offending and eventual punishment. The next section will highlight issues related to women's healthcare in jail and prison settings. One major issue is the impact of socioeconomic status and how living in poverty can lead to or further intensify health issues for women outside of prison and in turn effect women once they have been incarcerated. When folks are living in poverty, some of them without basic necessities like shelter, there is an increased likelihood that the experience of being poor will impact the factors involved with offending, eventual reentry, possible recidivism, and a myriad of other issues, like lack of positive familial bonding and socialization.

Healthcare

Transgender individuals often find obtaining healthcare difficult. Many face problems associated with the long-term care that identifying as transgender necessitates such as counseling for mental health concerns, obtaining hormone treatment, and, for some, eventual sex reassignment surgery. These costs can be extraordinary and we have seen transgender individuals search for other methods to obtain these services often times outside of the United States where costs are less expensive, or through illegally obtaining medication and services (Lenning & Buist, 2013). The cost of these healthcare expenses would be difficult for most, but because we have found that many transgender people experience socioeconomic challenges the costs are exacerbated and may very well contribute to the aforementioned obstacles in obtaining proper and legal health care.

The challenges of socioeconomic disadvantage also disproportionately impact cisgender women as well. Research has indicated that women often bring with them health issues and concerns once they enter the prison (Fearn & Parker, 2005). Additionally, the Bureau of Justice Statistics found that, "among state and federal inmates current medical problems were most commonly reported by those who were homeless in the year before arrest, who used a needle to inject drugs, and who reported receiving government assistance as compared to those who had not been homeless, who had not used a needle to inject drugs, and who did not receive government assistance" (Marschak, 2004, n.p.).

Regarding transgender women, being without a home and familial support may also contribute to offending as one in five trans youth, or 20 to 40%, experience homelessness in their lives (Tobin, Freedman-Gurspan, & Mottet, 2015). This homelessness may be the result of being kicked out of their homes because of their gender identity or fleeing from their homes because of abuse or violence. Wilber (2015, p. 11) has also noted that LGBQ, gender nonconforming, and transgender youth are disproportionately represented in the criminal legal system, noting that this population is "represented in the juvenile justice system at a rate close to three times higher than their percentage in the general population" which speaks to the cycle of violence. In general, the transgender community as a whole are incarcerated at disproportionate rates and for longer periods of time (Tobin et al., 2015).

Nijhawan, Salloway, Nunn, Poshkus and Clarke (2010) found that for cisgender women in prison, health indictors related to poverty and poor healthcare prior to incarceration. They note that "nearly one fourth of respondents reported being homeless, and more than half (56%) did not have health insurance before incarceration" (Nijhawan et al., 2010, p. 19). They go on to indicate that over 80% of their participants reported a mental health problem and 76% reported issues with drug or alcohol dependency (Nijhawan et al., 2010). Injection drug use was also found to be a major problem for women who are incarcerated, which could lead to riskier sexual behavior and in turn contribute to the high rates of women in prison who report having HIV, which is both higher than the general population and higher than male inmates in state prisons (Nijhawan et al., 2010).

As seen with cisgender inmates, poor healthcare follows transgender inmates from the streets to the correctional facilities that they are housed in as well. Not surprisingly, Sexton, Jenness, and Sumner (2010) found that the transwomen they interviewed in California prisons reported higher rates of homelessness, especially immediately before their incarceration. With further similarity to cisgender women in prison, the trans inmates in their study reported higher rates of mental health issues, substance abuse, and HIV/ AIDS infection.

Maruschak (2004) further reported that cisgender inmates are more likely to report medical problems than men who are incarcerated. Although this does not necessarily mean that women experience more medical issues than men in prison, it does indicate that because of the increased likelihood for women to report illness or health concerns there would be an increased need for medical treatment. Even though it would be difficult at best to assess the needs of all inmates regardless of sex or gender identity, we can safely claim that cisgender women and transgender women do have different medical needs than men. For instance, cisgender and post-operative transgender inmates require gynecological care and transgender women inmates often require hormonal therapy. In most prisons, a transgender inmate must be diagnosed with what was formerly known as Gender Identity Disorder (now Gender Dysphoria), in order to receive medical care specific to their transgender identity or to maintain a drug protocol (Brown, 2009). As previously mentioned, this can prove problematic for transgender inmates who, while identifying as women for what could be decades, may have never received an official diagnosis from a doctor or received their hormones legally or on a regular basis.

While it appears that the majority of cisgender women in prison are at the very least given physical exams upon entry and other routine care when incarcerated, results from the National Transgender Discrimination Survey found that 16% of male-to-female transgender inmates were denied "regular healthcare" while incarcerated. Additionally, 24% reported being denied hormone therapy (Grant et al., 2011). This denial of health care blatantly goes against the Supreme Court's ruling that "the government has an obligation to provide medical care to inmates" (Fearn & Parker, 2005, p. 6). While there has been a move to institute proper medical care and treatment for transgender inmates, these policies are often slow to be implemented, and again, transgender inmates still require a diagnosis to receive transition-related medical care. Although, we have seen some positive changes, like a move away from the "freeze-frame" policy, which prevented transgender inmates from starting any care related to their transition such as hormone therapy if they could not prove that they had begun treatment prior to being incarcerated (Glezer, McNeil, & Binder, 2013; Buist & Lenning, 2016). Sex reassignment surgery for transgender inmates is a topic rife for debate and we have seen more denials for surgery than surgeries granted with only one state (California) recently setting guidelines for sex reassignment surgeries for inmates.

Aside from the needs that transgender women have, perhaps the greatest health concern that women experience unique from male inmates are their reproductive needs. The next section will explore pregnancy and mothering in prison and how these issues impact both mothers and their children.

Pregnancy and Mothering

Just over 4% of the women entering prison or jail are pregnant, which is about 9,000 women at any given time, and over three-quarters of the women behind bars are mothers (US Department of Health & Human Services, 2012). Thus, incarcerated women experience a range of unique issues related to mothering, from being pregnant and giving birth behind bars, to raising children from a distance, to returning home to children who have experienced the absence of a parent. These experiences raise a host of physical, mental, and emotional issues, beginning with the health risks they face during pregnancy and childbirth.

Prenatal care is grossly inadequate in jails and prisons (McCoy-Grubb & del Carmen, 2016). This is in large part due to the paucity of resources dedicated to care for pregnant inmates and especially concerning given the high-risk nature of most inmate pregnancies, to include drug addiction and sexually transmitted diseases (McCoy-Grubb et al., 2016). The vast majority of US states do not require correctional authorities to provide pregnant in-mates with nutrition counseling, screenings for high-risk factors, or to make advance delivery arrangements with local hospitals (The Rebecca Project, 2010). In fact, basic medical exams are not compulsory as part of prenatal care in forty-three states (The Rebecca Project, 2010). Nevertheless, even though there are more pregnant inmates in jail than in prison, prison inmates are more likely than jail inmates to receive obstetric exams and other preg-nancy related care (US Department of Health and Human Services, 2012).

One of the most controversial issues regarding pregnant inmates is the use of shackles (handcuffs, leg cuffs, and belly bracelets) during both pregnancy and the birthing process. The use of shackles persists despite the fact that there is little disagreement that such practices are "degrading, barbaric, hu-miliating, and life threatening to both mother and child" (Griggs, 2012, p. 253). Only six states expressly prohibit restraining inmates during labor and delivery (The Rebecca Project, 2010), but evidence suggests that even in those states there is not enough oversight to ensure compliance (Roth & Bullock, 2016). Some may argue that shackling is necessary in order to prevent escape, however, as of this writing there have been no such reported cases of attempted escape of pregnant women before or during the birthing process.

As for issues related specifically to mothering, at least eight US states allow qualifying mothers to care for their newborn children for a period of 30 days to two years in segregated nurseries within the prison (Carlson 2009; Goshin, Byrne & Blanchard-Lewis, 2014). These programs support a very small number of inmates and are a relatively new part of the correctional landscape, making data scarce. Nevertheless, reviews of the programs that do exist show positive results. For example, the program in Nebraska, which allows 15 women to care for their children for up to 18 months, shows a 33.2% decrease in recidivism for participants in comparison to their pregnant peers who were not eligible to participate (Carlson, 2009). Positive effects on recidivism aside, the bond between mother and child is worthy of attention for, if no other reason, the child's development and emotional well-being.

While little is known about the long-term effects of maternal incarcera-tion on a child, two recent studies using the National Longitudinal Survey of Adolescent Health suggest that maternal incarceration can have a long-term effect on children (Burgess-Proctor, Huebner, & Durso, 2016; Muftic, Bouf-fard, & Armstrong, 2016). While both studies found that the children of incarcerated mothers were twice as likely to experience arrest, conviction, and incarceration as adults, Burgess-Proctor et al. (2016) point out that the effect of maternal incarceration has a stronger impact than does paternal incarceration, and that the impact is gendered—that is, girls experience more negative outcomes when their mother is incarcerated, and boys when their fathers serve time behind bars. Nevertheless, it is the incarceration of any parent (regardless of gender) that has the most statistically significant impact.

As briefly mentioned at the onset of this chapter, one major issue that mothers and their children encounter is the distance between them, which can make visitation difficult at best. This is also true in a more general sense for all women who are incarcerated. The lack of positive socialization and family life may be bridged within the jail and prison settings by developing positive relationships with other inmates. These connections are unique to women in prison and while some have argued that these relationships are not always positive and supportive, the bulk of the research indicates that they are indeed, supportive relationships for women in prison.

Pseudo-Families

Women are often said to be more social than men and, in turn, demonstrate a greater need to form relationships. This is true within the prison setting as well through the development of what is commonly referred to as pseudo-families, which are tightly bonded networks of women who take on various family member roles (i.e., mother, father, siblings, aunts and uncles, grand-parents, etc.). These relationships are developed for a variety of reasons, but often serve to develop friendship or familial relationships within the jail or prison setting in an attempt to quell the loneliness that one experiences while incarcerated.

The concept of the pseudo-family is often credited to Selling (1931) who identified several different types of pseudo-family relationships in girls' correctional institutions. Although he focused much attention on what he considered different stages of homosexuality (lesbianism, pseudo-homosexuality, mother and daughter relationship and friendship), not all of the relationships he focused on were sexual in nature. In short, he concluded that pseudo-families do exist within the institutional setting and essentially can manifest themselves in a variety of ways. One such way, according to a later examination of the concept, posited that these family structures were constructed for economic purposes (Heffernan, 1972). Certainly these relationships could prove economically beneficial within jail and prison such as allowing for shared commissary items. More recently, Forsyth and Evans (2003) concluded that pseudo-families function in a myriad of ways in addition to economic support, including as a means to provide emotional support. However, their research contends that pseudo-families for women may be more similar to gangs in a men's prison, and that continued focus on gender differences blinds the interpretation of the socialization (Forsyth & Evans 2003). While the authors state that they are not advocating for a return to male-centered criminological research, they are clearly advocating for less emphasis to be placed on the differences between women and men inmates, which we deem to be problematic at best.

Laura Bedard (2008), a former jail administrator and the first woman Deputy Secretary of the Florida Department of Corrections, has indicated that pseudo-families can vary in size, consisting of up to 20 members, and that the racial makeup of the families is often diverse. The families can be made up of women who take on a variety of family roles such as parents, children, siblings, and grandparents. Gender identity and presentation may play a role in the construction of these families as well, with women who appear more masculine in appearance often taking on the role of father, grandfather, son, or brother. In speaking directly to differences between women and men inmates Bedard (2008) clearly states that "research tells us that women come to prison for different reasons than men—they also bring a unique set of circumstances."

Recent work by Sexton and Jenness (2016) explores collective identity and collective efficacy among transgender women in California prisons. The authors mention early research from Sykes (1956) who posited that relationships in prison were often violent and manipulative, which speaks to Forsyth and Evan's (2003) stance that pseudo-families for women mirror gangs for men. However, much like the depth of research that highlights the potentially positive influence of familial relationships in prison, Sexton and Jenness' work delves deeper into the importance of community for transgender women housed in male prisons. They explore the concept of collective identity, which often implies some degree of commonality within or between groups or how someone does or does not identify with a particular group. For instance, not every transgender inmate will feel as though they identify with other transgender inmates simply because an individual is both transgender and an inmate.

Collective efficacy "is commonly conceptualized as having two components: (a) social cohesion and trust (SCT) and (b) informal social control (ISC). SCT measures commitment to a group and its members, while ISC measures expectations that one can depend on group members to intervene for the good of the group" (Sexton & Jenness, 2016, p. 5). In their research, Sexton and Jenness analyze this concept at the individual level. Although the transgender population is diverse (again, remembering that what is true for one may not be true for all) Sexton and Jenness' (2016, p. 16) findings indicate "relatively high levels of both collective identity and perceived collective efficacy." This particular research shows us that while the bonds between transgender women in male prisons may differ from the traditional pseudo-families that we see in women's correctional facilities, there is still a need to form similar connections with other inmates, with some of the participants in their research referring to each other as "family" (Sexton & Jenness, 2016, p. 17).

Additional commonalities between the experiences of cisgender and transgender women inmates is that while they may seek group relationships while in prison they are still part of the larger population of inmates within the prison. Regardless of identity, these folks are under correctional supervision and may indeed relate to other inmates simply because they are part of the environment. However, there is a greater need to find others who can provide a sense of community and family bonds which may be constructed and developed for a number of reasons. These bonds that are forged appear to be for very different reasons than the bonds that are formed between cisgender men in male prisons.

Returning to the impact of distance, for cisgender women in jails and prisons, we must keep in mind that because they represent just about seven percent of those incarcerated, there are fewer facilities in the country to house them. Therefore, this could mean that family members and friends need to travel hundreds of miles to visit, a problem exacerbated by poverty and likely explanatory of the types of relationships women form behind bars. Moreover, for transgender women serving time in male prisons, forming relationships with other transgender inmates may provide an understanding and acceptance that they do not experience inside prison and likely failed to experience prior to incarceration.

POLICIES

Many of the issues outlined above can be addressed through policy reform, beginning with improving the instruments used to classify women inmates prior to incarceration. Current classification systems are problematic for both cisgender and transgender women, for very different reasons. For cisgender women the problem is rooted in the fact that most classification systems were developed for men and thus are unresponsive to the unique needs of women (Salisbury, Van Voorhis, & Spriopoulos, 2009). Typically, classification systems take into account an inmate's potential risk factors (i.e., propensity toward misconduct) and their potential treatment needs. While these are both important issues to consider, they cannot be measured the same for men and women offenders, so to use the same classification instrument for men and women yields insufficient results. Classification systems that were designed with men in mind, for example, do not take into account the unique prior experiences of women that we discussed earlier and thus do not accurately assess their needs, which can result in overclassification (Van Voorhis, Wright, Salisbury, & Bauman, 2010).

In addition to issues relating to classification of inmates in jails and prison, gender-responsive techniques have been suggested in order to benefit women behind bars who, as previously mentioned, experience higher levels of past trauma and sexual victimization. King and Foley (2014) suggest that gender-responsive strategies and policy implementation is necessary within corrections, yet we rarely see such policies implemented. Gender-responsive strategies focus on the "design of the program, practice, or policy that addresses the specific circumstances of women's lives, their unique risk and need factors, and research on women that guides policy/practice" (King & Foley, 2014, p. 2). Those specific circumstances involve all of the factors discussed in this chapter such as mental health, substance abuse, past trauma, and overall healthcare. For instance, with such a high percentage of women in prison experiencing past sexual victimization and perhaps current victimization while in jail or prison, authorities should be aware of existing methods and policies that could have a negative impact on the women and in turn re-victimize them, such as strip searches (see George, 2015; King & Foley, 2014).

While we agree with King and Foley (2014) that we cannot unilaterally apply the same policies to both men and women, we would argue that their work highlights an even bigger issue in the debate on gender-responsive policies—namely that the policies considered by researchers and correctional authorities to be gender-responsive policies are indeed not *gender*-responsive at all, but are rather *sex*-responsive and are consistently discussed only in the context of meeting the needs of cisgender women in prison. To truly have gender-responsive policies would mean that transgender women were subject to the same policies as cisgender women, not the same as the men with whom they are currently housed. Ultimately, correctional policies for women must be both sex-responsive (e.g., policies that support healthy pregnancies) and gender-responsive (e.g., policies that support healthy gender transition).

ISSUES AND CHALLENGES

While incarceration poses issues for both cisgender and transgender inmates, and those tasked with overseeing them, we would argue that (at present) the challenges faced by transgender inmates are extremely complex and in many ways far more dangerous (emotionally and physically) than challenges faced by their cisgender counterparts. Moreover, their experiences are much less understood by criminologists. As previously mentioned, just as feminist criminology drew much needed attention to the experiences of girls and women in the criminal legal system, the development of queer criminology is in the early stages of doing the same regarding LGBTQ folks in the United States and abroad.

Though it is far from catching up to the impact that feminist criminology has made, queer criminology's influence has been gaining recognition and we are beginning to see a greater body of research on not only the LGBTQ experience in the criminal legal system, but specifically on the experiences of transgender inmates. This is an important step, as this particular topic presents many barriers to researchers such as gaining access to prisoners, the fact that prisoners are considered a protected class, and that researching the population requires additional permissions from human subject review boards. Thus, the work that we have underscored in this chapter is wholly important and highlights not only the issues that transgender women face in prison, but also provides insight to the issues and challenges that are faced by researchers as well.

As the prison landscape shifts, so must the trajectory of our research. Despite some evidence that responses to correctional issues must be gender-responsive, scholars agree that much more research is needed (e.g., Gover, Perez, & Jennings, 2008; Salisbury et al., 2009; Van Voohris et al., 2010). Though we need to continue to explore gendered issues (and not just those related to sex), we must also move beyond gender as the primary focus of our research to privilege intersectionality. It is true that gender can predict great differences in behavior, likelihood of arrest and conviction, sentencing, etc., but gender alone does not paint the entire picture. All women are defined by and experience life through the lens of their multiple identities, and feminist and queer criminologies (and ideally all criminologies) must continue to expand the scope of their inquiry.

FUTURE PROSPECTS

The United States cannot—and should not—sustain the cycle of mass incarceration that has come to define us to the rest of the world. We must address the alarming growth in female incarceration and reduce the number of women serving time behind bars. We should do this not only by addressing the prior experiences that lead women to crime (and incidentally are those experiences that lead them to recidivate), but also by promoting a conversation about the decriminalization of some behaviors and the more frequent implementation of non-carceral responses to crime.

In recent years there has been bipartisan movement to highlight the problems associated with continuing to incarcerate non-violent offenders. The discussion often focuses on non-violent drug offenders and how punishing those offenders with jail and prison sentences continues to fuel the incarceration binge in the United States, with little to no rehabilitative effectiveness. However, there has been no real discussion in the United States regarding issues of drug law reform or a change in how drug addiction for example should be addressed. For instance, how effective could it be in reducing incarceration in the United States if we decriminalized drug use and instead treated addiction via a medical model as opposed to a criminal legal model?

This speaks to how we punish. In fact, in the United States, "drug policies emphasize a punitive rather than rehabilitative response to substance abuse and addiction, they fail to address the actual cause of the illness, which only exacerbates the disease and results in relapse and recidivism" (McCray, 2012).

However, we continue to see the answer to criminal offending to be incapacitating the offenders in an often frivolous attempt to deter future behavior, however, with few legitimate opportunities outside of the carceral setting, incapacitating offenders' vis-a-vis incarceration has failed not only the incarcerated, but society as a whole as members of society continue to pay personal and financial costs for the cycle of incarceration. As recently as March of 2016 Barack Obama, speaking at the National Prescription Drug Abuse and Heroin Summit was quoted as saying that "for too long we've viewed drug addiction through the lens of criminal justice . . . the most important thing to do is reduce demand. And the only way to do that is to provide treatment—to see it as a public health problem and not a criminal problem" (as cited in Pratt, 2016). Additionally, research from the National Institutes of Health (2010) has stated that treating rather than punishing drug addiction reduces recidivism rates and is more cost effective than prison.

In a more general sense, there must be added attention given to the societal problems of deprivation that women experience at disproportional rates. Just as the investment in and access to education has long been an argument as a means to decrease the overall incarceration rate in this country, there must be a focus on legitimate opportunity once women are released from prison. Like men, cisgender and transgender women face a host of challenges prior to incarceration and upon leaving prison and reentering society, including underemployment or unemployment, lack of housing, insufficient social services, unrealistic post-supervision requirements, strained family reintegration, the reintroduction of previous negative stimuli (e.g., drugs, criminal peers), and community stigmatization. If up to 40% of trans folks experience homelessness in the United States and one in five (19%) of trans people are discriminated against in housing (Tobin et al., 2015), imagine the obstacles formerly incarcerated transwomen may face when trying to establish a legal residence once paroled or released from jail or prison. If one in four transgender people have been fired because of their gender identity and three fourths have reported some level of discrimination on-the-job (Tobin et al., 2015), imagine the odds of gainful employment for a transwoman who has a prison record.

This continues to make reentry and reintegration difficult upon release from prison. Instead, perhaps we should begin to seriously consider more cost effective non-carceral responses to crime including community corrections, which typically cost less than the average yearly expenditure per inmate which ranges from just over $28,000 to just above $41,000 (Kyckelhahn, [2012] 2014). While the average cost per inmate per year in the United States averages just under $30,000 a year, the annual cost of supervision by probation officers is approximately $3,347.41 (United States Courts, 2013). Although significantly higher than probation supervision, residential reentry centers are still more cost effective per year, averaging approximately three thousand dollars less annually.

CONCLUSION

Punishments and policies in corrections are often couched within the male experience. Little to no consideration is given to the unique factors that contribute to women offending that we have highlighted in this chapter. Factors and experiences that include physical and sexual abuse, and a myriad of healthcare related issues linked to experiences with poverty, drug abuse, HIV/AIDS, and mental illness. Women in prison are more likely to go long periods of time, perhaps their entire sentences, without seeing their loved ones because of the distance between where they have lived and where they are incarcerated. This is especially troubling for women who have children and the children themselves. Unlike the use of gang involvement in men's jails and prisons, the pseudo-family for women is unique and often indicative of positive familial relationships for women while they are incarcerated.

These previously mentioned factors are important to consider and take into account when studying incarcerated women, but many of these issues could be explored on their own. For instance, the disproportional impact that solitary confinement has on transwomen is of great importance for transgender women who are suffering in men's prisons, but the topic of solitary confinement in and of itself is one that should be addressed within corrections as a whole. The same can be said for issues regarding abuse, neglect, rape, drug use, and overall health issues that we continue to see time and again in the jail and prison settings. However, we cannot treat women like they are men and believe that we will achieve the same outcomes. Additionally, as we continue to address issues related to gender, we must identify that many of these "gender-responsive strategies" are rooted in sex-specific stereotypes of women and men. For instance, it is not uncommon to see programs in women's prison that teach women how to become a cosmetologist and in men's prisons programs that teach them how to become a welder. This is fine for some women and some men, but do these sex-specific programs fail the correctional clients in more ways than one? Who is more likely to make a higher wage upon release—a cosmetologist or a welder? Even if we were to address the problems related to these types of sex-specific policies and programs, we would still fail to meet the needs of transgender women.

As we mentioned at the forefront of this discussion, this chapter is unique from other inquiries about women behind bars because of our focus on *all* women. In doing so we have considered the commonalities that cisgender and transgender women face and exposed their differences. Consequently, it has become clear that there is so much more we have to learn if we are to truly address the over-incarceration of women and its consequences. It is true that the research we have highlighted only scratches the surface of what knowledge already exists, but it also reveals that there is much more work to be done. Most importantly, this work must be used to inform positive correctional reform for *all* of the women who are currently incarcerated and for those who may someday find themselves facing carceral punishment.

DISCUSSION QUESTIONS

1. What is the difference between cisgender and transgender women, and why is it important that we understand the experiences that both face behind bars?
2. How do incarceration rates differ for men and women in the United States? How do incarceration rates differ for women of different racial identities?
3. According to the research, what are the issues that transgender and cisgender inmates experience similarly and differently from each other?
4. When it comes to understanding women's experiences in prison, what challenges and issues do researchers face and/or need to consider?
5. What needs to be done in the future if we are to address the mass incarceration of women?

REFERENCES

American Psychiatric Association. (2013). Gender dysphoria. *Diagnostic and statistical manual of mental disorders* (5th ed.). Washington, DC: American Psychiatric Association.

Beck, A. J., Berzofsky, M., Caspar, R., & Krebs, C. (2013). *Sexual victimization in prisons and jails reported by inmates, 2011–12*. Washington, DC: Bureau of Justice Statistics.

Bedard, L. E. (2008, July 1). Making a difference: Managing the female offender population. *Corrections Today*. Retrieved from http://www.correctionsone.com/corrections/articles/1842846-Making-a-difference-Managing-the-female-offender-population/.

Bedard, L. E. (2009, October 2009). The pseudo-family phenomenon in women's prisons. *Corrections Today*. Retrieved from http://www.correctionsone.com/jail-management/articles/1956587-The-pseudo-family-phenomenon-in-womens-prisons/.

Belknap, J. (2001). *The invisible woman: Gender, crime, and justice*. Belmont, CA: Wadsworth, Thomson.

Britton, D. M. (2011). *The gender of crime*. Lanham, MD: Rowman & Littlefield

Brown, G. R. (2009). Recommended revisions to the World Professional Association for transgender health's standards of care section on medical care for incarcerated persons with gender identity disorder. *International Journal of Transgenderism, 11*(2), 133–39.

Buist, C. L., & Lenning, E. (2015). *Queer criminology*. New York: Routledge.

Carlson, J. R. (2009). Prison nurseries: A pathway to crime-free futures. *Corrections Compendium, 34*, 17–24.

Carson, A. (2015). *Prisoners in 2014*. Washington, DC: Bureau of Justice Statistics.

Chesney-Lind, M., & Shelden, R. G. (1998). *Girls, delinquency, and juvenile justice*. Belmont, CA: Wadsworth.

Chesney-Lind, M. (2002). *Imprisoning women: The unintended victims of mass imprisonment*. In M. Mauer and M. Chesney-Lind (Eds.), Invisible Punishment: The collateral consequences of mass imprisonment (pp. 79–94). New York: The New Press

Connell. R.W. (1987). *Gender and power*. Stanford, CA: Stanford University Press.

Fearn, N. E., & Parker, K. (2005). Health care for women inmates: Issues, perceptions and policy considerations. *Californian Journal of Health Promotion, 3*, 1–22.

Forsyth, C. J., & Evans, R. D. (2003). Reconsidering the pseudo-family/gang gender distinction in prison research. *Journal of Police and Criminal Psychology, 18*, 15–23.

George, E. (2015). *A woman doing life: Notes from a prison for women*. In R. Johnson and A. B. Martin (Eds.). New York: Oxford University Press.

Glezer, A., McNeil, D. E., & Binder, R. L. (2013). Correctional populations in the United States. U.S. Department of Justice: Bureau of Justice Statistics.

Goshin, L. S., Byrne, M. W., & Blanchard-Lewis, B. (2014). Preschool outcomes of children who lived as infants in a prison nursery. *The Prison Journal, 94*, 139–158.

Grant, J., Mottet, L., Tanis, J., Harrison, J., Herman, J. L., & Keisling, M. (2011). *Injustice at every turn: A report of the national transgender discrimination survey*. Retrieved from http://www.thetaskforce.org/static_html/downloads/reports/reports/ntds_full.pdf.

Griggs, C. L. (2012). Birthing barbarism: The unconstitutionality of shackling pregnant prisoners. *American University Journal of Gender, Social Policy & the Law, 20*, 247–271.

Gover, A. R., Perez, D. M., & Jennings, W.G. (2008). Gender differences in factors contributing to institutional misconduct. *The Prison Journal, 88*, 378–403.

Harlow, C. W. (1999). Prior abuse reported by inmates and probationers. U.S. Department of Justice: Bureau of Justice Statistics.

Hassine, V. (2011). *Life without parole: Living and dying in prison today*. New York: Oxford University Press.

Heffernan, E. (1972). *Making it in prison: The square, the cool, and the life*. New York: Wiley.

Jenness, V., & Fenstermaker, S. (2016). Forty years after Brownmiller: Prisons for men, transgender inmates, and the rape of the feminine. *Gender & Society, 30*, 14–29.

Jenness, V., Maxson, C. L., Matsuda, K. N., & Sumner, J. (2007). *Violence in California correctional facilities: An empirical examination of sexual assault. Report to the California Department of Corrections and Rehabilitation*. Irvine, CA: University of California, Irvine.

Johnson, R. (2002). *Hard time: Understanding and reforming the prison*. Belmont, CA: Wadsworth.

Kaeble, D., Glaze, L., Tsoutis, A., & Minton, T. (2015). *Correctional populations in the United States, 2014*. Washington, DC: Bureau of Justice Statistics.

King, E., & Foley, J. E. (2014). Gender-responsive policy development in corrections: What we know and roadmaps for change. Washington, DC: National Institute of Corrections. Retrieved from https://s3.amazonaws.com/static.nicic.gov/Library/029747.pdf.

Kyckelhahn, T. (2012). *State corrections expenditures, FY 1982–2010*. Washington, DC: Bureau of Justice Statistics.

Lenning, E., & Buist, C. L. (2013). Social, psychological & economic challenges faced by transgender individuals and their significant others: Gaining insight through personal narratives. *Culture, Health & Sexuality, 15*, 44–57.

Lynch, S., DeHart, D., Belknap, J., & Green, B. (2012). Women's pathways to jail: The roles & intersections of serious mental illness & trauma. U.S. Department of Justice: Bureau of Justice Assistance.

Mancini, C., Baker, T., Sainju, K. D., Golden, K., Bedard, L. E., & Gertz, M. (2016). Examining external support received in prison and concerns about reentry among incarcerated women. *Feminist Criminology, 11*, 163–190.

Maruschak, L. M. (2004). Medical problems of prisoners. Washington, DC: Bureau of Justice Statistics.

Mathias, C. (2014, November 18). New York's largest jail to open housing unit for transgender women. *Huffington Post.* Retrieved from http://www.huffingtonpost.com/2014/11/18/rik-ers-transgender-women_n_6181552.html.

McCoy-Grubb, L., & del Carmen, R. V. (2016). An analysis of court decisions, statutes, and administrative regulations related to pregnant inmates. *The Prison Journal, 96,* 355–391.

McCray, R. (2012). *Treating addiction as a disease, not a crime. ACLU Criminal Law Reform Project.* Retrieved from https://www.aclu.org/blog/treating-addiction-disease-not-crime.

Messerschmidt, J. (1993). *Masculinities and crime: Critique and reconceptualization of theory.* Lanham, MD: Rowman & Littlefield.

Millet, K. (1970). *Sexual politics.* Chicago, IL: University of Illinois Press.

Muftic, L. R., Bouffard, L. A., & Armstrong, G. S. (2016). Impact of maternal incarceration on the criminal justice involvement of adult offspring: A research note. *Journal of Research in Crime & Delinquency, 53,* 93–111.

National Institute of Health. (2010). *Addiction and the criminal justice system.* Washington, DC: U.S. Department of Health & Human Services. Retrieved from https://report.nih.gov/ nihfactsheets/ViewFactSheet.aspx?csid=22.

Nijhawan, A. E., Salloway, R., Nunn, A. S., Poshkus, M., & Clarke, J. G. (2010) Preventative healthcare for underserved women: Results of a prison survey. *Journal of Women's Health, 19,* 17–22.

Pratt, T. (2016, March 29). Obama: "Drug addiction is a health problem, not a criminal prob-lem." *The Guardian.* Retrieved from http://www.theguardian.com/us-news/2016/mar/29/ba-rack-obama-drug-addiction-health-problem-not-criminal-problem.

The Rebecca Project. (2010). *Mothers behind bars: A state-by-state report card and analysis of federal policies on conditions of confinement for pregnant and parenting women and the effect on their children.* Washington, DC: National Women's Law Center.

Renzetti. C. (2013). *Feminist criminology.* New York: Routledge.

Roth, R. & Bullock, M. (2016). *Breaking promises: Violations of the Massachusetts pregnancy standards & anti-shackling law.* Retrieved from http://theprisonbirthproject.org/wp-content/ uploads/2016/05/Breaking-Promises_May2016.pdf.

Ross, P. H., & Lawrence, J. E. (1998). Health care for women offenders. *Corrections Today, 60,* 122–129.

Salisbury, E. J., Van Voorhis, P., & Spiropoulos, G. V. (2009). The predictive validity of a gender-responsive needs assessment: An exploratory study. *Crime & Delinquency, 55,* 550–585.

Selling, L. S. (1931). The pseudo family. *American Journal of Sociology, 37,* 247–253.

The Sentencing Project. (2015). Fact sheet: incarcerated women and girls. Retrieved from http:/ /www.sentencingproject.org/wp-content/uploads/2016/02/Incarcerated-Women-and-Girls.pdf.

Sexton, L., & Jenness, V. (2016). "We're like community": Collective identity and collective efficacy among transgender women in prisons for men. *Punishment & Society, 11(3),* 1–34.

Sexton, L., Jenness, V., & Sumner, J. M. (2010). Where the margins meet: A demographic assessment of transgender inmates in men's prisons. *Justice Quarterly, 27,* 835–866.

Sykes, G. M. (1956). The corruption of authority and rehabilitation. *Social Forces, 11(3),* 257–62.

Tobin, H. J., Freedman-Gurspan, R., & Mottet, L. (2015). *A blueprint for equality: A federal agenda for transgender people.* Retrieved from http://www.transequality.org/issues/re-sources/a-blueprint-for-equality-a-federal-agenda-for-transgender-people-2015.

Toch, H. (1998). Hypermasculinity and prison violence. In L. H. Bowker (Ed.), *Masculinities and violence* (pp. 168–176). Thousand Oaks, CA: Sage Publications.

United States Courts. (2013, July 18). *Supervision costs significantly less than incarceration in the Federal system.* Retrieved from http://www.uscourts.gov/news/2013/07/18/supervision-costs-significantly-less-incarceration-federal-system.

US Department of Health and Human Services. (2012). *Best practices in the use of restraints with pregnant women under correctional custody.* Washington, DC: Bureau of Justice As-

sistance.   Retrieved   from   http://www.nasmhpd.org/sites/default/files/Best_Practices
_Use_of_Restraints_Pregnant(2).pdf.

Van Voorhis, P., Wright, E. M., Salisbury, E., & Bauman, A. (2010). Women's risk factors and
their contributions to existing risk/needs assessment: The current status of a gender-responsive supplement. *Criminal Justice and Behavior, 37,* 261–288.

Wilber, S. (2015). *Lesbian, gay, bisexual and transgender youth in the juvenile justice system.*
Retrieved from http://www.nclrights.org/wp-content/uploads/2015/09/AECF_LGBTinJJS_
FINAL2.pdf.

Part II

Security Issues

Chapter Five

Classification of Inmates

Mari B. Pierce

THE NATURE OF THE ISSUE

Once an individual has been convicted of a felony and receives a sentence (typically of more than one year) he or she will be moved to a prison to serve the sentence of incarceration. The judge does not traditionally sentence an individual to a specific facility, rather, a variety of circumstances determine the prison where each inmate will be housed to serve his or her sentence of incarceration. This is decided through inmate classification. Classification of an inmate refers to the process and procedures of identifying an inmate's custody level (Sun, 2013). Generally, an inmate convicted of a federal felony offense will be housed in a federal prison and an inmate convicted of a state offense will be housed in one of those state's prisons. The federal Bureau of Prisons and each state has a number of correctional facilities. Texas has the most state prisons, with 54 adult prisons. Hawaii has the fewest number of prisons of any state with four adult correctional institutions. Once an inmate is sentenced, determining which institution to send each inmate is not a random or arbitrary process, as institutions have varying security levels that meet different inmate needs.

To add to the complexity, sometimes the federal government contracts out with states to house their inmates and vice versa. Also, state or federal inmates are sometimes housed in privately funded correctional institutions, such as Corrections Corporation of America facilities, that contract to house offenders from various jurisdictions. For example, in addition to Texas' 54 adult state prisons, the Texas Department of Criminal Justice also houses inmates within six privately funded prisons. Placing inmates within private prisons is not the norm but it is also not uncommon. As of 2013, private prisons housed 8% of the nation's state and federal inmates (Bureau of Justice Statistics, 2014). Typically, prison inmates are sent to either a federal or state institution that houses inmates convicted of felonies within their jurisdiction. However, it is important to know and understand that there are sometimes exceptions to this standard. Federal, state, and private correctional facilities parallel each other but do not necessarily mirror each other.

Determining the type of facility and required level of supervision each inmate needs is not a simple process. The classification of inmates is important for the safety of the individual inmate, other inmates, correctional staff, and the community. Higher custody levels place more restrictions on inmates than lower custody levels (Berk, Ladd, Graziano, Baek, 2003). Therefore, the classification assignment impacts the services, educational and programming opportunities available to the inmate, the amount of freedom and privileges provided during his or her incarceration, and also the distance family and friends have to travel to visit their incarcerated loved one (Clear, 2003). The proper and appropriate classification of each inmate is vital.

TRENDS

As of December 31, 2014, an estimated 1,561,5000 were incarcerated in state and federal prisons throughout the United States (Bureau of Justice Statistics, 2015). Although always fluctuating, the state and federal total prison population decreased 1% from year end 2013 to year end 2014. This decrease in the national prison population was the second largest annual decline in the prison population in more than 35 years. The decline is attributed to fewer individuals being sentenced to periods of prison incarceration not an increase in individuals being released from prison. Even with a decline in newly sentenced inmates, 626,644 individual inmates were admitted to prisons in 2014 (Bureau of Justice Statistics, 2015). All of these individuals had to be classified and assigned to a correctional facility based on their individual security and management issues (Austin, 2003).

Historically, classification of inmates was not a formalized process. Rather, subjective classification was the standard. Subjective classification relies heavily on the opinions of prison staff to determine what level of security he or she needs and where to incarcerate the inmate. The California Department of Corrections and Federal Bureau of Prisons were the first to develop objective classification systems (Austin & Hardyman, 2004). It was not until the 1980s that correctional institutions routinely adopted objective, more formalized, classification systems (Austin, 2003). The move to objective classification was largely based on rising prison populations and increased violence within them (Austin & Hardyman, 2004). The most significant purpose for objective classification is predicting inmate misconduct (Berk & de Leeuw, 1999). The goal is to place each inmate in the least restrictive environment possible without risking community or institutional safety. Objective classification systems exist in the federal prison system and most state prison systems (Hardyman, Austin, & Tulloch, 2002).

The classification processes vary across institutions but often involve the computing of an inmate classification score. This score is based on factors such as length of sentence, behavior during prior incarcerations, age, crime seriousness, and educational and treatment needs. This classification score is used to determine the type of facility an inmate is suitable for during his or her incarceration. From this score, individual placement decisions are made. Although objective classifications have become normalized throughout correctional systems, the processes used to classify inmates is not standardized across these systems (Austin, 2003). The National Institute of Corrections suggest the following components in any objective classification system (Austin & Hardyman, 2004):

- a mission statement;
- classification goals and objectives;
- a dedicated classification unit and classification staff;
- centralized control over all prison transfers and housing decisions;
- reliable and valid classification instruments;
- classification instruments that have been tested;
- appropriate use of overrides;
- timely and accurate classification;
- formal housing plan and security/custody designation for each housing unit;
- adherence to the housing plan;
- accurate prisoner data;
- automated data systems;
- continuing monitoring and process evaluation; and
- impact evaluation.

The classification systems with fewer factors and less complicated processes, which are well-documented and recorded, and administered by trained staff, tend to be more reliable and valid than more complicated unofficial instruments (Austin, 2003).

Many objective classification systems still leave room for administrative discretion. Discretionary overrides, where an inmate is placed in a security level higher or lower than their classification score reflects, occurs in 5% to 15% of all classified prisoners (Austin, 2003). There are a number of reasons why this may occur. For example, an inmate may have an unresolved criminal charge. If convicted, this charge could result in the inmate moving to higher security classification than currently assigned. Therefore, the inmate may be placed in this higher security classification until the case is resolved.

Another possibility is that bed space is not currently available for the inmate in the assigned classification level. The inmate may need to be temporarily placed in a different security level until bed space becomes available in their assigned level.

In some systems, such as California, an inmate's conviction offense, such as sexual crime, or those serving life without the possibility of parole result in a required minimum classification level regardless of their assigned classification security score (Berk et al., 2003; Berk & de Leeuw, 1999). Sexual offenders place other inmates at potential risk especially in dormitory style housing. Also, the argument is that inmates serving life without the possibility of parole may have nothing to lose by participating in misconduct or attempting to escape (Berk et al., 2003). In addition, discretionary overrides can also occur based on classification officer judgement and experience. These decisions typically take into account factors not assessed in the classification system (Austin, 2003).

CURRENT RESEARCH

Misclassifying inmates can have serious consequences (Berk et al., 2003). Predicting prisoner behavior is difficult especially because serious and violent behaviors by inmates is rare (Austin, 2003). However, having valid classification systems is key to proper security assignment of inmates. Placement decisions are largely based on inmates' tendency to participate in misconduct (Berk & de Leeuw, 1999). Inmates placed in lower custody levels are seemingly less prone to misconduct than inmates placed in higher custody levels (Austin, 2003). In general, correctional institutions consider similar factors when assessing inmate's security needs: inmate age, gender, history of violence, history of mental illness, gang membership, program participation, prior institutional history, drug and alcohol history of use, history of attempted or successful escapes, sentence length, severity of offense, and time left of sentence (Austin, 2003; Berk et al., 2003; Wooldredge, 2003). However, studies have found that predictors such as gang membership, age of the inmate, one's history of involvement in the criminal justice system, and mental health diagnoses play a more significant role in predicting misconduct than traditional predictors, such as marital status, education level, military and employment history, drug and alcohol use, sentence length, time left to serve, and severity of the offense (Austin, 2003; Berk et al., 2003).

As placement decisions are largely based on inmates' perceived tendency to participate in misconduct, it is surprising so few identified studies examine this relationship. However, a few studies specifically do examine whether the security classification assignment impacts institutional misconduct. The findings are mixed. Two identified studies found that as security classifications increased, misconduct was also found to increase (Berk & de Leeuw, 1999; Worrall & Morris, 2011). Yet, Berecohea and Gibbs (1991) found that as security classifications increased misconduct decreased. Further, Bench and Allen (2003), Berk et al., (2003), Camp and Gaes (2005), and Cao, Zhao, and Van Dine (1997) found that security classifications had little to no effect on inmate misconduct. As the results of studies on the impact of security classification on institutional misconduct are mixed further research in this area is needed.

POLICIES

Once sentenced, the process of inmate classification varies based on the jurisdiction. For this chapter, we will specifically look at the classification processes for the Federal Bureau of Prisons (BOP) and the Texas Department of Criminal Justice, the largest state prison system (Bureau of Justice Statistics, 2015). In many instances, an offender is first sent to a reception center for initial classification. Once classified, the inmate is then transferred to the assigned prison to serve his or her sentence. Once assigned to a particular correctional institution, inmates will go through a further internal classification upon their arrival at the institution. This classification will determine specifically where the inmate will be housed within the institution (e.g., which exact cell or dormitory) and which programming, educational, or vocational services the inmate will be assigned (Austin, 2003). In order to help illustrate this process, we will examine the initial classification process for the Federal Bureau of Prisons and Texas Department of Criminal Justice. The federal prison system is the nation's largest prison system, making up 13% of all prison inmates. Texas has the largest state prison system (Bureau of Justice Statistics, 2015).

Inmate Classification within the Federal Bureau of Prisons

Federal prisons house inmates convicted of federal offenses. The Federal Bureau of Prisons (BOP), an agency within the US Department of Justice, was established in 1930. The Federal Bureau of Prisons is charged with housing and managing individuals convicted and sentenced to incarceration for crimes committed in the District of Columbia and for federal crimes. The most common federal offenses which result in incarceration are drug related and firearms related offenses (US Sentencing Commission, 1992–2014). As of May 2016, the Federal Bureau of Prisons had 195,709 federal inmates, with 81% of them being housed in one of the 122 BOP facilities throughout the United States.

Upon sentencing, the BOP is responsible for determining an inmate's security level and designating where the inmate will serve his or her sentence. Inmates are assigned to institutions based on:

- the level of security and staff supervision the inmate requires;
- the level of security and staff supervision the institution provides;
- the medical classification care level of the inmate and the care level of the institution;
- the inmate's program needs (e.g., substance abuse treatment, educational/vocational training, individual and/or group counseling, medical/mental health treatment); and
- various administrative factors (e.g., institution bed space capacity; the inmate's release residence; judicial recommendations; separation needs; and security measures needed to ensure protection of victims, witnesses, and the general public).

In summary, the initial classification assignment to an institution is based primarily on the inmates' security and program needs (Federal Bureau of Prisons, n.d.).

The initial classification is typically done by staff from the Designation and Sentence Computation Center in Grand Prairie, Texas. Security level decisions are based on the inmate's security point total. Points are assigned based on: the number of months until release; the severity of the offense; history of violence; prior institutional escapes or attempts; age; educational level; and drug or alcohol history. Public safety factors are also calculated. Examples of public safety factors include prior institutional behavior, gang involvement, and whether the inmate is a sexual offender. The security points total combined with the public safety factors determine the placement score for each inmate. The inmate is then assigned to a facility with a security level which corresponds with his or her placement score. The BOP attempts to house inmates within 500 miles of where the inmate is planning to reside upon release. Male institutions are classified as one of five security levels (minimum, low, medium, high, and administrative) while female institutions are classified as minimum, low, high, and administrative. Federal female institutions do not have a medium level classification (to view the Program Statement, which describes the inmate security and custody classification, see Federal Bureau of Prisons, 2006).

Minimum security institutions, also known as federal prison camps, are the lowest security level in the federal system. As of April 2016, 16.7% of federal inmates were classified as minimum security. These institutions have a relatively low staff-to-inmate ratio, have dormitory style housing, no perimeter fencing, and emphasize inmate participation programs and work. Low security facilities, known as federal correctional institutions, house the largest portion of the federal inmate population. As of April 2016, 38.1% of federal inmates were classified as low security. These institutions' staff-to-inmate ratio is higher than minimum security facilities and inmates are housed in either dormitory or cubicle style housing. These facilities do have a double-fenced perimeter, yet inmate participation programs and work is emphasized.

The next security level, medium, also called federal correctional institutions, house nearly 30% of all federally incarcerated individuals. Some US penitentiaries (which are traditionally high-security institutions) also house medium security inmates. These institutions have a higher staff-to-inmate ratio than low security facilities and have mostly cell housing. In addition, these facilities often have double fenced perimeters with electronic detection systems. Work and treatment programs are available to inmates housed in these facilities. High security level institutions, known as US penitentiaries, house 11.7% of the federal inmate population. These institutions have the highest staff-to-inmate ratio and house inmates in cells. Fencing is highly secure and there is close control of all inmate movement within the facility. The final category of federal prisons, administrative facilities, are institutions with special missions. Examples would be detention of pretrial offenders, inmates with serious medical problems, and inmates who are extremely dangerous or violent. Administrative facilities, except Administrative-Maximum Security Penitentiary (ADMAX), may hold inmates from any of the four security levels. United State Penitentiary Florence ADMAX is a "supermax" prison designed to hold federal inmates who are deemed unmanageable in any other federal facility.

Once assigned to a facility, custody classification reviews typically occur annually after the initial custody classification. Therefore, it is possible for an inmate's security level to change and for an inmate to relocate during the course of his or her incarceration (see Federal Bureau of Prisons, n.d.).

Inmate Classification within the Texas Department of Criminal Justice

The most recently available statistics indicate that the Texas Department of Criminal Justice (TDCJ) houses 136,450 state prison offenders in 54 state run prisons (known as units) throughout Texas. All inmates convicted and sentenced to more than 24 months are classified as TDCJ prison offenders. The most common state offenses which result in incarceration in a TDCJ prison are violent and drug offenses (Texas Department of Criminal Justice, 2014a). The Classification and Records Office schedules and processes inmate intakes into the state prisons.

Prison offenders are fingerprinted, and undergo a physical examination and a mental health screening. In addition, prison offenders receive educational testing, a substance abuse assessment, and an intake interview. This information, combined with the offender's current institutional behavior, prior institutional behavior, current sentenced offense, and prior criminal history, aid the State Classification Committee in determining the initial classification and custody level designation for each inmate. In brief, individuals are housed based on their safety, security, and treatment needs. The intake process typically takes a few weeks (Texas Department of Criminal Justice, 2014b). Once the security classification decisions are made the inmates' program needs, such as mental health service or substance abuse treatment, and home are also considered before the final prison assignment (Seiter, 2013).

The Texas Department of Criminal Justice has six prison offender custody levels (general population levels one, two, three, four, five, and administrative segregation). Inmates assigned to general population levels one, two, and three have a history of good disciplinary histories and have served a significant portion of their sentence. Nearly 80% of the Texas state prison population are categorized as general population levels one, two, or three (Texas Department of Criminal Justice, 2014a).

General population level one is the lowest custody level. Inmates within this custody level are housed in dormitory style housing on the prison grounds but outside of the secure internal perimeter. Inmates within this custody level are permitted to work outside the secure perimeter without armed supervision. Inmates in general population level two are housed in either dormitories or cells surrounded by a secure perimeter. General population level three is the next prison offender custody level. Inmates within level three reside in either dormitories or cells within the main prison complex. These inmates are serving sentences of 50 years or greater and are normally employed within the secure perimeter. General population level four inmates are typically housed in cells. These inmates have had either two or more non-assaultive major disciplinary convictions within the last six months or one disciplinary conviction for an assault of a staff member or a fellow inmate without a weapon within the last year. When permitted to work on the prison grounds but outside the secure perimeter, inmates in general population levels two, three, and four are always under direct supervision of armed officers (Texas Department of Criminal Justice, 2014a; 2014b).

General population level five inmates are those with a history of assaultive or aggressive behaviors. These inmates have one or more disciplinary convictions for assault against a staff member or a fellow inmate with a weapon within the past two years, two or more disciplinary convictions for assault against a staff member of a fellow inmate without a weapon within the last year, or one or more disciplinary convictions for extortion of sexual abuse within the past two years. Inmates in general population level five are required to live in cells. Inmates in the highest security level, administrative segregation, are either dangerous toward other offenders or staff or they are in being housed in segregation for their own protection. Inmates in administrative segregation are isolated from inmates in the general population. Nearly 5% of the Texas state prison population reside in administrative segregation. These inmates are required to live in cells and typically only leave their cell for showers or recreation (Texas Department of Criminal Justice, 2014a; 2014b).

Classification committees will periodically review the custody level of inmates to reassess classification decisions. Inmates may also request an institutional transfer within their classification level. Therefore, it is possible for an inmate's security level to change or for an inmate to be relocated during the course of his or her incarceration. As some prisons house inmates from various security levels within the same institution it is also possible for an inmate to move across security levels but remain at the same correctional institution. (To view the Texas Department of Justice *Offender Orientation Handbook,* see Texas Department of Criminal Justice, 2016.)

The Texas Department of Criminal Justice prison offenders' classification process illustrates how a state correctional system classification process can look. However, it is important to note that not all state correctional classification processes systems mirror Texas' system. Although most states use custody levels (i.e., minimum, medium, maximum custody) or level systems (Level I, II, III, and IV) the classification systems within states varies (Austin, 2003). Illustrating how one state's system works will permit you to apply this knowledge to understanding your own state's correctional classification system.

ISSUES/CHALLENGES

As previously mentioned, an inmate's initial classification assignment is not absolute. Rather, classification committees regularly, typically yearly, review the custody level of inmates to reassess classification decisions. Reassignment can occur in either direction. However, reassignment to more restrictive housing can cause unique challenges within correctional institutions. Reclassifying an inmate to a different security level will likely result in a change in the housing assignment, which will take the inmate away from his or her known social and community network. In addition, reclassification will likely alter the educational and programming opportunities available to the inmate and the amount of freedom and privileges afforded. In addition, the distance the inmate is housed from loved ones who may visit, and the length of or number of allotted visits may also be changed. The reclassification of inmates also impacts tax payers, as the daily cost of housing an inmate in

higher security levels is more expensive than housing inmates at lower security levels (Henrichson & Delaney, 2012).

Those assigned to the highest security units, commonly referred to as
administrative segregation, are typically placed there due to violent or disor-
derly conduct within the institution. Inmates classified in segregation endure
the most restrictions and least amounts of freedom of all incarcerated individuals. It is not uncommon for these inmates to be housed in single-occu-
pancy cells for up 23 to 24 hours per day. These inmates may reside either
within a secure unit within an existing correctional facility or the entire
facility may be dedicated to administrative segregation (Frost & Monteiro,
2016). Although due process rights are afforded to inmates receiving segregation, or solitary confinement, for short-term disciplinary reasons these
same rights are not afforded to inmates being assigned to administrative
segregation for purposes of classification (O'Keefe, 2008). Many correctional systems do however have protocols for review of assignments to segregation units (Metcalf et al., 2013).

In the past few years, community concern has risen about the expanding
use of assignment to segregation units among the United States' inmate
population. A myriad of court cases have examined the use of solitary confinement and administrative segregation, the most notable being *Ruiz v.
Johnson* (1999). David Ruiz was an inmate within administrative segregation
within the Texas Department of Criminal Justice. Gary Johnson, at the time,
was the Texas Department of Criminal Justice Director of the Institutional
Division. Ruiz challenged the conditions of his confinement in administrative segregation arguing that the conditions violated the Eighth (right against
cruel and unusual punishment) and Fourteenth (right to equal protection
under the law) Amendments of the US Constitution. Although the deciding
justices did not explicitly define administrative segregation as cruel and unusual punishment subsequent cases on the issue continue to arise.

In 2006, the Commission on Safety and Abuse in America's Prisons
noted the increased use of solitary confinement and recommended decreased
reliance on its use (Gibbons & Katzenbach, 2006). Since then, a number of
states have worked to reduce the number of inmates assigned and placed in
administrative segregation (see Hager & Rich, 2014; Shames, Wilcox, &
Subramanian, 2015). Hananel (2015) further contends that US Supreme
Court involvement in this issue may likely be approaching. Even President
Obama (2015) called for a US Justice Department investigation into the
practice of administrative segregation. Increased focus on inmates within
segregation units will likely spur conversations about security classifications,
in general. (See Frost and Monteiro [2016] for the full National Institute of
Justice report, *Administrative Segregation in U.S. Prisons*.)

FUTURE PROSPECTS

Classification of inmates is still in its early stages. American Prisons have been around since the mid-1800s but widespread use of objective classification is not yet 40 years old. Studies have suggested that more inmates could be placed in less restrictive custody levels without affecting safety (Baird, 1993; Worrall & Morris, 2011). State and federal prisons populations were at historic high in 2009 but have shown continued decline each year since (Bureau of Justice Statistics, 2015). Nonetheless, the nearly 1.5 million inmates housed in correctional facilities need to be managed. Correctional systems without objective classification system need to work to design them. For those with classification processes, just as inmate classifications are routinely evaluated, so too should the classification processes within the institutions especially because prison populations are much higher than when classification schemes first emerged. The National Institute of Corrections is a resource available to correctional agencies to help them develop, revise, and assess correctional classification processes (see nicic.gov). Assessing not only the inmates, but also the classification system, could help assure the proper management of the countless inmates who pass through our nations prisons.

DISCUSSION QUESTIONS

1. Explain the difference between subjective and objective classification systems. What advantages and disadvantages do you see for each type of system?
2. What are discretionary overrides in the classification process? Explain how they might be used.
3. Identify five predictors of inmate behavior. How might these be used to predict behavior?
4. Compare the Federal Bureau of Prisons and Texas Department of Criminal Justice's classification systems to those of your home state. Identify similarities and differences between the systems.
5. Discuss your thoughts on classifying administrative segregation. Do you believe it is a form of cruel and unusual punishment?

REFERENCES

Austin, J. (2003). *Findings in prison classification and risk assessment.* Washington, DC: National Institute of Corrections.
Austin, J., & Hardyman, P. L. (2004). *Objective prison classification: A guide for correctional agencies.* Washington, DC: US Department of Justice, National Institute of Corrections.

Baird, C. (1993). Objective classification in Tennessee: Management, effectiveness, and planning issues. In *Classification: A tool for managing today's offenders*. Laurel, MD: American Correctional Association.

Bench, L. L., & Allen, T. D. (2003). Investigating the stigma of prison classification: An experimental design. *The Prison Journal, 83*(4), 367–382.

Berecochea, J. E., & Gibbs, J. B. (1991). Inmate classification: A correctional program that works? *Evaluation Review, 15*(3), 333–363.

Berk, R. A., & de Leeuw, J. (1999). An evaluation of California's inmate classification system using a generalized regression discontinuity design. *Journal of American Statistical Association, 94*(448), 1045–1052.

Berk, R. A., Ladd, H., Graziano, H., & Baek, J. (2003). A randomized experiment testing inmate classification systems. *Criminology & Public Policy, 2*(2), 215–242.

Bureau of Justice Statistics. (2015). *Prisoners in 2014*. Washington, DC: US Bureau of Justice Statistics.

Bureau of Justice Statistics. (2014, September 16). *In 2013 the state prison population rose for the first time since 2009* (Press Release). Washington, DC: US Bureau of Justice Statistics.

Camp, S. D., & Gaes, G. G. (2005). Criminogenic effects of the prison environment on inmate behavior: Some experimental evidence. *Crime and Delinquency, 51*(3), 425–442.

Cao, L., Zhao, J., & Van Dine, S. (1997). Prison disciplinary tickets: A test of the deprivation and importation models. *Journal of Criminal Justice, 25*(2), 103–113.

Clear, T. R. (2003). Inmate classification. *Criminology & Public Policy 2*(2), 213–214.

Federal Bureau of Prisons. (n.d.). *Federal Bureau of Prisons*. Retrieved from https://www.bop.gov/.

Federal Bureau of Prisons. (2006). *Program statement*. Washington, DC: Federal Bureau of Prisons.

Frost, N. A., & Monteiro, C. E. (2016). *Administrate segregation in U.S. prisons*. Washington, DC: US Department of Justice, National Institute of Justice.

Gibbons, J. J., & Katzenbach, N. D. B. (2006). *Confronting confinement: A report of the commission on safety and abuse in America's prisons*. Retrieved from http://archive.vera.org/sites/default/files/resources/downloads/Confronting_Confinement.pdf.

Hager, E., & Rich, G. (2014, December 23). *Shifting away from solitary*. Retrieved from https://www.themarshallproject.org/2014/12/23/shifting-away-from-solitary.

Hananel, S. (2015, August 11). *Justice Kennedy provides hope to solitary confinement foes*. Retrieved from http://www.businessinsider.com/ap-justice-kennedy-provides-hope-to-solitary-confinement-foes-2015-8.

Hardyman, P. L., Austin, J., & Tulloch, O. C. (2002). *Revalidating external classification systems: The experience of seven states and model for reclassification reform*. Washington, DC: The Institute of Crime, Justice and Corrections at the George Washington University.

Henrichson, C., & Delaney, R. (2012). *The price of prisons: What incarceration costs taxpayers*. Retrieved from http://archive.vera.org/sites/default/files/resources/downloads/Price_of_Prisons_updated_version_072512.pdf.

Metcalf, H., Morgan, J., Oliker-Friedland, S., Resnik, J., Spiegel, J., Tae, H., . . . Holbrook, B. (2013). *Administrative segregation, degrees of isolation, and incarceration: A national overview of state and federal correctional policies*. Retrieved from https://www.aclu.org/files/assets/Administrative%20Segregation,%20Degrees%20of%20Isolation,%20and%20Incarceration.pdf.

O'Keefe, M. L. (2008). Administrative segregation from within: A corrections perspective. *The Prison Journal, 88*(1), 123–143.

Seiter, R. P. (2013). *Corrections: An introduction* (4th ed.). Upper Saddle River, NJ: Pearson.

Shames, A., Wilcox, J., & Subramanian, R. (2015). *Solitary confinement: Common misconceptions and emerging safe alternatives*. Retrieved from https://www.vera.org/publications/solitary-confinement-common-misconceptions-and-emerging-safe-alternatives.

Sun, K. (2013). *Correctional counseling: A cognitive growth perspective* (2nd ed.). Burlington, MA: Jones and Bartlett Publishers.

Texas Department of Criminal Justice. (2016). *Texas Department of Criminal Justice offender orientation handbook.* Retrieved from http://www.tdcj.state.tx.us/documents/Offender_Orientation_Handbook_English.pdf.

Texas Department of Criminal Justice. (2014a). *Texas Department of Criminal Justice statistical report, fiscal year 2014.* Retrieved from https://www.tdcj.state.tx.us/documents/Statistical_Report_FY2014.pdf.

Texas Department of Criminal Justice. (2014b). *Texas Department of Criminal Justice annual review.* Retrieved from http://www.tdcj.state.tx.us/documents/Annual_Review_2014.pdf.

US Sentencing Commission. (n.d.). *Quick facts: Federal offenders in prison – January 2015.* Retrieved from http://www.ussc.gov/sites/default/files/pdf/researchand-publications/quickfacts/QuickFacts_BOP.pdf.

Wooldredge, J. (2003). Keeping pace with evolving prison populations for effective management. *Criminology & Public Policy, 2*(2), 253–258.

Worrall, J. L., & Morris, R. G. (2011). Inmate custody levels and prison rule violations. *The Prison Journal, 91*(2), 131–157.

Chapter Six

Prison Gangs and Security Threat Groups

Beverly R. Crank and Catherine D. Marcum

Anecdotally and statistically, prisons have a reputation of being a hot bed of violent activity. A single pod can contain a variety of criminal offenders, from petty thieves to murderers. Many inmates were raised in a subculture of violence, where aggression and violent behavior were accepted and even encouraged. For those inmates not physically intimidating, or from a "softer" lifestyle, hearing the clang of a cell door shut and seeing a crowd of tattooed, hardened offenders can evoke feelings of fear and struggle for survival. Bringing these two contradicting lifestyles together in a close environment often facilitates the need for protection in this dangerous environment. An inmate can find this in a prison gang.

The purpose of this chapter is to examine the prevalence of prison gangs in our American correctional facilities, as well as their effect on the safety and welfare of those incarcerated and employed in the facilities. The nature of the issue will first be examined, followed by a discussion of current trends in which gangs are most prominently featured. Current research on the effects of the prison gang will be presented, including consideration of violent behavior on the administration and recidivism of gang members. This text also will investigate the current correctional policies in place to address the increasing presence of prison gangs, as well as the challenges associated with ensuring safety in a secure facility. Lastly, future directions for our corrections system will be explored as we try to reactively manage past events and look proactively to decreasing the negative effect these groups have on a prison population.

Nature of the Issue

Prison gangs, or security threat groups (STGs), are cohesive groups of prisoners with an identified leader that participate in criminal activities while incarcerated (Huff, 1996). There is an overrepresentation of gang presence in prison facilities compared to those in the general population. The National Gang Intelligence Center (2011) estimated that approximately 230,000 gang members reside in state and federal prisons in the United States. With the total incarcerated population approximating at 2.2 million (Kaeble, Glaze, Tsoutis, & Minton, 2016), this equates to prison gang members composing 10.5% of the incarcerated population.

Prison gang members are often identified gang members before incarceration. Loyalty to a gang is expected no matter an individual's location or life circumstances, so a stint behind bars does not cease membership. Clemmer (1940) and Irwin and Cressey (1962) described this as an issue of importation, as established street gang members bring their loyalties and beliefs into prison with them to help develop the prison subculture. An expectation of violence and aggression is present, just as it was on the outside. Approximately one-third of prisoners were street gang members before joining a prison gang (Varano, Huebner, & Bynum, 2011).

Other members of a prison gang may join as a result of incarceration or simply for protection. Joining a prison gang and continued active participation with the group is also a result of adapting to the environment and merging into the prison subculture. Prisons are total institutions, a place where every move a person makes is regulated, controlled, and observed. As a result of the deprivation of liberties and freedoms (Sykes, 1958), inmates conform to the prison subculture by forming new attitudes and values, in order to adapt to the central focus of violence. Clemmer (1940) asserted that prisoners assimilate into the prison subculture and adopt the pro-violence, antiauthority attitudes that are prevalent. In other words, men who enter prison facilities quickly become aware that an inmate will be safe and successful in prison if they use aggression and dominance to establish a reputation. For those who are unable to protect themselves, membership in a prison gang appears to be an obvious answer to ensure safety.

As gang members are released into the community, it is often difficult to determine if membership originated in a street gang or a prison gang. Well-known street gangs, such as the Bloods and Crips, actually first became active in prison after many members were incarcerated (McGloin, 2005). Gangs capitalize on confinement and use prisons as a way of recruiting new members and solidifying gang mentality and culture. Winterdyk (2009) found that more than half of prisoners who join prison gangs were not members of a gang on the outside.

TRENDS

The recent rise in the number of prison gangs corresponds to the overall growth of the incarcerated population. In other words, "prison gangs expanded as prisons did" (Pyrooz, Decker, & Fleisher, 2011, p. 14). According to a study conducted by Winterdyk and Ruddell (2010), from 2004 through 2009, there was an increase in the overall proportion of STG members, and prison officials reported that over this time period, these gangs increased in their levels of destructiveness and sophistication.

Violence/aggression is not the only characteristic associated with prison gang membership. Racist attitudes are especially prevalent in male prisons, and this is not an exception when it comes to gang membership. In fact, prison gangs often fuel racism and prejudice. While prison administration does not promote prejudicial behavior or segregation, male prison gangs most often affiliate by race and ethnicity and have negative feelings toward at least one other race. Not surprisingly, this equates to a formidable amount of interracial conflict and violence among prison gangs. While some gangs of different races will align to fight a common enemy, no one can be completely trusted. There are dozens of recognized gangs in the corrections system. However, according to the Florida Department of Corrections (2016), the following are the six most prevalent prison gangs recognized nationally, each separated by race and ethnicity.

Neta, composed of Puerto Rican males, are represented by the colors red, white, and blue, and generally wear beads or bandanas in these colors to demonstrate membership (Florida Department of Corrections, 2016). The emblem for Neta is a heart pierced by two Puerto Rican flags with a shackled hand and the middle and index finger crossed, and members will salute each other with the crossed fingers on their right hands over their heart. Members of Neta are often secretive and will deny membership to prison administration, so it is difficult to identify them. However, they are willing to perform "hits" for other security threat groups while incarcerated. Their most notable enemy is the Latin Kings (Florida Department of Corrections, 2016).

Mexican Mafia (EME), another Hispanic prison gang, originated as a Los Angeles street gang (Florida Department of Corrections, 2016). According to the Federal Bureau of Prisons, they are the most active prison gang in federal penitentiaries, and support ethnic solidarity and control drug trafficking. They are represented by an eagle or snake (as seen on the Mexican flag), along with the initials EME. The Mexican Mafia has an extremely volatile relationship with La Nuestra Familia ("kill or be killed" mentality), forcing the Federal Bureau of Prisons to separate confirmed members. During incarceration, they will offer protection to members of La Costra Nostra and collaborate with the Aryan Brotherhood to advance gang interests (Florida Department of Corrections, 2016).

Texas Syndicate (TS) is composed of Mexican-American males, originating in the 1970s in Folsom Prison in California (Florida Department of Corrections, 2016). Membership is currently increasing, attributing this rise to the inclusion of members from Latin American countries such as Colombia. Members are called "carnals," branding themselves with tattoos including the TS symbol. They have multiple enemies, including Aryan Brotherhood, La Nuestra Familia, and Mexican Mafia. They are heavily involved in extortion, drug trafficking, and internal discipline inside the prison (Florida Department of Corrections, 2016).

The final Hispanic-based gang, *La Nuestra Familia (NF)*, was originally formed for protection against the Mexican Mafia (Florida Department of Corrections, 2016). They are well known for bringing contraband into prisons and are organized separately in prison compared to outside the prison walls. A sombrero with a dagger, the number 14, and red rags are commonly used to mark gang members. They are enemies with the Mexican Mafia, Aryan Brotherhood, and Texas Syndicate. While often associated with the Black Panthers simply because they have similar enemies, it is a love–hate relationship between the two gangs (Florida Department of Corrections, 2016).

The most notable African American based gang is the *Black Guerilla Family (BGF)*, which was founded by Black Panther member George Jackson (Jackson died in 1971 as a result of the attempted escape of the "San Quentin Six") (Florida Department of Corrections, 2016). It is the most politically organized prison gang, formed with the idea to overthrow the US government and eradicate racism. They are extremely anti-government, using the letters "BGF" or cross sabers and a shotgun as their symbolic representation. They have a good working relationship with La Nuestra Familia, and often recruit Bloods or Crips into their ranks during incarceration. Aryan Brotherhood and Texas Syndicate are their mortal enemies based on their strong hatred for the race, which often leads to acts of violence (Florida Department of Corrections, 2016).

Lastly, the *Aryan Brotherhood* is composed solely of Caucasian males (Florida Department of Corrections, 2016). They mark themselves with Neo-Nazi symbols, such as swastikas, or the numbers "666." Most are incarcerated for property crimes and just try to make it through their sentence without conflict. While promoting "white power," they do align themselves with the Mexican Mafia, and therefore are opposed to La Nuestra Familia. However, their main enemy is any gang composed of African Americans, specifically Black Guerilla Family. A significant act of violence or hit is often necessary to secure membership into the Aryan Brotherhood (Florida Department of Corrections, 2016).

CURRENT RESEARCH

Prison gang members are often attracted to gang membership for protection from victimization, as well as domination of other races. Individuals are also attracted to participating in the prison gang due to the money and power associated with membership (Fong, 1990), and will use violence and intimidation to control staff and other inmates (Huff, 1996; Irwin, 1980). This can make life extremely uncomfortable and tense for individuals who are not identified gang members, or have attempted to leave a gang. The mentality "blood in, blood out" signifies that the only way to disengage from a gang is through your own death, and not voluntarily dropping out. In fact, Stevens (1997) asserted that where prison gangs are most active, 73% of inmates not declaring gang membership requested a transfer to another facility and 87% requested protective custody.

Prison gang culture plays an integral role in the ability of prison administration to control inmates. Increased gang activity inside prison walls leads to larger frequencies of administrative infractions and criminal activity by inmates (Drury & DeLisi, 2010; Gaes, Wallace, Gilman, Klein-Saffran, & Suppa, 2002). This heightened amount of offending behavior also decreases the ability of prison staff to ensure safety and a controlled environment in the prison (Griffin & Hepburn, 2006). Generally more of an issue in male facilities, prison gangs manage criminal enterprises in prisons. Organized activities fueled by prison gangs are, but not limited to, the following: extortion, gambling, contraband, prostitution, rape, and assault.

Membership in a prison gang also increases the likelihood that an individual will recidivate once released (Dooley, Seals, & Skarbek, 2014). Participating in a prison gang indicates a commitment to a criminal lifestyle, as the mantra is often "blood in, blood out." In other words, members are involved in gang life their entire lifetime. Individuals who attempt to leave gang life, or "degang," are met with violent or fatal attempts on their lives and families. Many of those who try to leave must relocate to get away from potential harm.

Recidivating behavior is also influenced by deviant peer association. Spending time with individuals who have long criminal histories and serious offending behaviors, such as gang members, increases the likelihood a person will recidivate after release (Bayer, Hjalmarsson, & Posen, 2009). In addition, gang membership expands a person's social network to other members in the gang community, hence giving the opportunity to learn more criminal behaviors and improve skills for theft, drug trafficking, and violence (Gambetta, 2009). Members of prison gangs also have higher levels of recidivism as they are more likely to get arrested based on increase attention by law enforcement (Dooley et al., 2014). Inmates identified as gang members are often tracked and followed more by law enforcement; hence, more opportunity for arrest.

It should be noted that although gang members are disproportionately represented in prisons, overall research focusing on prison gangs is lacking (Pyrooz, Decker, & Fleisher, 2011). Pyrooz and colleagues (2011) note two primary reasons for our limited understanding surrounding prison gangs. First, from an administrative perspective, outside access to prisons is limited. Correctional personnel review research proposals, but may only grant access to prison data for a very limited number of researchers, and usually only if there is some relevance or benefit to the correctional agency. In addition, researchers must seek approval from institutional review boards, both from their own institution and the correctional agency, before proceeding with research. Second, there are methodological limitations to gang research. The validity of the data is questionable, as the sources of such information is limited to prison inmates, staff, or records. In addition, definitions and policies vary considerably among prisons, which is a challenge from a research standpoint (Pyrooz, Decker, & Fleisher, 2011, p. 12–13).

POLICIES

Identifying gang members can be a challenge for prison officials. Typically, an assessment is performed upon arrival to determine if an individual belongs to a gang. Some methods of identifying gang members include signs or symbols displayed, information found in correspondences, tattoos, prior official records, association with other gang members, and self-admission of gang membership. Once "validated" as a gang member, an inmate may receive a form from prison officials containing information surrounding the basis of this validation, which typically does not disclose the source (Toch, 2007).

Most prisons have staff who are assigned to investigate gang activity within the prison. However, some of the challenges staff face include a constantly changing environment (as inmates rotate in and out of the prison), the ability to compel inmates to provide information, the need to collect information and maintain informant safety, and the never ending workload these investigators face (Wilkinson & Delgado, 2006).

Prison administrations have attempted a number of strategies for gang intervention. Some of the most common methods include monitoring facilities (75.7% of all facilities), monitoring mail (75%), use of informants (59.5%), transfers (58.1%), segregation (55.4%), interrupting communications (46.6%), and lockdowns (41.2%) (Knox, 2012; Pyrooz et al., 2011). Interestingly, 4.7% of correctional facilities report the strategy of ignoring the existence of gangs (Knox, 2012). Unfortunately, knowledge surrounding the effectiveness of such interventions is limited, due to the research limitations noted in the preceding section. However, in one national survey of prisons, officials rated the perceived effectiveness of different gang management strategies with segregation being rated as highly effective (75%), followed by restrictions on visits (64.7%), access to communication (42.9%), and the use of specialized housing units (50%) (Winterdyk & Ruddell, 2010). Further, this study revealed searching an STG member's mail and monitoring their phone calls were perceived by prison officials as very effective strategies in controlling gang members.

One of the most common strategies for controlling gangs is the use of administrative segregation units (ad seg) or secured housing units (SHU). The purpose is to isolate known gang members and leaders from other inmates. These inmates typically spend 23 hours per day locked in their single cell. Roughly 55.4% percent of correctional facilities nationwide report using some form of segregation (Knox, 2012); however, its effectiveness is questionable. Further, implementation of such policies are costly and segregated members are unlikely to receive treatment and services (Di Placido, Simon, Witte, Gu, & Wong, 2006). A counterargument is that containing gang members and removing them from the general population may help prevent the recruitment of new members, as Knox (2005) reported that 11.6% of male inmates and 3.7% of female inmates joined their first gang during confinement.

Most correctional agencies now use databases that provide information on known gang members and their activities. These databases provide information on gang members' known locations and affiliates, as well as identifying information such as photos, and information on scars, marks, and tattoos. The use of databases increases communication among correctional and law enforcement agencies, and also improves data accuracy (Pyrooz et al., 2011; Wilkinson & Delgado, 2006). According to Wilkinson and Delgado, this relationship between community law enforcement and correctional agencies is "crucial to investigatory success" (p. 40). Despite these methods of controlling gangs, many challenges still exist as discussed below.

ISSUES AND CHALLENGES

There are a number of challenges and negative impacts of gangs on prison administration. One of the most obvious challenges is that the presence of prison gangs are associated with higher violence within an institution. Similar to chronic street offenders, who make up a small percentage of the offending population but are responsible for the majority of crime, prison gang members also make up a small percentage of the prison population, but are thought to be responsible for the majority of prison violence. For instance, a study by the Washington State Department of Corrections estimated that gang members comprise 18% of the inmate population, but are responsible for 43% of violence in prisons (Orr & Kunzi, 2008). Some argue that gang-related crimes are even underreported, as inmates are unwilling to "snitch" on other inmates (Di Placido et al., 2006). Further, Gaes and colleagues (2002) note in their study on prison gang violence and misconduct that gang affiliation is associated with institutional misconduct, even after controlling for other individual characteristics that have been found from prior research to increase the likelihood of violent misconduct.

Relatedly, the issue of prison staff safety is a serious concern. According to the 2012 National Gang Crime Research Center (NGCRC) National STG Survey, roughly 25% of correctional facilities report that gang members have assaulted staff, and 49% of correctional facilities report that gang members have threatened staff (Knox, 2012). This is of concern given reports of homicides of off-duty correctional officers by gang members (Winterdyk, 2009). What is interesting is the lack of disciplinary rules in place to prevent gang recruitment. In the same NGCRC survey, 41.4% of facilities reported having no rules that prohibit gang recruitment. Knox describes that in "many prisons and jails in America it is still 'open season' for gang members to freely recruit other gang members" (para. 26) without concern for disciplinary sanctions.

Another prominent issue involving prison gangs related to staff and inmate safety are illegal drugs. Prison gangs often seek to control the prison economy and one of the most lucrative items smuggled into prisons are drugs (Wilkinson & Delgado, 2006). As gangs grow in terms of membership and organization, so does their control and power over the entire prison population. Drug trafficking is a serious concern, as it compromises staff safety and the daily operations of correctional facilities. Additionally, gangs provide other "services," such as gambling and prostitution (Fleisher, 1989). These services pose significant safety concerns, as struggle over territory can quickly lead to turf wars among rival gangs (Fleisher & Decker, 2001).

In addition to the above, another contemporary issue in prison gangs is the concern of radicalization. For instance, Hamm (2008) reports that "prisoner radicalization grows in the secretive underground of inmates subcultures through prison gangs and extremist interpretations of religious doctrines that inspire ideologies of intolerance, hatred and violence" (p. 17). In a recent study by the National Institute of Justice (NIJ), gang intelligence officers noted that most inmates are radicalized by other radical inmates, instead of outside influences (Hamm, 2008).

Gangs often use religious programs and "call-outs" in prison, in order to meet and conduct gang business (Hamm, 2008; Knox, 2012). Through interviews with former rival gangs, Hamm finds instances of Crips and Bloods joining forces under Islamic banners, and even some Neo-Nazi groups becoming Sunni Muslims. He further notes internal conflict among prison Islamic groups, with the Nation of Islam against the Sunnis and the Sunnis against the Shiites. In addition, Prison Islam is referred to as encompassing "gang values and fierce intra-group loyalties based on 'cut-and-paste' interpretations of the Koran—against all the other forms of inmate Islam" (Hamm, 2008, p. 17). In a report by the NGCRC, 23.6% of correctional facilities indicate the presence of Islamic inmates forming a separate gang (Knox, 2012).

This radicalization poses a huge security risk for prison administrators. As one prison chaplain noted "some of these inmates are very fertile ground for jihad" (Hamm, 2008, p. 18). And although such radicalization does exist, recruitment for terrorism is uncommon (Hamm, 2008). However, the current threat is the potential for these small radical groups to join terroristic networks and plan acts upon release (Hamm, 2008). For example, through the use the US Postal Service, the Maoist International Movement (MIM) spreads communist ideology among inmates in efforts to radicalize them and organize resistance against the government. The percentage of facilities reporting inmate contact with MIM is low (approximately 4.6%), but there is the potential for this to spread throughout prisons and jails (Knox, 2012).

Ethnicity in gang membership is becoming more fluid, as the demand for new members grows and protection is needed (Hamm, 2008). However, the existence of white racial extremism is still ever present in correctional facilities, and correctional workers reportedly are very pessimistic about the prospects of solving the racial problem (Knox, 2012). Further, Knox reports that few program resources exist to deal with racial tensions.

Finally, as described by Knox (n.d.), another contemporary gang management issue is the use of social media to disseminate gang information. Just like ordinary, law-abiding citizens, gang members also have a presence on social media, especially Facebook. For instance, the Five Percenters are described as a domestic extremist Islamic gang that is present in a number of prisons. They are well represented on Facebook and can be found simply by searching for "Five Percenter." The issue with gangs using Facebook in particular is that a user must be logged into their own account in order to report a page. There is no option to report a group just because they are a gang, instead, the closest option would be reporting due to "violence or harmful behavior." Gang investigators are torn in terms of gang presence on Facebook. On one hand, such Facebook pages may facilitate at-risk youths joining gangs. On the other hand, gang investigators are well aware of gang members' presence on social media and use this to their advantage in terms of investigations (see Knox, n.d., for an overview). The use of Facebook and other social media sites by gangs should come as no surprise; however, the dilemma is should these pages be shut down or should they remain open for investigation.

As noted in the previous section, gang membership has a strong correlation with recidivism (Dooley et al., 2014; Huebner, Varano, & Bynum, 2007; McShane, Williams, & Dolny, 2003). This is a great concern to public safety as gang members are released back into the community. Many validated inmates are segregated prior to release, with little reentry policies in place to ease the transition. Upon reentry, gang members may find that their community and even former gangs have changed. Gang members are no longer subject to institutional control, and with that, are no longer provided with their basic needs, such as housing, food, and medications (Pyrooz et al., 2011). With little to no skills (or desire) for potential employment, gang members may soon find themselves returning to prison (Pyrooz et al., 2011).

FUTURE DIRECTIONS

When considering the future directions of gang research, the life course importation model may aid in our current understanding of prison gangs. This model takes into consideration events and factors from early childhood (e.g., abuse, victimization, family criminality, poor parenting, poverty, and psychosocial traits), which lead to later delinquency and antisocial behavior, as well as misconduct while confined (see DeLisi, Trulson, Marquart, Drury, & Kosloski, 2010). For instance, in one study, DeLisi and colleagues (2010) found that sexual abuse and time served were positively associated with gang activity. Gang involvement also was predictive of poor inmate compliance. It is argued that this theoretical framework may further our understanding of desistance from crime by including time spent in an institutional setting.

In terms of policy implications, some scholars suggest the potential of gang renunciation programs, in order to provide a safe place for those interested in leaving gang life. Currently, very few resources exist and gang members often do not embrace such programming (Pyrooz et al., 2011). The few programs in existence vary significantly. In some renunciation programs, inmates disclose information about gang activities and their involvement to STG investigators, and then they may be transferred to a unit or facility that is safe for ex-gang members (Winterdyk & Ruddell, 2010). Some facilities (2.1%) even report gang tattoo removal services for inmates wishing to renounce gang life (Knox, 2012).

The Connecticut Department of Corrections offers a Gang Management Program, which has served as a model for other states. Their intensive close custody program requires gang members to renounce their gang membership in order to successfully complete the program. In this program, gang members work on listening and communication skills and work together in 12 member "squads" throughout the entire five and a half month program (Gaseau, 2003). They must also sign a letter of intention to renounce their gang affiliation. Despite the promise of this renunciation program, Di Placido and colleagues (2006) argue that participation in "self-improvement" programs may be less threatening and more acceptable to peers than outright renunciation programs, as the costs of renunciation can be high for former gang members.

In addition, cognitive behavioral therapy may hold promise in rehabilitating gang members, if designed in accordance with the risk, needs, and responsivity principles. For example, the ABC Program uses cognitive behavioral treatment targeted at those who pose as significant management problems or have a history of extensive violence (Di Placido et al., 2006). Criminogenic factors, such as criminal thinking patterns, aggression, and substance use, are addressed through individual and group therapy. In addition, individuals may be provided with life skills training, and may be required to work on areas, such as family dynamics, education, and community support. The use of this program has shown significant reductions in recidivism and the rate of institutional misconduct (see Di Placido et al., 2006)

The future for gang problems in facilities looks dire. According to the NGCRC survey from 2012, facilities expect that gang problems including violence will continue to increase, more gang members will abuse their religious rights, correctional officer assaults will rise, and the problem of radical militantism among Islamic inmates is expected to grow (Knox, 2012). Further, in Winterdyk and Ruddell's (2010) study, approximately 75% of prison officials reported that STG membership increase over the previous five years. Additionally, approximately 44% of respondents indicated an increase in female STG members. It is yet to be determined if the rise of prison gang membership has continued to increase since 2010.

Although a number of strategies are employed by prisons, including policies and procedures, investigations, intelligence, security resources, and willingness to cooperate with community law enforcement agencies, none of these strategies have been found to be consistently effective in managing STGs (Winterdyk & Ruddell, 2010). As noted by Winterdyk and Ruddell, some interventions may be successful in one jurisdiction and not in another, or some strategies may work better for certain types of prison gangs. The key for future directions in the management of STGs is improved intelligence gathering and dissemination (Winterdyk & Ruddell, 2010). Sharing this information with community law enforcement may aid in the prosecution of known gang members with the hope that increased legal consequences of associating with an STG will deter some and incapacitate others, thereby preventing future crimes (Winterdyk, & Ruddell, 2010).

DISCUSSION QUESTIONS

1. Describe the trends in prison gang membership overtime. In the future, is gang membership expected to increase or decrease?
2. Based on your reading, what do you think is the best strategy for controlling gangs in a prison environment? If you were a warden, how would you address the issue of prison gangs in your prison?
3. What are some of the contemporary issues discussed in the reading surrounding prison gangs? How do you suggest combating these issues?
4. Is there any hope in the rehabilitation of gang members? If so, what specifically may prove beneficial?
5. How does community law enforcement and correctional systems collaborate in terms of information surrounding gangs? Why is such collaboration beneficial?

REFERENCES

Bayer, P., & Hjalmarsson, R., & Posen, D. (2009). Building criminal capital behind bars: Peer effects in juvenile corrections. *The Quarterly Journal of Economics, 124*(1), 105–147.

Clemmer, D. (1940). *The prison community.* New York: Holt, Rinehart and Winston.

Connecticut Department of Corrections (2016). *Gang management program.* Retrieved from http://www.ct.gov/doc/cwp/view.asp?a=1492&Q=305970.

DeLisi, M., Trulson, C. R., Marquart, J. W., Drury, A. J., & Kosloski, A. E. (2010). Inside the prison black box: Toward a life course importation model of inmate behavior. *International Journal of Offender Therapy and Comparative Criminology.* Advance online publication. doi: 10.1177/0306624X10383956.

Di Placido, C., Simon, T. L., Witte, T. D., Gu, D., & Wong, S. C. (2006). Treatment of gang members can reduce recidivism and institutional misconduct. *Law and Human Behavior, 30,* 93–114.

Dooley, B., Seals, A., & Skarbeck, D. (2014). The effect of prison gang membership on recidivism. *Journal of Criminal Justice, 42,* 267–75.

Drury, A., & DeLisi, M. (2010). The past is prologue: Prior adjustment to prison institutional misconduct. *The Prison Journal, 90*(3), 331–352.

Fleisher, M. S. (1989). *Warehousing violence.* Newbury Park, CA: Sage.

Fleisher, M. S., & Decker, S. H. (2001). An overview of the challenge of prison gangs. *Corrections Management Quarterly, 5,* 1–9.

Florida Department of Corrections. (2016). *Major prison gangs.* Retrieved from http://www.dc.state.fl.us/pub/gangs/prison.html.

Fong, R. (1990). The organizational structure of prison gangs: A Texas case study. *Federal Probation, 54,* 36–43.

Gaes, G., Wallace, S., Gilman, E., Klein-Saffran, J., & Suppa, S. (2002). The influence of prison gang affiliation on violence and other prison misconduct. *The Prison Journal, 82,* 359–385.

Gambetta, D. (2009). *Codes of the underworld: How criminals communicate.* Princeton, NJ: Princeton University Press.

Gaseau, M. (2003). *Connecticut program turns gang members around.* Retrieved from http://www.corrections.com/articles/11234-connecticut-program-turns-gang-members-around.

Griffin, M., & Hepburn, J. (2006). The effect of gang affiliation on violent misconduct among inmates during the early years of confinement. *Criminal Justice and Behavior, 33,* 419–448.

Hamm, M. S. (2008). Prisoner radicalization: Assessing the threat in U.S. Correctional Institutions. *NIJ Journal, 261,* 14–19.

Huebner, B. M., Varano, S. P., & Bynum, T. S. (2007). Gangs, guns, and drugs: Recidivism among serious, young offenders. *Criminology & Public Policy, 2,* 187–222.

Huff, C. (1996). The criminal behavior of gang members and nongang at-risk youth. In C. R. Huff (Ed.), *Gangs in America* (2nd ed.), (pp. 75–102). Newbury Park, CA: Sage.

Irwin, J. (1980). *Prison in turmoil.* Boston, MA: Little, Brown, and Co.

Irwin, J., & Cressey, D. (1962). Thieves, convicts, and the inmate culture. *Social Problems, 10,* 142–155. DOI: 10.2307/799047.

Kaeble, D., Glaze, L., Tsoutis, A., & Minton, T. (2016). *Correctional populations in the United States, 2014.* US Department of Justice, Office of Justice Programs, Bureau of Justice Statistics, NCJ 249513.

Knox, G. W. (n.d.). *Gang members on Facebook: Should we look the other way?* National Gang Crime Research Center. Retrieved from http://www.ngcrc.com/gangface.html.

Knox, G. W. (2005). *The problem of gangs and security threat groups (STG's) in American prisons today: Recent research findings from the 2004 prison gang survey.* National Gang Crime Research Center. Retrieved from http://www.ngcrc.com/corr2006.html.

Knox, G. W. (2012). *The problem of gangs and security threat groups (STG's) in American prisons and jails today: Recent findings from the 2012 NGCRC National Gang/STG Survey.* National Gang Crime Research Center. Retrieved from http://www.ngcrc.com/corr2012.html.

McGloin, J. (2005). Policy and intervention considerations of a network analysis of street gangs. *Criminology and Public Policy, 4,* 607–635. DOI: 10.1111/j.1745 –9133.2005.00306.x.

McShane, M. D., Williams, F. P., & Dolny, M. (2003). Effect of gang membership on parole outcome. *Journal of Gang Research, 10,* 25–38.

National Gang Intelligence Center. (2011). *National gang threat assessment 2011: Emerging trends.* Washington, DC, 30.

Orr, D. A., & Kunzi, T. (2008). *Security threat groups in Washington state prisons: An exploratory search for best practices.* Washington State Department of Corrections. Retrieved from http://app.leg.wa.gov/ReportsToTheLegislature/Home/GetPDF? fileName=Gang%20 Intervention%20Study%20Report_2c565712–0106–497d-b0c7–1004a2c4a691.pdf.

Pyrooz, D. C., Decker, S. H., & Fleisher, M. (2011). From the street to the prison, from the prison to the street: Understanding and responding to prison gangs. *Journal of Aggression, Conflict and Peace Resolution, 3,* 12–24.

Stevens, D. (1997). Origins of prison gangs in North Carolina. *Journal of Gang Research, 4,* 23–35.

Sykes, G. (1958). *The society of captives: Study of a maximum security prison.* Princeton, NJ: Princeton University Press.

Toch, H. (2007). Sequestering gang members, burning witches, and subverting due process. *Criminal Justice and Behavior, 32,* 274–288.

Varano, S., Huebner, B., & Bynum, T. (2011). Correlates and consequences of pre-incarceration gang involvement among incarcerated and youthful felons. *Journal of Criminal Justice, 39,* 30–38. DOI: 10.1016/j.jcrimjus.2010.10.001.

Wilkinson, R. A., & Delgado, A. (2006). Prison gang and drug investigations: An Ohio Approach. *Corrections Today, 68*(2), 36–40.

Winterdyk, J. (2009). *Prison gangs: A review and survey of strategies.* Ottawa, Ontario, Canada: Correctional Service of Canada.

Winterdyk, J., & Ruddell, R. (2010). Managing prison gangs: Results from a survey of U.S. prison systems. *Journal of Criminal Justice, 38,* 730–736.

Chapter Seven

Solitary Confinement

Restrictive Housing, Segregation, and the Isolation of Inmates

Jody Sundt

The number of inmates held in solitary confinement has increased dramatically in the last two decades. A recent study conducted by Yale University and the State Association of Correctional Administrators estimates between 80,000 and 100,000 inmates were held in solitary confinement, disciplinary segregation, or protective custody in 2014 (Liman-ASCA, 2015). Many thousands more experience solitary confinement in jails and detention facilities. These surprising numbers—coupled with longstanding unease about the legality and morality of the practice—have contributed to an emerging consensus that the United States must reform the use of solitary confinement.

President Obama voiced his concerns about the use of solitary confinement during a speech he gave in 2015:

> I've asked my Attorney General to start a review of the overuse of solitary confinement across American prisons. The social science shows that an environment like that is often more likely to make inmates more alienated, more hostile, potentially more violent. Do we really think it makes sense to lock so many people alone in tiny cells for 23 hours a day, sometimes for months or even years at a time? That is not going to make us safer. That's not going to make us stronger. And if those individuals are ultimately released, how are they ever going to adapt? It's not smart. (White House Office of the Press Secretary, 2015)

Similar views are shared by growing number of conservative and liberal politicians, civil rights groups, correctional leaders, and judges (Frost & Monteiro, 2016).

This chapter examines the use of solitary confinement in the United States. We will explore the nature of social isolation in prison and how this controversial practice is currently used as a punishment and as a strategy for managing inmates. The chapter reviews the research on solitary confinement, highlighting important findings and conclusions about its effect on inmate health, prison safety, and recidivism. Finally we will consider important reforms being made to solitary confinement and what role it may have in the future.

THE NATURE OF SOLITARY CONFINEMENT

The nature of solitary confinement is difficult to describe. Each jail and prison system defines and uses the practice differently. To makes matters more confusing, isolation is also referred to by many different names. The lack of agreed upon definitions, names, and standard practices inhibit our ability to understand and assess the use of solitary confinement. This is something to remember when trying to draw conclusions about solitary confinement or make recommendations about it use.

There are three primary types of restrictive housing: disciplinary segregation, protective custody, and administrative segregation.[1] We can distinguish between types of restrictive housing by their purposes. Disciplinary or punitive segregation is used to punish inmates who violate prison or jail rules. It is a sanction for *past behavior*. The purpose of protective custody is to isolate inmates who are at risk of being victimized or may be a danger to themselves. Administrative segregation is used to isolate inmates who are considered too dangerous or disruptive to be housed in the general inmate population. Protective custody and administrative segregation are strategies for preventing *future behavior*. Finally, a "supermax" is a stand alone prison or unit within a prison designed for the purpose of administrative segregation (Riveland, 1999).

Regardless of purpose or name, restrictive housing typically involves "limited interaction with other inmates, limited programming opportunities, and reduced privileges" (Beck, 2016, p. 2). Inmates in segregation spend a minimum of 23 hours per day in their cells (Metcalf & Resnik, 2012). Most facilities allow inmates three to five hours per week of recreation and two to three short showers a week. The conditions in solitary confinement are austere.

As an illustration, the court described Ohio's supermax prison in the 2005 Supreme Court case *Wilkinson v. Austin*.

[A]lmost every aspect of an inmate's life is controlled and monitored. Inmates must remain in their cells, which measure 7 by 14 feet, for 23 hours per day. A light remains on in the cell at all times, though it is sometimes dimmed, and an inmate who attempts to shield the light to sleep is subject to further discipline. During the one hour per day that an inmate may leave his cell, access is limited to one of two indoor recreation cells.

[The] cells have solid metal doors with metal strips along their sides and bottoms which prevent conversation or communication with other inmates. All meals are taken alone in the inmate's cell instead of in a common eating area. Opportunities for visitation are rare and in all events are conducted through glass walls. It is fair to say [Supermax] inmates are deprived of almost any environmental or sensory stimuli and of almost all human contact. (pp. 214–215)

The conditions described in the Ohio supermax are typical of the nature of segregation units found in other US prisons (Metcalf & Resnik, 2012).

The nature of solitary confinement is also evident at the federal supermax prison, US Administrative Maximum (ADX) Penitentiary, in Florence, Colorado. Inmates incarcerated at ADX have spent an average of 3.8 years in solitary confinement (McGinnis et al., 2014). Some federal inmates have spent decades in isolation (*Silverstein v. Federal Bureau of Prisons*).

TRENDS IN THE USE OF SOLITARY CONFINEMENT

In the early 1980s, prisons began to rely more heavily on solitary confinement as a strategy to address prison violence. For example, Texas experimented with a policy of placing all known or suspected gang members in administrative segregation to interrupt a spike in inmate violence (Ralph & Marquart, 1991). Similar efforts to address gang problems were attempted in California, which "locked-down" several prisons in response to violence (Irwin, 2004). By the end of the 1990s, the use of supermax prisons increased dramatically. In 1984, there was only one supermax prison in the United States. Fifteen years later, King (1999) identified 35 jurisdictions with a supermax prison. A recent report about the federal prison system found that the number of inmates held in restrictive housing increased dramatically from 439 in 2004 to 10,747 in 2014 (McGinnis et al., 2014).

As noted above, an estimated 100,000 adult prison inmates were held in restrictive housing in 2014 (Liman-ASCA, 2015). Some states are reforming their policies and dramatically reducing reliance on restrictive housing. For example, Colorado, Kansas, Maine, Mississippi, Ohio, and Illinois have recently closed supermax prisons. Colorado reduced its segregated population substantially. In 2011, more than 7% of the Colorado prison population was held in administrative segregation. By 2014, just 1% of Colorado prisoners were in solitary confinement (Liman-ASCA, 2015).

The decline in the use of solitary confinement in some jurisdictions is related to two other recent trends. First, the number of successful lawsuits and legal settlements challenging the use of solitary confinement has jumped in the last several years. Between 2010 and 2015, federal class action lawsuits led to changes in the use of solitary confinement in 10 states (Schlanger & Fettig, 2015). Second, there has been a recent flurry of policy activity reforming solitary confinement. Fourteen states and the federal government have revised policies or passed legislation on the use of solitary conferment since 2010 (Schlanger & Fettig, 2015).

Legislative activity and successful lawsuits are evidence of the growing consensus that solitary confinement is overused and harmful to certain groups of prisoners. The momentum for change received a boost in early 2016 when the Obama Administration issued new rules governing solitary confinement in the federal prisons system and banned the use of solitary confinement for juveniles (Shear, 2016). Given the broad support for change, we can expect to see more reforms in the future aimed at reducing the use of solitary confinement and reducing the social isolation of inmates held in restrictive housing.

CURRENT RESEARCH

Solitary confinement is hard to study. One of the challenges noted above is the lack of clear definitions and the significant variation in conditions and practices between locations. There is also a lack of quality data. Most departments of corrections do not track information about the use of solitary confinement and the data that are collected may be unreliable or difficult to obtain. Original data collection is also difficult in high security prisons. Organization may deny or limit researchers' access. Paradoxically, researchers that gain access to inmates in isolation may dilute the effect of social isolation simply by interacting with inmates (Smith, 2006). Inmates may also be unwilling to disclose mental health problems and other stigmatized and prohibited behaviors or they may exaggerate symptoms.

There are three primary areas of social science research on solitary confinement. These include the effects of solitary confinement on inmate health and wellbeing, inmate misconduct and prison safety, and recidivism. The effect of solitary confinement on inmates' wellbeing has received the most research attention and is also the most controversial. Fewer studies exist on the effect of solitary confinement on prison and public safety. So far, the evidence suggests that solitary confinement does not create safer prisons and is associated with higher rates of recidivism.

Inmate Health and Wellbeing

The effect of solitary confinement on inmate wellbeing has been a subject of debate and concern since the 1800s. The founders of the first prisons in the United States believed that isolation in penitentiaries would encourage repentance and reform. Failing genuine inmate change, advocates of the penitentiary model believed that isolation could impose physical order, slow the spread of disease, and prevent inmates from corrupting one another (Rothman, 1971). Serious problems with isolation were apparent from the start. For example, an experiment with total social isolation in New York State had a devastating effect. After 18 months of solitary confinement several prisoners had committed suicide and many more experienced mental breakdowns. The governor of New York visited the prison and declared that the results of the experiment were so dire and the punishment so severe that he immediately released 26 of the inmates (Smith, 2006). New York subsequently abandoned the use of solitary confinement in favor of a model of incarceration that required inmates to work, pray, and eat together, but in enforced silence (Rothman, 1971).

By the middle of the 1800s, the use of isolation was widely condemned. In 1847 Francis Gray published a study of the American prison system. Gray concluded that the experiment with isolation was a failure.

> [I]t appears that the system of constant separation as established here, even when administered with the utmost humanity, produces so many cases of insanity and of death as to indicate most clearly, that its general tendency is to enfeeble the body and the mind. (as cited in Smith, 2006, p. 461)

By the end of the 1800s, the United States had abandoned the practice of long-term isolation and soundly rejected its use.

Research continues to document the physical and mental health consequences of solitary confinement and catalog a consistent set of problems associated with restrictive housing. Smith (2006) provides an extensive review of this research. He documents a wide range of symptoms experienced by inmates in isolation. Physical symptoms associated with solitary confinement include dizziness, difficultly sleeping, severe headaches, digestive problems, increased pulse, and oversensitivity to stimuli. Psychological symptoms include difficulty concentrating, confusion, memory loss, hallucinations, paranoia, panic attacks, depression, anger, and impulsivity (Smith, 2006, pp. 488–493).

The symptoms observed among isolated inmates are consistent with research that examines hospitalizations and suicides. For example, a study by Sestoft and colleagues found that inmates who had spent four weeks in solitary confinement were 20 times more likely to be hospitalized for a psychiatric problem than similar inmates not subject to solitary confinement (as cited in Smith, 2006, p. 479). Reeves and Tamburello (2014) found that suicides were concentrated in restrictive housing and single cells more generally. The risk of suicide among inmates in single cell detention was more than 400 times higher than the risk to general population inmates in double-cells. Self-mutilation is also concentrated in isolation cells and may be extreme, including self-amputations. Research like these studies show that the symptoms observed among inmates in solitary confinement have real health consequences.

Some studies have not found evidence of serious mental health effects associated with administrative segregation (e.g., O'Keefe, Klebe, Stucker, Sturm, & Leggett, 2011). There is also a great deal of litigation surrounding the mental health effects of solitary confinement because inmates have a constitutional right to appropriate health care. Nevertheless, the bulk of the evidence from different authors, over different time periods, and in different prisons and jails finds an association between mental health problems and solitary confinement (Smith, 2006).

People react differently to solitary confinement. Some people experience severe problems after short periods of time in isolation whereas others adapt to extended time in solitary confinement with relatively few health effects (Smith, 2006). One way to make sense of this pattern is to think about solitary confinement as a risk factor. It does not automatically lead to a particular outcome but increases the chances that it will occur. As an illustration, you know that driving without a seat belt on does not automatically lead to a fatal car accident but it does increase the odds. We can think about time in solitary confinement in the same way. "[T]he health risk rises for each additional day in solitary confinement" (Smith, 2006, p. 495).

Scholars argue that the key feature of solitary confinement is social isolation. Environmental and sensory deprivations within solitary confinement may exacerbate the effects of social isolation. Similarly, the duration of exposure to social isolation and how prisoners interpret and think about their isolation may condition the effects it has. For example, solitary confinement where lights are kept on 24 hours a day and inmates are not allow to cover their head to sleep at night is more distressing than conditions that allow for access to natural light patterns (Schlanger & Fettig, 2016). Staff hostility may also exacerbate psychological and physical problems of isolated inmates (Smtih, 2006). These studies suggest some predictions. We can expect more mental and physical health problems when the degree of social isolation is greater, when conditions are more depriving, and when the few social interactions inmates have are negative. They also help us think about why we might see different results across studies.

Inmate Misconduct and Prison Safety

The purpose of punitive segregation is to punish inmates who break the rules. The aim of administrative segregation is to create a safer prison system by removing inmates from the general population who have may be disruptive or dangerous. Finally, protective custody is supposed to prevent vulnerable inmates from being hurt or manipulated by more aggressive inmates. If isolation is effective at achieving these goals we should see a relationship between solitary confinement and improved prison safety.

Despite the severe restrictions placed on inmates in solitary confinement, research consistently finds that restrictive housing is the most dangerous place in prison (Appelbaum et al., 2011; Bidna, 1975; Kratcoski, 1988; Proporino, 1986; Sorensen, Cunningham, Vigen, & Woods, 2011). A study of New York prisoners found that inmates punished in solitary confinement were seven times as likely to harm themselves as comparable inmates held in the general population (Kaba et al., 2014). Similarly, Sorensen et al. (2011) report that more than half of all serious assaults against staff in Texas occurred in segregated housing despite the fact that only a small fraction of the total inmate population was held there. Paradoxically, solitary confinement appears to contribute to the very problems it is attempting to prevent (Rhodes, 2004).

Research also raises doubts about the ability of solitary confinement to improve prison safety by deterring or incapacitating dangerous and disruptive inmates. Deterrence is the idea that the threat of punishment can prevent crime. The experience of solitary confinement may be so awful that inmates are convinced to never again do something that might result in a return to segregation. Incapacitation is the idea that removing the "bad apples" from the general population makes everyone else safer and help prisons run more smoothly.

Although inmates have described their experience in solitary confinement as torture (see, e.g., Manning, 2016), research finds that placement in punitive segregation does not appear to be an effective deterrent. For example, Huebner (2003) found that the proportion of inmates in a prison facility who had received solitary confinement as a punishment for a rule violation was unrelated to the frequency of assaults. This is consistent with the results of studies that look at how inmates behave after they are released from punitive segregation and return to the general inmate population. Morris (2015) used a sophisticated method to compare a group of inmates sent to punitive segregation to a matched group who remained in the general population. He found that punitive segregation had no effect on the likelihood, timing, or pattern of violent misconduct (Morris, 2015). Similarly, Labrecque (2015) and Lucas (2015) found that placement in disciplinary segregation and the length of time inmates spent in solitary confinement (up to 30 days) were unrelated to future misconduct. When Labrecque (2015) looked at different types of inmates, however, he found that gang members and mentally ill inmates were more, not less, likely to engage in misconduct after spending in time segregation.

Studies also raise doubts about whether segregating disruptive or violent inmates makes prisons safer overall. Two studies by Sundt and colleagues found that supermax prisons and administrative segregation had no effect on overall inmate safety (Briggs, Sundt, & Casetellano, 2003; Sundt, Castellano, & Briggs, 2008). The effect of administrative segregation on staff safety was mixed, sometimes improving correctional officer safety, sometimes making it worse, but mostly having no effect. Further questions about the utility of solitary confinement were raised by a national study of 247 prisons from 40 states. Wooldredge and Steiner (2015) found that the use administrative segregation was associated with increased rates of assaults and misconduct, even after taking into account the characteristics of inmates and the prisons were they were incarcerated.

Although we need more research to reach stronger conclusions, the research to date does not support the claim that solitary confinement makes prisons or correctional officers safer. Useem and Piehl (2006) remind us that "[p]risons cannot operate by force alone" (p. 90). Perhaps the lack of evidence that administrative segregation makes prison safer should not surprise us. Prisons are political communities that depend on inmate cooperation and belief in the fairness and legitimacy of regimes. Yet Beck (2015) found that prisons and jails with poor climates, where inmates do not trust correctional officers, rely more heavily on restrictive housing. Although Beck was not able to say whether poor climate was the cause or effect of heavy use of restrictive housing, this is a troubling finding regardless of the direction of influence. It is important that research look more carefully at this issue in the future to learn more about how prison policies affect prison safety.

Recidivism

As prisons began to expand the use of extended solitary confinement, critics of the practice warned of the potential danger of releasing inmates—some whom spent years in isolation—directly to the community. Critics' worst fears appeared to come true in 2013, when a Colorado inmate released directly from a supermax prison assassinated Tom Clements, who was the Executive Director of the Colorado Department of Corrections, on the doorstep of his home (Healy, 2013). Research confirms that inmates held in supermax prisons are higher-risk and commit more crime after they are released than inmates housed in general population prisons (Lovell, Johnson, & Cain, 2007; Mears & Bales, 2007; Motiuk & Blanchette, 2001). But does this mean that solitary confinement causes inmates to commit more crimes after they were released from prison?

The answer to this question is not settled yet, but two studies have tested the effect of solitary confinement on recidivism. A study of Washington State prisoners found that inmates released directly from supermax were more likely to commit a new crime compared to a matched group of similar inmates who were released from a general population prison (Lovell et al. 2007). A similar study of Florida inmates found that inmates incarcerated in supermax prisons were more likely to commit a violent crime after release, but how long they spent in segregation and whether they were released directly from solitary confinement did not make a difference (Mears & Bales, 2009).

We do not know enough to draw conclusions about whether spending time in solitary confinement increases the chance that inmates will commit more crime. What is clear, however, is that inmates in isolation are much less likely to participate in treatment programs and get help preparing for their eventual release because they are in restrictive housing. It is ironic that the inmates who need these services the most are the least likely to have access to them.

In summary, the research on solitary confinement raises important doubts. Evidence is mounting that solitary confinement does not improve prison safety and may backfire. Some prison officials are questioning whether the focus on segregation and control detracts from the public safety mission of prisons (Mohr & Raemisch, 2015). Added to these doubts is evidence that time spent in solitary confinement can do lasting physical and psychological harm to some inmates.

POLICIES GOVERNING SOLITARY CONFINEMENT

The policies governing solitary confinement are diverse and corrections officials have wide discretion in how they use this practice. There is a consensus among corrections officials that the main purpose of segregation is to improve prison safety (Mears & Castro, 2006; Metcalf et al., 2013). Beyond this, however, there is little agreement about who should be placed in isolation, why, for how long, or under what conditions. The lack of specific, consistent, and transparent policies around the use of solitary confinement has contributed to calls for reform (Turner, 2014; Metcalf & Resnik, 2012).

Who Belongs in Segregation?

Advocates of supermax prisons argue that long-term solitary confinement is needed to control the "worst of the worst"—predatory convicts, gang members, and notorious murders. Indeed, the supermax model originated at the

US Penitentiary at Marion in 1983 when two correctional officers were brutally murdered by members of a prison gang serving life sentences. Following the attacks, the Marion prison was placed on "lockdown" and inmates were confined to their cells. What began as a temporary response to a crisis became a permanent policy and marked the creation of the "supermax." One of the inmates involved in this incident, Tommy Silverstein, has served more than 30 years in solitary confinement. In 2014, he lost a federal appeal challenging his extended confinement in isolation (*Silverstein v. Federal Bureau of Prisons*). The court ruled that he still posed a serious risk to prison safety.

Although prison officials argue that administrative segregation is needed to manage dangerous inmates, research finds that a substantial proportion of the inmates held in solitary confinement do not pose a serious security risk and have not committed serious infractions. According to Turner (2014), "[Segregation] has increasingly been used with prisoners who do not pose a threat to staff or other prisoners but are placed in segregation for minor violations that are disruptive but not violent, such as talking back (insolence), being out of place, failure to report to work or school, or refusing to change housing units or cells" (p. 2). Research by the Vera Institute found that, in one state, 60% of inmates released from segregation during one year had been placed in solitary confinement for a minor rule violation (Turner, 2014). Similarly, researchers from Yale University note "[i]n our exchanges about administrative segregation, several correctional experts discussed the risk of overuse based on what is colloquially known as being 'mad' at a prisoner, as contrasted with being 'scared' of that individual." (Liman-ASCA, 2015, p. 8).

David Lovell and his colleagues (2000) classified supermax inmates into seven categories that described patterns of institutional behavior. The first group consisted of inmates seeking protection and safety. For these inmates, supermax provided informal protective custody without the stigma that can be associated with asking for formal protective custody. The second group consisted of inmates who had poor impulse control. Many of the inmates in this group had diagnoses for a host of physical, cognitive, emotional, and behavioral problems. A third group consisted of inmates who were "paying the price" and viewed supermax as the "cost of doing business" in prison. Inmates described as socially inept made up the fourth group. This group has a history of trouble adapting to incarceration and exhibit progressively poor adjustment. A fifth group included inmates who were described as being "at war with the system." For these individuals, supermax was a type of "stalemate." Two additional groups were identified that consisted of mentally ill inmates who were either in route to treatment from supermax or are in route to supermax from treatment. The inmates "paying the price" and those "at war" most closely resemble the idea of the "worst-of-the-worst" but they made up a small proportion of those held in supermax.

Other research indicates that the mentally ill and other vulnerable populations are disproportionately located in solitary confinement. In a follow-up study Lovell (2008) found that 45% of supermax inmates in Washington State had a serious mental illness. A national survey conducted by the Bureau of Justice Statistics reports a similar pattern. Twenty-nine percent of prison inmates and 22% of jail inmates with symptoms of serious mental illness had spent time in restrictive housing in the previous year, rates significantly higher than the general population of inmates (Beck, 2016). The Bureau of Justice Statistics study may underestimate the prevalence of seriously mentally ill inmates in segregation because many of these individuals did not participate in the survey because they were too ill or were not allowed out of isolation (Beck, 2016).

Mentally ill inmates are particularly vulnerable to the effects of solitary confinement. Inmates with personality disorders, brain damage, developmental disabilities, and chronic depression are also at high risk for mental health problems while incarcerated in solitary confinement. In *Madrid v. Gomez* (1995) the court ruled California's supermax prison at Pelican Bay imposed cruel and unusual punishment on mentally ill inmates. "For these inmates, placing them in [administrative segregation] is the mental equivalent of putting an asthmatic in a place with little air to breathe." Although the courts have been unwilling to rule that solitary confinement is intrinsically cruel and unusual, they are more sympathetic to the argument that it is cruel to certain classes of inmates like the mentally ill and developmentally disabled.

There is also growing agreement that juveniles do not belong in solitary confinement. In addition to the federal government, Alaska, Colorado, Mississippi, Nevada, New York, Oklahoma, and West Virginia prohibit the use of solitary confinement for juveniles (Frost & Monteiro, 2016). When juveniles are placed in isolation, best practice guidelines hold that the director or warden should make this decision and that the youth should talk to a counselor within two hours of being isolated. A survey of youth in detention found that more than a third of juveniles reported spending time in isolation and half of these individuals were held for longer than 24 hours (Sedlak & McPherson, 2010). Although the researchers did not measure who made the decision to place the youth in isolation, 52% who spent longer than 2 hours in isolation report that they had not talked to a counselor at any time since arriving at the facility where they were incarcerated.

Placing suspected and known gang members in administrative segregation is also very controversial. As mentioned, above this practice gained popularity in the mid-1980s and used by California, Arizona, and the Federal Bureau of Prisons. There is evidence that inmates affiliated with gangs are at a higher risk of engaging in prison violence, although other factors such as an inmate's age has a stronger influence on whether an inmate is violent (Griffin & Hepburn, 2006). Critics argue that it is not appropriate to isolate someone who has not committed an offense and are only suspected of being a gang member. Toch (2007) compared the identification and punishment of gang members in administrative segregation to the persecution of witches by medieval inquisitors. He notes several parallels including guilt by association, reliance on secret evidence, the blending of the judge and prosecutor role, and calls for confessions and renunciations. The practice of holding known or suspected gang members in administrative segregation for indefinite periods of time was successfully challenged in California. In 2015, the California Department of Corrections and Rehabilitation entered into a settlement agreement to end this practice (St. John, 2015).

There is more agreement about who does not belong in solitary confinement than about who does. In addition, the research shows that many inmates end up in solitary confinement who probably do not belong there either because they are vulnerable or because they do not pose a security risk. To understand why the net has widened to include larger numbers of less serious inmates in restrictive housing it is useful to consider the policies that govern getting in and out of solitary confinement.

Getting In and Out

Most jurisdictions in the US give broad discretion to corrections administrators to decide why to place an inmate in segregation. Metcalf et al. (2013) report that most jurisdictions specify a list of factors that are considered when someone is placed in administrative segregation. The criteria are wide-ranging and often include "catch all" language. Nebraska, for example, lists 19 factors "including but not limited" to "[a]ny other information regarding the inmate that the classification authority deems appropriate" (as cited in Metcalf et al., 2013, p. 8).

Other states do not attempt to list specific criteria for placement in administrative segregation but instead provide general authority to do so. For example, New York's policy simply states: "Administrative segregation admission results from a determination by the facility that the inmate's presence in general population would pose a threat to the safety and security of the facility" (as cited in Metcalf et al., 2013, p. 9).

In contrast, some jurisdictions like Delaware limit the authority to place an inmate to specific, high-ranking individuals with the prison system. "The Watch Commander, or higher authority, may order immediate Administrative Segregation when it is necessary to protect the offender or others. This action is reviewed within 72 hours by the facility Warden" (cited in Metcalf et al., 2012, p. 10). Other states such as Virginia have narrowed the use of administrative segregation by clearly and narrowly defining "segregation qualifiers." Examples include "aggravated assault on staff" and "aggravated assault on an inmate w/weapon or resulting in serious injury w/o weapon" (cited in Metcalf et al., 2013, p. 10). States with narrow, specific policies that limit the authority to place an inmate in solitary confinement tend to have fewer inmates in isolation.

The Liman Project found few rules governing how inmates could get out of segregation. Some states have no written policies while others allow for "periodic review." A handful of states have "step-down" programs where inmates gain additional time out of their cell and privileges for good behavior.

> In sum, a wide net of authority permits institutions to place prisoners into segregation. The 2013 policies made plain that, in most jurisdictions getting into administrative segregation was relatively easy to do, and that getting out of segregation was not a focus of the rules. (Liman-ASCA, 2015, p. 9)

This combination of policies helps to explain why the number of inmates held in isolation has grown.

Duration of Confinement

There are few studies or reports on the average length of time inmates spend in solitary confinement. Indeed, critics of solitary confinement argue that the lack of transparency is a purposeful strategy to avoid public scrutiny and accountability. Disciplinary segregation tends to be limited to a 30-day sanction, but inmates may stay in disciplinary segregation longer for breaking rules while in isolation. In addition, inmates may serve consecutive periods of time in disciplinary segregation that add-up to much longer than 30 days. Inmates in administrative segregation may be held indefinitely or until the end of their sentence. Some states require that inmates spend a minimum number of days in administrative segregation but very few jurisdictions place limits on the maximum time inmates can be kept in isolation (Liman-ASCA, 2015). Thus, the "length of time spent in isolation can vary from a few days to many years" (Metcalf et al., 2013, p. 1).

Beck (2015) reports that 18% of prison inmates and 17% of jail inmates spent time in restrictive housing between 2011 and 2012. "Approximately 10% of all prison inmates and 5% of jail inmates said they had spent 30 days or longer in restrictive housing." Prison inmates who spent time in solitary confinement during the year served an average of 8.6 months in restrictive housing. The average length of time jail inmates spent in restrictive housing was 3.5 month.

The Liman project attempted to gather information about how long inmates were being held in administrative segregation. Twenty-four jurisdictions (out of 51) provided information to the researchers. In 11 jurisdictions, the majority of inmates were held for 90 days or less. Eighteen jurisdictions reported holding inmates in segregation for longer than 3 years (Liman-ASCA, 2015). Although these data are limited and do not allow us to draw conclusions about the average length of stay in administrative segregation, the results reinforce the conclusion that a subset of inmates are spending very long periods of time in isolation. The United Nations Standard Minimum Rules for the Treatment of Prisoners (2015), also known as the Nelson Mandela Rules, hold that isolation for longer than 15 days is "cruel, inhumane, and degrading treatment."

REFORMING SOLITARY CONFINEMENT

The US Senate Committee on the Judiciary held bipartisan hearings in 2012 and 2014 amid growing concerns about the use of solitary confinement. These were the first, national legislative hearings ever held on solitary confinement in the United States. Testimony was presented from a coalition of correctional officials, former inmates and their family members, researchers, civil rights lawyers, and religious leaders. Participants spoke to the harmful effects of solitary confinement, how solitary confinement can be reformed, and how we can make sure that it is used more wisely.

Specific recommendations for reforming the use of solitary confinement were presented by the Vera Institute of Justice (Turner, 2014) and the Texas Public Policy Foundation (Levin, 2014). These recommendations are summarized in Table 7.1. The Vera Institute describes itself as a non-partisan whereas the Texas Public Policy Foundation describes itself as a conservative organization. Despite different orientations, there is substantial overlap in their recommendations. The suggestions focus on ways to reduce the use of solitary confinement and prepare inmates for their eventual return to general population prisons and to the community. There is also agreement that individuals who need some type of protective custody should not be placed in solitary confinement.

Mississippi was one of the first states to fundamentally rethink its use of administrative segregation and implement reforms like those outlined in Table 7.1. In 2007, the Mississippi Department of Corrections (MDOC) faced a crisis. A lawsuit was working its way through the courts challenging the conditions in the administrative segregation unit, excessive use of force, the treatment of seriously mentally ill inmates, and the lack of a rational classification system. In addition, the administrative segregation unit erupted in violence and gang warfare that resulted in multiple stabbings and inmate deaths. In response, the MDOC leadership and the civil rights advocates came together to find solutions (Kupers et al., 2009).

Table 7.1.   Recommendations for Reforming Solitary Confinement

Vera Institute of Justice	Texas Public Policy Foundation
1. Reduce intakes to segregation by using alternative sanctions for all but the most serious violations.	1. End the practice of releasing inmates directly from solitary confinement.
2. Review currently segregated population to identify needed policy changes.	2. Create oversight mechanisms to review decisions to keep an inmate in solitary confinement beyond 72 hours.
3. Provide tiered incentives to reduce segregation time for sustained good behavior.	3. Provide inmates isolated for non-violent misconduct a means to earn their way out of solitary confinement.
4. Limit the violations for which segregation is a sanction and reduce segregation time for categories of violations.	4. Eliminate rules that make all inmates in solitary confinement ineligible for any programing and allow access to constructive reading materials.
5. Increase protective custody (PC) bed availability to prevent prisoners from remaining at higher custody levels longer than necessary.	5. Improve training for prison personnel in de-escalation techniques, mental illness, and mental retardation.
6. Create or expand "missioned" general population housing targeted to the needs of prisoners who are mentally ill, developmentally delayed, or at risk for sexual victimization or other bodily harm.	6. Require agencies to include an estimate of the cost of solitary confinement in their budget proposals.
7. Increase programming for prisoners in segregation.	7. Implement prison management models that create incentives for positive behavior and self-improvement and approximate community.

8. Improving basic physical conditions.

9. Increase mental health and social work staff across facilities and special needs/protective custody units to enhance the delivery of treatment and programs and reduce disruptions.

10. Implement transition programs and housing to transition segregation prisoners to the general population prior to their release from custody.

8. Create a matrix of sanctions that must be used prior to placing an inmate in solitary confinement, unless that inmate has engaged in violent misconduct.

9. Restore parole for nonviolent offenders and allow them to earn time off their sentence based on their performance.

10. Create separate, smaller, "missioned" housing for inmates in protective custody, for mentally ill inmates, and for inmates with developmental disorders.

11. Reexamine prison construction and renovation plans to ensure that unnecessary solitary confinement cells are not added.

12. Improve availability of data.

Source: Turner (2014) and Levin (2014). Recommendations edited for length and clarity.

Significant reforms were made in the MDOC. First, the prison established a new classification system that used objective, specific criteria for placement. When implemented, the MDOC found that 80% of the inmates held in administrative segregation did not meet the new criteria for placement there. The population in supermax dropped from 1,000 inmates to less than 150. Second, the MDOC mandated a 90-day review and a written case-plan that identified how the inmates could earn their release. Most inmates would be released from segregation within 12 months. Third, the MDOC created a new unit for seriously mentally ill inmates that included intensive treatment, better training for all staff, the use of treatment teams that consisted of treatment and security staff, and a "step-down" program that moved inmates from single-cells with little out of cell time to increasing levels of group interaction. In addition to reducing the number of inmates in isolation and the duration of their stay, the changes also saved the state millions of dollars, and importantly reduced the use of force and violent misconduct (Kupers et al., 2009).

As discussed above, there is strong momentum to reform solitary confinement. Across the political spectrum each branch of government recognizes the need for reform and greater accountability for our prison policies. We can anticipate that more states will follow the lead of Mississippi and Colorado in the next several years.

THE FUTURE OF SOLITARY CONFINEMENT

We can think about the expansion of supermax prisons and the proliferation of solitary confinement as part of the same trend that led to build-up in the prison population. "Mass incarceration" was the result of policy decisions to punish a wider range of behaviors for longer periods of time (Travis, Western, & Redburn, 2014). The population in restrictive housing grew for the same reasons: a broad range of misbehavior and troublesomeness was punished for increasingly long periods of time. During the 1980s and 1990s, our correctional system embraced a policy of incapacitation. The sentiment at the time was that we should get-tough on criminals; "lock 'em up and throw away the key." Prisons experienced a crisis of crowding as they struggled to respond to the rapid rise in the inmate population and the mission of prisons shifted from inmate reform to containment and control (Cullen, Van Voorhis, & Sundt, 1996). Within this context, supermax prisons made sense. Isolation was an expedient, efficient way to respond to complex problems like overcrowding, gang activity, and severe mental illness (see, e.g., Raemisch, 2014). In a system where the goal was to warehouse inmates, there was little reason to look critically at what was happening behind prison walls.

Likewise, the same trends that are raising doubts about mass incarceration have raised the alarm about solitary confinement. We are more aware now of the limits of incarceration (Travis et al., 2014). And, the public is willing to consider policies for downsizing prisons (Sundt, Cullen, Thielo, & Johnson, 2015). Importantly, we have also gained perspective on the high financial and human costs of incarceration. We are more committed to evidence-based practices and expect a better return on our public safety investments. Perhaps most important, we have confronted the fact that the vast majority of prisoners—approximately 95%—come back to the community. "We can no longer slam the cell door and turn our backs on the impact our policies have on the incarcerated and the safety of our nation" (Durbin, 2012).

The momentum to reform the use of solitary confinement is high. It is likely that we will see more states ban its use for juveniles, pregnant women, and the seriously mentally ill. It is possible that we will see federal legislation or a Supreme Court decision prohibiting all but emergency isolation for groups of vulnerable prisoners. Although a universal ban on solitary confinement is unlikely, the trend to reduce the number of inmates in segregation and the length of time they spend in segregation will shrink the use of isolation. We are especially likely to see fundamental changes to how inmates who need protective custody are treated.

In the future, the nature of solitary confinement and the policies governing its use may be very different than they are today. We may not recognize the restrictive housing units of the future as "supermax" or "administrative segregation." Indeed it is likely that extreme social isolation and particularly harsh conditions found in many of our current segregation prisons will no longer exist. These painful conditions do not serve a legitimate purpose and the evidence is mounting that they can have devastating effects.

Prisons have a responsibility to manage the risks that inmates pose and maintain order. "The very nature of our prisons," observes Cohen (2008), "means we must have some means by which to separate prisoners on the basis of those who are at risk from those who create those risks" (p. 1017). Prisons need strategies to manage dangerous inmates and a way to separate those who cannot be safely supervised in general population prisons. Some type of restrictive housing may be a necessary tool to manage prisons safely. Prisons also have a responsibility to treat inmates with dignity and prepare them to return to society better prepared than when they arrived. In the future, we must find a better way to balance these goals.

DISCUSSION QUESTIONS

1. The size of a solitary confinement cell is approximately 7 feet by 13 feet, which is slightly smaller than an average parking spot. Inmates have limited access to readings materials, personal items, visits, showers, recreation, natural sunlight, and food. Imagine what it would feel like to spend a week in isolation. What would you miss the most? How would you cope? (Download the "Guardian VR" app to experience solitary confinement in virtual reality. Information is available at: http://gu.com/p/4t6xe/sbl.)
2. Surprisingly little research exists about solitary confinement. What would you most like to know about solitary confinement? How could this question be studied? What ethics problems might arise when trying to study this question?
3. What are the intended and unintended effects of solitary confinement? What are the implications of your observations?
4. Views differ about the maximum length of time that should inmates be held in isolation. The "Mandela Rules" hold that prisoners should not be kept in solitary confinement for longer than 15 days. However, courts in the United States have upheld decisions to keep inmates in solitary confinement for decades. Where do you stand? How long

should an inmate be kept in solitary confinement before the practice becomes "cruel and unusual?"

5. Compare and contrast the recommendations of the Vera Institute of Justice and the Texas Public Policy Foundation for reforming solitary confinement. What are the areas of agreement? How do the recommendations differ?

NOTES

1. Death row is another type of restrictive housing. Death row holds inmates who are awaiting execution. Inmates on death row experience many of the same problems as inmates held in other types of social isolation. In other important ways, however, death row is unique and will not be discussed in this chapter. To learn more about death row see *Death Work: A Study of the Modern Execution Process* by Robert Johnson.

REFERENCES

Appelbaum, K. L., Savageau, J. A., Trestman, R. L., Metzner, J. L., & Baillargeon, J. (2011). A national survey of self-injurious behavior in American prisons. *Psychiatric Services, 62*, 285–290.

Beck, A. J. (2016). *Use of restrictive housing in US prisons and jails, 2011–12.* Washington, DC: Bureau of Justice Statistics.

Bidna, H. (1975). Effects of increased security on prison violence. *Journal of Criminal Justice, 3*, 33–45.

Briggs, C. S., Sundt, J. L., & Castellano, T. C. (2003). The effect of supermaximum security prisons on aggregate levels of institutional violence. *Criminology, 41*, 1341–1376.

Cullen, F. T., Van Voorhis, P., & Sundt, J. L. (1996). Prisons in crisis: The American experience. In P. Francis and R. Mathews (Eds.), *Prisons 2000* (21–52). UK: Palgrave Macmillan.

Durbin, D. (2012, June 19). *Opening statement. Reassessing solitary confinement: The human rights, fiscal, and public safety consequences.* US Senate Committee on the Judiciary. Available at www.judiciary.senate.gov

Frost, N. A., & Monteiro, C. E. (2016). *Administrative segregation in US prisons.* Washington, DC: National Institute of Justice.

Griffin, M. L., & Hepburn, J. R. (2006). The effect of gang affiliation on violent misconduct among inmates during the early years of confinement. *Criminal Justice and Behavior, 33*(4), 419–466.

Healy, J. (2013). Colorado reels after killing of top official over prisons. *New York Times* retrieved from www.nytimes.com

Huebner, B. M. (2003). Administrative determinants of inmate violence: A multilevel analysis. *Journal of Criminal Justice, 31*(2), 107–17.

Irwin, J. (2004). *The warehouse prison: Disposal of the new dangerous class.* New York: Oxford University Press.

Kaba, F., Lewis, A., Glowa-Kollisch, S., Hadler, J., Lee, D., Alper, H., & Venters, H. (2014). Solitary confinement and risk of self-harm among jail inmates. *American Journal of Public Health, 104*(3), 442–447.

King, R. D. (1999). The rise and rise of supermax: An American solution in search of a problem? *Punishment & Society, 1*, 163–186.

Kratcoski, P. C. (1988). The implications of research explaining prison violence and disruption. *Federal Probation, 52*, 27–40.

Kupers, T. A., Dronet, T., Winter, M., Austin, J., Kelly, L., Cartier, W., . . . & Vincent, L. C. (2009). Beyond supermax administrative segregation: Mississippi's experience rethinking prison classification and creating alternative mental health programs. *Criminal Justice and Behavior, 36(10),* 1037–1050.

Labrecque, R. M. (2015). *The effect of solitary confinement on institutional misconduct: A longitudinal evaluation* (doctoral dissertation, University of Cincinnati).

Levin, M. A. (2014, February 25). *Testimony. Reassessing solitary confinement II: The human rights, fiscal, and public safety consequences.* US Senate Committee on the Judiciary. Available at www.judiciary.senate.gov.

Liman Program & Association of State Correctional Administrators. (2015). *Time-In-Cell: ASCA-Liman 2014 National Survey of Administrative Segregation in Prison.* New Haven, CT: Yale Law School.

Lovell, D. (2008). Patterns of disturbed behavior in a supermax population. *Criminal Justice and Behavior, 35*(8), 985–1004.

Lovell, D., Cloyes, K., Allen, D., & Rhodes, L. (2000). Who lives in super-maximum custody? A Washington State study. *Federal Probation, 64,* 33–38.

Lovell, D., Johnson, L. C., & Cain, K. C. (2007). Recidivism of supermax prisoners in Washington State. *Crime & Delinquency, 53*(4), 633–656.

Lucas, J. W. (2015). *The deterrent effect of disciplinary segregation on prison inmate misconduct* (doctoral dissertation, Walden University).

Manning, C. E. (2016). Solitary confinement is "no touch" torture, and it must be abolished. *The Guardian* retrieved from www.theguardian.com.

McGinnis, K., Austin, J., Becker, K., Fields, L., Lane, M., Maloney, M., & Felix, T. (2014). *Federal Bureau of Prisons: Special Housing Unit Review and Assessment.* Arlington, VA: CNA.

Mears, D. P., & Bales, W. D. (2009). Supermax incarceration and recidivism. *Criminology, 47*(4), 1131–1166.

Mears, D. P., & Castro, J. L. (2006). Wardens' views on the wisdom of supermax prisons. *Crime & Delinquency, 52*(3), 398–431.

Metcalf, H., Morgan, J., Oliker-Friedland, S., Resnik, J., Spiegel, J., Tae, H., . . . & Holbrook, B. (2013). *Administrative segregation, degrees of isolation, and incarceration: A national overview of state and federal correctional policies.* Hartford, CT: Liman Public Interest Program, Yale Law School.

Metcalf, H., & Resnik, J. (2012, June 19). *Written statement. Reassessing solitary confinement: The human rights, fiscal, and public safety consequences.* US Senate Committee on the Judiciary. Available at www.law.yale.edu.

Mohr, G. C., & Raemisch, R. (2015, Feb. 13). Restrictive housing: Taking the lead. *Corrections Today.* Retrieved from www.aca.org.

Morris, R. G. (2015). Exploring the effect of exposure to short-term solitary confinement among violent prison inmates. *Journal of Quantitative Criminology,* 1–22.

Motiuk, L. L., & Blanchette, K. (2001). Characteristics of administratively segregated offenders in federal corrections. *Canadian Journal of Criminology, 43,* 131.

O'Keefe, M. L., Klebe, K. J., Stucker, A., Sturm, K., & Leggett, W. (2011). One year longitudinal study of the psychological effects of administrative segregation. Final report to the US Department of Justice. Washington, DC: U.S. Department of Justice.

Porporino, F. J. (1986). Managing violent individuals in correctional settings. *Journal of Interpersonal Violence, 1,* 213–237.

Raemisch, R. (2014, February 21). My night in solitary, *New Tork Times,* p. A25.

Ralph, P. H., & Marquart, J. W. (1991). Gang violence in Texas prisons. *The Prison Journal, 71,* 38–49.

Reeves, R., & Tamburello, A. (2014). Single cells, segregated housing, and suicide in the New Jersey Department of Corrections. *Journal of the American Academy of Psychiatry and the Law Online, 42*(4), 484–488.

Rhodes, L. A. (2004). *Total confinement: Madness and reason in the maximum security prison* (Vol. 7). Berkeley and Los Angles: University of California Press.

Riveland, C. (1999). *Supermax prisons: Overview and general considerations.* Washington, DC: National Institute of Corrections.

Rothman, D. J. (1971). *The discovery of the asylum.* Piscataway, NJ: Transaction Publishers.

Schlanger, M., & Fettig, A. (2016, May 26). Eight principles for reforming solitary confinement. *The American Prospect.* Available at: www.prospect.org.

Sedlak, A. J., & McPherson, K. S. (2010, May). *Conditions of confinement: Findings from the survey of youth in residential placement.* Bulletin. Washington, DC: Office of Juvenile Justice and Delinquency Prevention.

Shear, M. (2016, January 25). Obama bans solitary confinement of juveniles in federal prisons. *New York Times.* Available at www.nytimes.com.

Smith, P. S. (2006). The effects of solitary confinement on prison inmates: A brief history and review of the literature. *Crime and Justice, 34*(1), 441–528.

Sorensen, J. R., Cunningham, M. D., Vigen, M. P., & Woods, S. O. (2011). Serious assaults on prison staff: A descriptive analysis. *Journal of Criminal Justice, 39*, 143–150.

St. John, P. (2015, September 1). California agrees to move thousands of inmates out of solitary confinement. *Los Angeles Times.* Retrieved from www.latimes.com.

Sundt, J., Castellano, T. C., & Briggs, C. S. (2008). The sociopolitical context of prison violence and its control: A case study of supermax and its effect in Illinois. *The Prison Journal, 88*, 94–122.

Sundt, J., Cullen, F. T., Thielo, A. J., & Jonson, C. L. (2015). Public willingness to downsize prisons: Implications from Oregon. *Victims & Offenders, 10*(4), 365–378.

Toch, H. (2007). Sequestering gang members, burning witches, and subverting due process. *Criminal Justice and Behavior, 34*(2), 274–288.

Travis, J., Western, B., & Redburn, S. (eds.) (2014). *The growth of incarceration in the United States: Exploring the causes and consequences.* Washington, DC: The National Academies Press.

Turner, N. (2014, February 25). *Written testimony. Reassessing solitary confinement II: The human rights, fiscal, and public safety consequences.* US Senate Committee on the Judiciary. Available at www.vera.org.

United Nations standard minimum rules for the treatment of prisoners (the Nelson Mandela rules) (2015, December 17). General Assembly resolution A/RES/70/175 available at www.undocs.org.

US Government Accountability Office. (2013). Improvements needed in Bureau of Prisons' monitoring and evaluation of impact of segregated housing. Washington, DC: US Government Accountability Office.

Useem, B., & Piehl, A. M. (2006). Prison buildup and disorder. *Punishment & Society, 8*, 87–115.

White House Office of the Press Secretary. (2015). *Remarks by the President at the NAACP Conference.* Washington, DC: The White House, Office of the Press Secretary.

Williams, T. (2015, May 28). Prison officials join movement to curb solitary confinement. *New York Times.* Available at www.nytimes.com.

Wooldredge, J., & Steiner, B. (2015). A macro-level perspective on prison inmate deviance. *Punishment & Society, 17*, 230–257.

CASES CITED

Madrid v. Gomez, 889 F. Supp. 1146 (N.D. Cal. 1995).

Silverstein v. Federal Bureau of Prisons, No. 12–1450 (D.Ct. No. 1:07-CV-02471-PAB-KMT) (Colo.) (2014).

Wilkinson v. Austin, 545 U.S. 209 (2005).

Part III

Programming

Chapter Eight

Psychological Prison Programs

Emily Lasko and Chad Posick

NATURE OF THE ISSUE

Programming inside prison is a relatively new phenomenon. Centuries old prisons (e.g., dungeons and debtors prisons) were hardly concerned with rehabilitation and more with isolation and punishment. Prisons were "the abandonment of an offender," states Peters (1995), "confined and left to starve to death, shaded into another category of physical punishment: the punishment of the body by death, mutilation, or beating (p. 3)." The early prisons in the United States after the enlightenment period of the 1700s were only slightly better—being less concerned with "correcting" the individual than they were with providing a place where the prisoner could repent and find God in order to reform themselves. This model of prison led to the penitentiary, a quiet, drab place where the wayward individual could reflect on their sins and come to form a relationship with God.

Shortly after the traditional penitentiary, the Auburn prison in New York decided to use a new model where prisoners would work during the day and be separated (and barred from talking to one another) at night. The idea here was not to offer the prisoners a chance to learn skills and help them re-enter society after their sentence but to profit off of their productivity. In the South, the lease system similarly profited off the labor of prisoners but instead of mostly manufacturing work inside the prison, prisoners worked outside in agricultural settings. Prisoners were "leased" to work on farms and plantations for free so that the owner, as well as the criminal justice system, could profit (Spierenburg, 1987).

These models of prison changed, especially in the early 1940s, when the promise of science to reform, or "correct," people with defects of the body and brain was realized by society and the criminal justice system. Advances in medicine and neuroscience suggested that criminal behavior had a basis in brain functioning that could be addressed through psychological treatment. This is one of the first periods where one can see the impact of psychology on prison programming. These early prison programs relied heavily on behavior modification techniques, token economies, and aversion therapies (in cases of sex offenders) primarily because the goal was to decrease deviant behaviors through counter-conditioning and contingencies (Jennings & Deming, 2013). For example, reality therapy, developed by Glasser (1965), was once a popular treatment modality in correctional facilities. It was based around the inmate involving himself in the "here and now," rejecting his irresponsible behavior, and learning more adaptive ways to fulfill his needs without any attention given to past behaviors or events (Burkhead, 2007). Reality therapy-based programs began to fall out of favor following the introduction of cognitive therapy by Beck in the 1980s (Jennings & Deming, 2013) and was completely discontinued by 1999.

However, after the now infamous Martinson (1974) report that many took to suggest that "nothing works," programming gave way to warehousing massive numbers of prisoners with few or no resources directed toward programming. Known as the "crime control period," an expansion was seen in the number of prisoners incarcerated as well as the amount of time those individuals were incarcerated. Many believe that we are still in a period of crime control but prison programming is gaining back at least some traction, especially programs that are psychological in nature which are often found to "work" for prisoners (see Cullen & Gendreau, 2001).

TRENDS

Psychological prison programming was championed in the 1970s by a group of American and Canadian criminologists who can be credited with bringing about the new "what works" in reducing crime and recidivism (Cullen, 2005). In particular, Francis Cullen reinvigorated correctional rehabilitation with his book *Reaffirming Rehabilitation* in 1982. In the book, Cullen argued that some interventions failed to reduce recidivism and rehabilitate prisoners. However, he argued that there are proven and promising programs that exist for some people some of the time. Along with Canadian criminologists Paul Gendreau and Andrew Bonta, Cullen championed the "what works" movement in offender rehabilitation (Cullen, 2005).

This movement largely came to fruition in 1990 when the Risk-Need-Responsivity model (RNR model) was introduced as a theoretical framework that provided a better option for dealing with crime by placing greater emphasis on rehabilitative efforts for offenders. This framework outlines the major known causes of re-offending and suggests three overarching principles (risk, need, and responsivity) for reducing criminal activity. These principles delineate broadly who should receive treatment services, the characteristics of those in need of services (i.e., "criminogenic needs"), and the strategies by which the treatment should be delivered (Polaschek, 2012).

Programs adhering to this model have been shown to reduce recidivism by up to 35% and can generalize across settings, criminal behaviors, and offender subtypes. Adherence to the model is also associated with reduced offending related to violent offenses, prison misconduct, gang-related activity, and sexual offenses (Andrews & Bonta, 2010). The RNR model has been identified by numerous meta-analytic studies as successfully addressing the principles that are likely some of the most important in the effectiveness of correctional programs (Polaschek & Daly, 2013).

Since the resurgence catalyzed by Cullen, Gendreau, and Bonta, other prominent criminologists have picked up the torch for the rehabilitation movement. Many of these researchers latched onto the success of psychological programming which focused on how the brain interprets the environment and social interactions (cognition) and responds to those interpretations (behavior). Cognitive behavioral therapy (CBT) was, and remains, one of the strongest rehabilitation programs likely because it is psychological in nature—focusing on the restructuring of thought (the cognitive aspect) and on how people respond to their thoughts (the behavioral aspect). CBT is able to address these psychological factors and influence the way the brain operates (Vaske, Galyean, & Cullen, 2011).

Along with CBT, the Motivational Interviewing Model, most known for its utility in substance abuse programs, has gained popularity in prisons over the years primarily because it does not rest on the assumption that offenders are motivated to change. This and more recent changes in programming approaches tend to reflect the movement away from independent cognitive or behavioral models and toward multidimensional evidence-based approaches (Jennings & Deming, 2013). The next section of this chapter will review proven and promising psychological prison programs for offender rehabilitation.

CURRENT RESEARCH

CBT–based programs have been the primary modality used in prison programs for the past few decades, focusing on both the offenders' problem behaviors and the maladaptive thinking patterns exhibited by offenders. CBT programs acknowledge how cognitions, emotions, and behaviors interact and target the antisocial and socially maladaptive thinking patterns and the behaviors that are the ultimate product of those patterns. Dialectal Behavior Therapy, a specific form of CBT, has more recently been incorporated into some programs to target self-injurious and other violent behaviors (Scott & Gerbasi, 2005). Several meta-analytic studies looking at the efficacy rate for prison-based CBT programs have found them to be highly effective. For instance, Pearson et al. (2002) compared 69 experimental and quasi-experimental studies and found that CBT programs were significantly more effective in reducing recidivism (approximately 30% mean reduction) than behavioral ones. Wilson et al. (2005) analyzed 20 studies comparing CBT to no treatment control groups and found recidivism reductions of about 20–30% in CBT groups compared to control groups.

A meta-analysis conducted by Landenberger and Lipsey (2005) examined 58 studies of CBT programs that were directed toward changing cognitive distortions and teaching new cognitive skills utilizing traditional CBT-associated therapeutic strategies (i.e., monitoring thought processes, identifying and challenging problematic cognitions, etc.). They found an average recidivism reduction of about 25% and the odds of remaining out of prison in the following year was about one and a half times greater for CBT-treated offenders compared to those in control groups. These findings were also dependent on the risk level of the offender, how well the treatment had been implemented, anger issues, and interpersonal problem-solving skills. Substantial variation still exists in the magnitude of the effects, which could likely be due to any number of factors including age, gender, criminal history, or quality of treatment. However, Andrews et al. (1990) have posited a viable explanation—the "risk principle." The principle suggests that effective treatment will have a greater impact on higher risk offenders if only due to the larger margin of room for improvement compared to lower-risk offenders.

Originally developed by Little and Robinson (1988), Moral Reconation Therapy (MRT) is a CBT-based program that draws on the theoretical ideas originally put forth by Kohlberg's theory of the six stages of moral development. Higher levels of moral reasoning involve abstract thinking and perspective taking, areas in which offenders tend to be deficient. It is suggested that individuals who reach those higher levels of moral development are less likely to engage in behaviors that are harmful to others and, thus, are less likely to engage in criminal activities. Now used in over 40 state prisons and jails as well as international correctional facilities, the purpose of MRT is to improve social, moral, and behavioral deficits in offenders with the ultimate goal of increasing their moral reasoning abilities and improving social behavior (Burkhead, 2007; Wilson, Bouffard, & Mackenzie, 2005).

MRT sessions are typically one to two hours in length and held in small groups (10 to 15 offenders) biweekly. The sessions consist of exercises and lessons completed via a structured workbook which is standardized and distributed to each member (Burkhead, 2007). The exercises are highly varied, including discussions of the sources of internal distress, issues they may be having within the prison environment, identification of goals, reflection of good and bad events in one's life, and the specific behaviors that made those events turn out as such. The components of the therapeutic techniques utilized attempts to draw a connection between the offender's thought processes and his behavior. Efficacy studies have shown that MRT results in a 41% recidivism rate after five years compared to 56% for those not involved in MRT and a reduction from 20% to 10% in rate of rearrest (Wilson, Bouffard, & Mackenzie, 2005). MRT has additionally been studied with felony drug offenders, also yielding significant positive effects (Little, Robinson, & Burnette, 1991; 1993). Despite some mixed results, research generally shows strong evidence in support of the long-term positive benefits of MRT, including reduced recidivism (Burkhead, 2007).

Now implemented widely across the United States and internationally, Reasoning and Rehabilitation (R&R, AKA Cognitive Skills Training) programs were originally developed by Ross and Fabiano (1985) based on the premise that offenders have cognitive and social competency deficits that are the likely result of a tumultuous upbringing and poor early socialization (Burkhead, 2007). The focus of the program is on restoring these deficits, targeting skills such as problem solving, Theory of Mind development, critical reasoning, self-control, and instilling prosocial values. In order to accomplish these goals, the program incorporates a wide variety of traditional CBT therapeutic techniques such as role-playing, modeling, reasoning exercises, and discussions as well as audio-visual presentations, games, and puzzles. The versatile nature of R&R has allowed it to be utilized with many offender groups including high-risk offenders, substance users, and juveniles (Burkhead, 2007; Wilson, Bouffard, & Mackenzie, 2005).

Studies have generally found that those who participate in R&R programs led by trained probation officers have significantly lower recidivism rates and likelihood of reoffending (Wilson, Bouffard, & Mackenzie, 2005). A large, five-year study conducted by Robinson (1995) found that all effects (reduced recidivism, rearrest) favored those who were in R&R programs compared to control groups. Overall, their research is supportive and optimistic, but additional research is needed to determine generalizability to settings and instructors.

All CBT-based programs focus on cognitive restructuring, however some programs, such as MRT and R&R, focus more heavily on restoring deficits whereas others place more emphasis on identifying alternatives to maladaptive cognitions and behaviors. For instance, Strategies for Thinking Productively (Baro, 1999) aims to identify key thinking patterns that may lead to criminal behavior and devise alternative patterns of assessing the situation. These types of programs were found to have a significant positive effect over traditional self-help programs (such as Alcoholics and Narcotics Anonymous). Regardless of these differences, the goals of CBT programs remain the same in altering cognitive styles to reduce criminalistic behaviors and the research tends to support their effectiveness.

Evidence suggests that the positive effects of CBT programs are actually substantially stronger than education, vocation, and work programs (Burkhead, 2007). A survey evaluating cognitive behavioral intervention programs of all types showed that in general they are capable of reducing recidivism rates by about 8% on average, the most effective programs being MRT, R&R, and Thinking for a Change. These programs also showed efficacy with sex offenders (15% reduction) (Aos, Miller, & Drake, 2006). The preponderance of evidence suggests that the CBT approach leads to significant positive effects regardless of the specific program and across generations and populations (Landenberger & Lipsey, 2005).

According to the Federal Bureau of Prisons (2016), almost half of all incarcerated persons have committed drug offenses. As such, programs oriented toward drug offenders are exceedingly popular. One such program, "Changing Course," has been found to significantly lower recidivism rates of inmates who were identified to have substance abuse problems (Proctor et al., 2012). The program utilizes components of the transtheoretical model of change (Prochaska & Velicer, 1997) through providing resources for self-directed change. Activities and resources mainly include visualization and journaling techniques.

Therapeutic communities have become an increasingly popular modality of substance abuse treatment in correctional settings. Collectively, these programs operate under a "self-help" model but may incorporate theories, ideas, and techniques from a number of overarching therapeutic models to accommodate the individual inmate and provide the best treatment. In these communities, the inmates ("residents") are responsible for their own active participation in the program and for interacting regularly with staff and each other (Scott & Gerbasi, 2005). As the inmates progress through the program they may acquire greater responsibility and independence, additionally allowing them to learn conflict resolution skills, improved social skills, and prosocial behaviors. Research has demonstrated the efficacy of these programs as well as certain "dosage" effects such that the longer the inmates are active in the program, the more the likelihood of re-offense decreases (Burkhead, 2007).

Delaware was one of the first states to implement this type of program in 1988. The KEY/Crest substance abuse program is a program that focuses on providing treatment while offenders are transitioning back into the community. The program is targeted toward inmates who have been incarcerated for longer periods of time, and inmates typically become involved during the last year of incarceration. Inmates receive daily treatment, which includes counseling, peer counseling, workshops, and a work-release portion of the program. Multiple studies have found the program to be effective in both lowering recidivism and enabling offenders to remain drug-free post-incarceration (Inciardi et al., 2004; Martin et al., 1995; Martin et al., 1999).

A survey conducted by Aos, Miller, and Drake (2006) evaluated several types of programs that have been implemented in correctional facilities across the United States and internationally, looking at the effect of each type of program on recidivism rates. Results indicated that, for substance use programs in general, recidivism was reduced by about 5–11%, dependent on the specific program. The most effective of the programs, however, were those that continue treatment into the community and drug courts, with 10 and 11% reduction rates respectively (Aos, Miller, & Drake, 2006).

Women in Prison

In recent years, prisons and jails have reported substantially higher growth rates of incarcerated women compared to men (Morash, Bynum, & Koons, 1998; Scott & Gerbasi, 2005). The majority of these women tend to be minorities who are unmarried and often unemployed. Moreover, about two-thirds of incarcerated women have children who are under the age of 18 (Scott & Gerbasi, 2005). Women tend to enter prison with a different set of needs and issues than those of men due in large part to a higher rate of sexual, physical, and emotional victimization outside of prison and, if they have children, the responsibility they have for them. Although women are more likely to suffer from trauma at the time of incarceration, there tends to be a notable lack of necessary screening related to such issues. Furthermore, alcohol dependence poses more of a danger to women than men in prison because, due to their physiology and likely comorbid substance use and/or mental illness, women are more likely to suffer the negative repercussions sooner than men (e.g., cirrhosis, heart disease) (Scott & Gerbasi, 2005).

Considering these differences in needs and the gendered nature of prisons, it makes practical sense to offer certain psychological programs in women's prisons. Programs using a cognitive behavioral framework that focuses more on increasing self-esteem and social functioning are likely to be the most effective and least damaging for women who have a history of abuse or trauma, with specific goals such as empowerment and fully processing traumatic experiences (Scott & Gerbasi, 2005). Research has also found that staff who can act as strong female role models and with whom women offenders can identify provide the opportunity to form a support network, which may be a crucial element in a successful program (Morash, Bynum, & Koons, 1998).

One program called "Seeking Safety" is an intervention program that utilizes cognitive-behavioral therapy for people with Post-Traumatic Stress Disorder (PTSD) and substance disorders. Although the program itself is not gendered, Lynch et al. (2012) conducted a study evaluating Seeking Safety as a 12-week intervention program by conducting follow-up interviews 12 weeks after the program ended. Lynch et al. (2012) found that women's PTSD scores were lower compared to the PTSD of women who were wait-listed for the program.

"Forever Free" is a substance abuse treatment program specifically targeted toward incarcerated women. The program is six months long and meant for women in the last six months of their prison sentence. Women in the program are housed separately, engage in counseling, workshops, 12-step programs, drug testing, and other behaviorally-focused activities. Women are then given the option to join a community-based program after their sentence. Hall and colleague's (2004) evaluation of the program found that, although women had often used drugs since their release, they reported *less* drug use than those who had not participated in the program. Additionally, women who participated in the program were more likely to be employed and were less likely to be re-incarcerated compared to women who had not participated in the program.

Other programs offered to women that have shown beneficial effects include the Women's Opportunity Resource Center and the Turning Point Alcohol and Drug Program. The Resource Center primarily focuses on helping women learn the skills necessary to find jobs and remain drug-free once released from prison. The emphasis is on acquiring life skills and learning how to use community resources, although GED classes and referrals to alcohol and drug counseling are also offered. The Turning Point Alcohol and Drug Program is targeted toward substance abusers to provide life skills training, information about substance abuse, interpersonal skill development, and anger management. Groups are separated by gender such that the women's sect addresses issues that are more often encountered by women, such as sexual abuse and other sex-oriented crimes (Morash, Bynum, & Koons, 1998).

Juveniles

For most juvenile-targeted programs, "juvenile" is defined as a person less than 21 years old. Serious juvenile offenders are those who have committed violent offenses or those who have a long history of offending. In these cases, there are several major treatment options, ranging from psychological and therapeutic techniques (such as cognitive-behavioral therapy) to educational treatment. A meta-analysis of 17 experimental or quasi-experimental design studies by Garrido and Morales (2007) found that both chronic and violent juvenile offenders who received some kind of treatment (cognitive-behavioral, educational) had lower recidivism rates than juveniles who did not receive some kind of treatment while incarcerated.

A subsect of CBT known as Mode Deactivation Therapy (MDT) has demonstrated higher effectiveness in treating antisocial children and adolescents than more traditional forms of CBT, particularly regarding personal distress, pre-existing psychopathology, and externalizing behaviors. MDT, based upon the work of Aaron Beck, examines aspects of personality that may lead to criminality and delinquency, intending to restructure cognitions into more adaptive ways of thinking (Beck, Steer, & Brown, 1996). Thodor and Cautilii (2011) examined the effectiveness of MDT with high risk adolescent males. The main components utilized in therapy sessions were imagery and relaxation techniques in order to improve cognitive ability and reduce emotional dysregulation. The ultimate goal of the therapy is to channel the antisocial responses that have become automatic into more prosocial behaviors. Results showed a considerable reduction in overall antisociality which was also associated with a reduction in recidivism, specifically related to aggressive and sex offenses (Thoder & Cautilli, 2011).

Developed by Goldstein and Glick (2001), Aggression Replacement Training (ART) was designed specifically for juvenile offenders, but research has shown that it can be applied to many other populations and settings. The focus of ART is on teaching prosocial behavior, anger management skills, and moral reasoning ability as a replacement for antisocial behaviors. A variant program, known as EQUIP, combines ART with Positive Peer Culture which involves group meetings that serve to motivate youth to remain actively involved in one another's healing processes. Research has yielded positive results in support of the program (Burkhead, 2007). Moreover, Curulla (1991) evaluated the effectiveness of ART programs in learning disabled offenders and found a significant positive effect for the program participants.

Project Broader Urban Involvement and Leadership Development (BUILD) is a violence prevention program targeted toward juveniles in detention programs and facilities. The juveniles deal with a variety of issues, such as violence (particularly gang violence), substance abuse, and other crimes. The BUILD program began in 1993 in the Nancy B. Jefferson Alternative School of the Cook County Juvenile Temporary Detention Center located in Chicago, Illinois. The program is targeted toward both males and females and, in its original implementation, had only one teacher for the BUILD curriculum. The original BUILD curriculum focused on four themes: self-esteem enhancement, communication skills, problem-solving techniques, and goal-setting/decision-making (Lurigio et al., 2000; Thompson & Jason, 1986).

Today, the BUILD curriculum has expanded to involve pre- and post-implementation evaluations and includes program dimensions designed to develop a wider variety of life skills, including leadership development and civic engagement. The modern BUILD curriculum promotes participation in sports, provides academic tutoring, and encourages field trips. Full sessions of the curriculum are 10 weeks, although youth may also attend as few as one workshop. Of 25 programs listed in the National Institute of Justice *Crime Solutions* database, BUILD is the only one considered "effective," meaning that it has substantial evidence in its favor that many other programs do not yet have.

Suicide Prevention

Suicide is consistently one of the leading causes of inmate deaths in both prisons and jails with the risk averaging three times that of the general public. Juvenile offenders tend to be at an even higher risk, especially if placed in adult facilities (US Marshal Service; Daniel, 2006). Since the 1980s, after the deinstitutionalization of mental institutions, the number of suicides has increased exponentially, averaging approximately 400 per year not accounting for those that often go unreported due to fear of litigation or the violent nature of an act that may cause a suicide to appear to be a murder or fight (aka "invisible suicides") (Daniel, 2006; Scott & Gerbasi, 2005; Kupers & Toch, 1999).

The initial screenings of incoming inmates are often inadequate at identifying offenders who are at high-risk for suicide which, when compounded with contributing factors that are innate to prisons (e.g., environmental factors and inmate crises), creates a virtual perfect storm for suicide attempts (Scott & Gerbasi, 2005). Although specific causes of prison suicides vary, they typically reflect the two major themes of an environment that is conducive to suicidal ideation and an inmate undergoing a personal crisis about which they are helpless. Common factors contributing to the conducive environment tend to be the sudden loss of autonomy and privacy, the disconnection from loved ones and the comforts of home, daily threats and confrontations, rape, cell isolation, overcrowding, and lack of basic necessities (food, clothes, activity). Preexisting mental illness and substance abuse are also fairly commonplace in prisons, which also tend to become exacerbated the longer the imprisonment (Kupers & Toch, 1999; Scott & Gerbasi, 2005; Daniel, 2006). Furthermore, an inmate's cell in and of itself can provide the means by which they can attempt suicide, utilizing vent grates, hinges, or bunk frames as anchors for hanging. This is often the reason inmates are much more likely to commit suicide when they are isolated in single cells (Daniel, 2006).

Many states have successfully implemented prevention programs in their jails and prisons, yielding favorable results. For instance, New York saw a significant decrease in statewide jail suicides after the implementation of a comprehensive prevention program and Texas reported a 50% decrease after increasing and improving staff training as well as requiring the regular maintenance of suicide prevention policies. However, despite the standards set forth by the APA and National Commission on Correction Health Care (NCCHC) for what constitutes a comprehensive prevention program, most prisons are still lacking in the execution of many elements that are explicitly stated (Scott & Gerbasi, 2005).

Hall and Gabor (2004) recently evaluated the Samaritans of Southern Alberta (SAMA) program implemented in Canadian prisons. SAMA places the responsibility of identifying at-risk inmates with their peers, other inmates specifically chosen or who volunteered for this role. The program rests on the assumption that, due to their proximity, inmates can play an essential role in identifying suicide risk, alerting the correctional officers and mental health workers, as well as providing support to their peers. The findings from this program evaluation showed that these inmates were more often approached and appreciated by their peers, but the actual impact of the program on number of suicides could not be determined (Hall & Gabor, 2004).

A French prevention program, known as CDS, was created based on evidence that more knowledge of suicide results in the underestimation of risk, conversely, actual exposure to a suicide attempt results in the overestimation of risk. The program consists of a team of trained inmates whose duty it is to identify and provide support to those prisoners who are at-risk of committing suicide. The recruited inmates must first undergo testing to ensure they meet specific criteria to be determined mentally stable. The program was in place for one year with a sample of 54 inmates and 17 corrections professionals across different prisons. The results of the study were compared to prisons without the program and findings revealed that inmates in the prisons with the program were more likely to believe that support should come from other inmates and more likely to believe that they are able to identify at-risk peers compared to the control groups who were more likely to believe support should come from correctional officers or mental health professionals (Auzoult & Abdellaoui, 2013).

New Developments

Armed with knowledge about the biosocial basis of behavior, individuals have designed psychological programs inside prisons that account for the role of certain practices on the body. A growing research base highlights the promise of meditative practices (especially mindfulness meditation) on improving biological and neurological functioning. Practicing mindfulness is correlated with stress reductions through structural changes in the amygdala (Hölzel et al., 2009) and increased gray matter in the hippocampus leading to better emotion regulation (Hölzel et al., 2011). Practicing mindfulness has also been shown to produce lasting changes in certain brain waves associated with emotional reactivity and cognition (Gillespie, 2012). Recent evaluation studies on mindfulness meditation in prison show that it has reduced substance use among prisoners re-entering society (Bowen et al., 2006), reduced hostility and mood disorders in male and female prisoners (Samuelson, Carmody, Kabat-Zinn, & Bratt, 2007), and decreased the number of disciplinary infractions in prison both in the short and long terms (Perelman et al., 2012). Mindfulness programs that were implemented in Massachusetts correctional facilities targeted hostility, self-esteem, and mood disturbance and found that the meditational practices produced therapeutic benefits for the inmates (Gillespie et al., 2012). Mindfulness practices may hold a key for improving self-regulation and reducing mood disorders that are associated with antisocial behavior by targeting specific brain regions associated with these faculties. It is likely with the increased precision and cost-effectiveness of fMRI technology that mindfulness will receive additional research in the future.

POLICIES

As previously discussed, in the mid-1970s, the United States moved to a more punitive focused goal of imprisonment rather than rehabilitative in order to give them what they deserved and contain them to keep them from infecting society. This "get tough" policy approach rejected rehabilitation and promoted harsh punishment (Andrews & Bonta, 2010). A "side effect" of this punitive approach was that sentences increased in length and the scope of incarceration was expanded so more people were being arrested who originally would not have been (e.g., drug offenders)—resulting in an increase in psychological strains and social costs. Additionally, this approach was costly, leading to overcrowding in jails and prisons across the country with little to no rehabilitative programming.

From a policy standpoint, warehousing individuals without rehabilitation is an untenable approach. On the other hand, small improvements can make a huge impact on criminal justice costs. Cohen (1998) conservatively calculated that the average high-rate offender would cost society around two million dollars in the long run. If rehabilitation programs could prevent just a small number of high-frequency offenders from continuing their behavior such programs would pay for themselves quickly. This says nothing about the intangible benefits related to the reduction in violence for the community when a persistent offender desists from crime.

However, as previously noted, no matter how well-intentioned a prison is and how well-developed a program is, there will be no benefits if the program is not faithfully implemented and carried out. Therefore, prison policies must be put into place to ensure that the correct procedures exist to reduce disciplinary infractions and recidivism. A passage from Cullen and Gendreau (2000, p. 142) is instructive:

> The lack of training for human service workers, the use of less effective treatment modalities, the failure to develop and utilize well-designed and comprehensive treatment manuals, and the failure to monitor therapeutic integrity—these and other problems are not inherent in correctional rehabilitation but are due to policy decisions that can be rectified.

Through policy, prisons can *do something* about problem behavior to make prisons and society safer.

As long as policy clearly lays out what should happen in offender rehabilitation, there is likely to be some return on efforts. Again, Cullen and Gendreau (2000) nicely lay out the recommendations that research has highlighted over the years. By following the four principles of effective rehabilitation, real-world change can be had: (1) interventions should target the known predictors of crime and recidivism for change; (2) the treatment services should be behavioral in nature; (3) treatment interventions should be used primarily with higher risk offenders, targeting their criminogenic needs (dynamic risk factors) for change; and (4) a range of other considerations, if addressed, will increase treatment effectiveness (e.g., community follow-up intervention, highly trained staff).

ISSUES AND CHALLENGES

The United States consistently reports incarceration rates between four and eight times those of other nations (Haney, 2002). In effect, many prisons often have problems with overcrowding, staff and resource shortage, deterioration of facilities, and resorting to punitive approaches to discipline such as isolation and "supermax" confinement which only results in increased tensions, fear, and a more dangerous environment (Haney, 2002). To compound these issues, most inmates are being released from prison and returning to their former neighborhoods, which inevitably has a negative impact on any attempts they may make at rehabilitation as well as the local economies (Andrews & Bonta, 2010). These problems often contribute to and exacerbate suicidal tendencies and other mental health issues of offenders, which is why it is suggested that assessment of risk should be an ongoing process throughout incarceration, although this is rarely carried out. Additionally, the standards of prevention programs including determination of risk prior to incarceration, communication between staff and inmates, and creating an environment conducive to engaging with treatment programs are often not fully followed (Daniel, 2006). In order to maximize the effectiveness of treatment programs the problematic prison policies and the deleterious conditions of confinement must be addressed. Significant changes must also be made within the structure of prisons and in the way in which prisoners transition from prison to home (Andrews & Bonta, 2010).

Another challenge that plagues treatment programs in prisons is determining which type of program will be most effective for which offenders based on various factors including personality features and risk of re-offending. There is evidence showing that risk assessment tools such as the PCL-R SV can be useful in progressive correction systems in prioritizing the placement of high-risk offenders in specialized treatment interventions (Polaschek & Daly, 2013). The personality traits related to the three main facets of psychopathy (boldness, meanness, and disinhibition) have been debated over by experts in the field in the context of correctional treatment, as it is currently unclear whether these traits should be targeted for change or simply "worked around." For instance, a randomized controlled trial conducted by Swogger et al. (2016) examined the efficacy of using a brief motivational intervention (BMI) program in concert with the standard care provided to offenders with substance use in a pretrial jail diversion program. The results of the trial found that offenders high in the interpersonal/affective traits (Factor 1) of psychopathy who participated in the combined treatment showed more frequent substance use at the follow-up. In contrast, those scoring low on these traits showed a decrease in substance use frequency, suggesting that using a BMI approach with high F1 individuals may actually be counterproductive to rehabilitative efforts. However, valid arguments have been put forth for the effectiveness of providing high-risk offender populations with their own specialized interventions, as was found in a study conducted by Young et al. (2012).

Using a revised version of the R&R treatment paradigm, psychiatric patients diagnosed with a severe personality disorder, a history of violent offending, and who exhibited PCL-R Factor 2 traits and/or ADHD symptoms participated in 15 sessions of the manualized treatment. Those who were treated with the revised R&R intervention showed great improvements in problem-solving abilities and emotional stability as well as reduced ADHD symptoms, violent attitudes, and anger problems. It is suggested that this revised R&R intervention may actually be more effective in addressing anger-related problems specifically, compared to the original (Young et al., 2012). Further, due to the plethora of traits associated with psychopathy and the diversity of co-occurring severe personality disorders, trait-change using specialized treatments need not be limited to solely psychopathic traits (Polaschek & Daly, 2013).

The increase in use of the previously mention RNR model is promising but one major assumption of the model, and a drawback of it, is that the government is responsible for resources and accountability of correctional rehabilitation and that correctional programs are not mandated to address the psychological or physical health needs of prisoners if addressing those needs does not lead to reduced involvement in crime (Polaschek, 2012). Probation officers often don't follow the risk principle, rarely attend to criminogenic needs of clients, and rarely use CBT strategies in execution of model-based programs (Andrews & Bonta, 2010). Reducing offending should be the main focus for identified psychopathic and other high-risk inmates who are treated in correctional facilities, but due to the common belief that these individuals are extremely difficult to handle and often "untreatable" this is not always the case (Polaschek & Daly, 2013). In fact, evidence has shown that high PCL-R scoring offenders can benefit from risk-reducing treatment and appear to do so by changing dynamic risk factors (e.g., substance abuse, impulsivity, etc.).

FUTURE PROSPECTS

In 2009, following the economic crash in 2008, another surprise struck the United States—something that has not been seen since the early 1970s—the US imprisonment rate decreased from 506 per 100,000 people in 2008 to 504 per 100,000 people in 2009. This reduction has been seen each year since (Carson, 2015). The United States still vastly outnumbers similar nations in their use of incarceration, but the tide may be turning and the use of alternatives to incarceration are likely to increase. Another likely scenario is that the US criminal justice system might begin to finally take offender rehabilitation seriously and focus on what happens to individuals who are incarcerated and re-entering society.

Evidence from neuroscientific research shows that there are associations between certain brain regions and specific antisocial behaviors (Gillespie et al., 2012). In particular, the orbitofrontal (OFC) and prefrontal (PFC) cortices are typically associated with moral reasoning, impulsivity, and violent behavior as well as contingency learning and the appraisal of risk while the amygdala is involved in attention, learning, and emotion. The prefrontal cortex is responsible for exerting behavioral control thus inhibiting the amygdala. In light of this evidence, it is likely that an increase in therapeutic approaches will be aimed at improving prefrontal control over the amygdala in individuals with behavioral issues—often characteristic of offender populations—mindfulness techniques can potential help achieve this as well as certain biofeedback applications (Gillespie et al., 2012; Howard, 2013). Biofeedback is the real-time visual presentation of physiological changes occurring within one's own body (e.g., brain waves, heart rate, blood pressure, skin conductance) which can lead to improved emotional control and self-regulation in addition to addressing an offender's emotional regulation issues (Gillespie et al., 2012). It is well-established that biofeedback procedures used to self-regulate certain brain waves in healthy people can be effective in reducing impulsivity—most notably, but not exclusively, in children with ADHD (Howard, 2013). A limited number of studies to date have tried this with adult patients with similar but more serious behavioral issues and have shown favorable results.

In all, psychological rehabilitation programs inside American prisons have been shown to be effective in reducing problem behaviors and increasing the chances of success after leaving prison. Coupled with new evidence on cognition and brain functioning, psychological programs targeting the brain are likely to increase in the future. With the reduction in cost and complexity of psychological testing of prisoners, the psychological approach to offender rehabilitation might not only become more effective but less costly as well.

DISCUSSION QUESTIONS

1. Explain how the psychological movement of rehabilitation re-emerged in the United States.
2. Name three psychological approaches to offender rehabilitation that have received empirical support.
3. Discuss one positive policy development and one negative policy development related to the psychological treatment of offenders.
4. Name two major challenges to the psychological treatment of incarcerated individuals.
5. What do you think the future holds for the psychological treatment of those who are incarcerated in the United States?

REFERENCES

Andrews, D. A., & Bonta, J. (2010). Rehabilitating criminal justice policy and practice. *Psychology, Public Policy, and Law, 16*(1), 39–55.

Andrews, D. A., Zinger, I., Hoge, R. D., Bonta, J., Gendreau, P., & Cullen, F. T. (1990). Does correctional treatment work? A clinically relevant and psychologically informed meta-analysis. *Criminology*, 28, 369–404.

Aos, S., Miller, M., & Drake, E. (2006). Evidence-based public policy options to reduce future prison construction, criminal justice costs, and crime rates. *Federal Sentencing Reporter, 19*, 275–90.

Auzoult, L., & Abdellaoui, S. (2013). Perceptions of a peer suicide prevention program by inmates and professionals working in prisons. *Crisis, 34,* 289–292.

Baro, A. L. (1999). Effects of a cognitive restructuring program on inmate institutional behavior. *Criminal Justice and Behavior, 26*(4), 466–84.

Beck, A. T., Steer, R. A., & Brown, G. K. (1996). *Beck depression inventory-II*. San-Diego CA: Harcourt-Brace.

Bowen, S., Witkiewitz, K., Dillworth, T. M., Chawla, N., Simpson, T. L., Ostafin, B. D., Larimer, M. E., Blume, A. W., Parks, G. A., & Marlatt, G. A. (2006). Mindfulness meditation and substance use in an incarcerated population. *Psychology of Addictive Behaviors*, 20(3), 343–347.

Burkhead, M. D. (2007). *The treatment of criminal offenders: A history*. Jefferson, NC: McFarland Publishing.

Carson, E. A. (2015). Prisoners in 2014. NCJ 248955, Washington, DC: US Department of Justice. Office of Justice Programs. Bureau of Justice Statistics.

Cohen, M. A. (1998). The monetary value of saving a high-risk youth. *Journal of Quantitative Criminology, 14*(1), 5–33.

Cullen, F. T. (2005). The twelve people who saved rehabilitation: How the science of criminology made a difference. *Criminology, 43*(1), 1–42.

Cullen, F. T., & Gendreau, P. (2000). Assessing correctional rehabilitation: Policy, practice, and prospects. *Criminal Justice, 3*(1), 299–370.

Cullen, F. T., & Gendreau, P. (2001). From nothing works to what works: Changing professional ideology in the 21st century. *The Prison Journal, 81*(3), 313–338.

Cullen, F. T., & Gilbert, K. E. (1982). *Reaffirming rehabilitation.* Cincinnati, OH: Anderson.

Curulla, V. L. (1991). *Aggression replacement training in the community for adult learning disabled offenders.* Unpublished manuscript. (Available from Curulla, Special Education, University of Washington, Seattle, WA).

Daniel, A. E. (2006). Preventing suicide in prison: a collaborative responsibility of administrative, custodial, and clinical staff. *Journal of the American Academy of Psychiatry and the Law Online, 34*(2), 165–175.

Federal Bureau of Prisons. (2016). *Offenses.* Retrieved from https://www.bop.gov/about/statistics/statistics_inmate_offenses.jsp.

Garrido, V., & Morales, L. A. (2007). Serious (violent or chronic) juvenile offenders: A systematic review of treatment effectiveness in secure corrections [Monograph]. *Campbell Systematic Reviews, 3*(7).

Gillespie, S. M., Mitchell, I. J., Fisher, D., & Beech, A. R. (2012). Treating disturbed emotional regulation in sexual offenders: The potential applications of mindful self-regulation and controlled breathing techniques. *Aggression and Violent Behavior, 17*(4), 333–343.

Glasser, R. (1965). *Reality therapy: A new approach to psychotherapy.* New York: Harper Perennial.

Goldstein, A. P. & Glick, B. (2001). Aggression replacement training: Application and evaluation management. In G. A. Bernfield, D. P. Farrington & A. W. Leschied (Eds.). *Offender rehabilitation in practice* (pp. 121–48). Chichester: Wiley.

Hall, B., & Gabor, P. (2004). Peer suicide prevention in a prison. *Crisis, 25*(1), 19–26.

Hall, E. A., Prendergast, M. L., Wellisch, J., Patten, M., & Cao, Y. (2004). Treating drug-abusing women prisoners: An outcomes evaluation of the Forever Free Program. *The Prison Journal, 84*(1), 81–105.

Haney, C. (2003). The psychological impact of incarceration: Implications for post-prison adjustment. In J. Travis & M. Waul (Eds.). *Prisoners once removed: The impact of incarceration and reentry on children, families, and communities* (pp. 33–66). Lanham, MD: Rowman & Littlefield Press.

Hölzel, B. K., Carmody, J., Evans, K. C., Hoge, E. A., Dusek, J. A., Morgan, L., Pitman, R. K. & Lazar, S. W. (2009). Stress reduction correlates with structural changes in the amygdala. *Social Cognitive and Affective Neuroscience, 5,* 11–17.

Hölzel, B. K., Carmody, J., Vangel, M., Congleton, C., Yerramsetti, S. M., Gard, T., & Lazar, S. W. (2011). Mindfulness practice leads to increases in regional brain gray matter density. *Psychiatry Research: Neuroimaging, 191*(1), 36–43.

Howard, R., Schellhorn, K., & Lumsden, J. (2013). A biofeedback intervention to control impulsiveness in a severely personality disordered forensic patient. *Personality and Mental Health, 7*(2), 168–173.

Inciardi, J., Martin, S., & Butzin, C. (2004). Five-year outcomes of therapeutic community treatment of drug-involved offenders after release from prison. *Crime and Delinquency, 50*(1), 88–107.

Jennings, J. L., & Deming, A. (2013). Effectively utilizing the "behavioral" in cognitive behavioral group therapy of sex offenders. *International Journal of Behavioral Consultation and Therapy, 8*(2), 7–13.

Kupers, T. A., & Toch, H. (1999). *Prison madness: The mental health crisis behind bars and what we must do about it.* San Francisco, CA: Jossey-Bass.

Landenberger, N., & Lipsey, M. (2005). The positive effects of cognitive-behavioral programs for offenders: A meta-analysis of factors associated with effective treatment. *Journal of Experimental Criminology, 1,* 451–476.

Little, G. L., & Robinson, K. D. (1988). Moral reconation therapy: A systematic step-by-step treatment system for treatment resistant clients. *Psychological Reports, 62*(1), 135–51.

Little, G. L., Robinson, K. D., & Burnette, K. D. (1991). Treating drug offenders with moral reconation therapy: A three-year recidivism report. *Psychological Reports, 69*(3 suppl), 1151–54.

Little, G. L., Robinson, K. D., & Burnette, K. D. (1993). Cognitive behavioral treatment of felony drug offenders: A five-year recidivism report. *Psychological Reports, 73*(3 suppl), 1089–90.

Lurigio, A., Bensinger, G., Thompson, S. R., Elling, K., Poucis, D., Selvaggio, J., & Spooner, M. (2000). *A process and outcome evaluation of Project BUILD: Years 5 and 6.* Unpublished Report. Chicago, IL: Loyola University.

Lynch, S. M., Heath, N. M., Matthews, K. C., & Cepeda, G. J. (2012). Seeking safety: An intervention for trauma-exposed incarcerated women. *Journal of Trauma & Dissociation, 13,* 88–101.

Martin, S., Butzin, C., & Inciardi, J. (1995). Assessment of a multistage therapeutic community for drug-involved offenders. *Journal of Psychoactive Drugs, 27*(1), 109–116.

Martin, S., Butzin, C., Saum, C., & Inciardi, J. (1999). Three-year outcomes of therapeutic community treatment for drug-involved offenders in Delaware: From prison to work release to aftercare. *The Prison Journal, 79*(3), 294–320.

Martinson, R. (1974). What works?—Questions and answers about prison reform. *National Affairs-Public Interest,* (35), 22–54.

Morash, M., Bynum, T., & Koons, B. (1998). Women offenders: Programming needs and promising practices. NCJ 171668, *Research in brief.* Washington, DC: US Department of Justice, Office of Justice Programs, National Institute of Justice.

Pearson, F. S., Lipton, D. S., Cleland, C. M., & Yee, D. S. (2002). The effects of behavioral/ cognitive-behavioral programs on recidivism. *Crime & Delinquency, 48*(3), 476–96.

Perelman, A. M., Miller, S. L., Clements, C. B., Rodriguez, A., Allen, K., & Cavanaugh, R. (2012). Meditation in a Deep South prison: A longitudinal study of the effects of Vipassana. *Journal of Offender Rehabilitation, 51*(3), 176–198.

Peters, E. M. (1995). Prison before the prison. In N. Morris, & D. J. Rothman, (Eds.). *The Oxford history of the prison: The practice of punishment in Western society* (pp. 3–46). New York: Oxford University Press.

Polaschek, D. L. (2012). An appraisal of the risk–need–responsivity (RNR) model of offender rehabilitation and its application in correctional treatment. *Legal and Criminological Psychology, 17*(1), 1–17.

Polaschek, D. L., & Daly, T. E. (2013). Treatment and psychopathy in forensic settings. *Aggression and Violent Behavior, 18*(5), 592–603.

Prochaska, J., & Velicer, W. (1997). The transtheoretical model of health behavior change. *American Journal of Health Promotion, 12,* 38–48.

Proctor, S. L., Hoffman, N. G., & Allison, S. (2012). The effectiveness of interactive journaling in reducing recidivism among substance-dependent jail inmates. *International Journal of Offender Therapy and Comparative Criminology, 56*(2), 317–332.

Robinson, D. (1995). The impact of cognitive skills training on post-release recidivism among Canadian federal offenders. Canada: Correctional Research and Development, Correctional Service of Canada. Retrieved from: http://www.csc-scc.gc.ca/research/r41e-eng.shtml.

Ross, R., & Fabiano, E. (1985). *Reasoning and rehabilitation: Manual.* Retrieved from: http://www.cognitivecentre.ca/.

Samuelson, M., Carmody, J., Kabat-Zinn, J., & Bratt, M. A. (2007). Mindfulness-based stress reduction in Massachusetts correctional facilities. *The Prison Journal, 87*(2), 254–268.

Scott, C. L., & Gerbasi, J.B. (Ed.). (2005). *Handbook of correctional mental health.* Arlington, VA: American Psychiatric Publishing.

Spierenburg, P. (1987). From Amsterdam to Auburn an explanation for the rise of the prison in seventeenth-century Holland and nineteenth-century America. *Journal of Social History*, *20*(3), 439–461.

Swogger, M., Conner, K., Caine, E., Trabold, N., Parkhurst, Prothero, L., & Maisto, S. (2016). A test of core psychopathic traits as a moderator of the efficacy of a brief motivational intervention for substance-using offenders. *Journal of Consulting and Clinical Psychology, 84(3),* 248–258.

Thoder, V. J., & Cautilli, J. D. (2011). An independent evaluation of mode deactivation therapy for juvenile offenders. *International Journal of Behavioral Consultation and Therapy*, *7*(1), 40–45.

Thompson, D., & Jason, L. A. (1986). *Effective school-based intervention: The evaluation of BUILD's gang membership prevention program, Final Evaluation Report.* Chicago, IL: Dysfunctioning Child Center of Michael Reese Hospital.

US Marshals Service. *Suicide Prevention and Recommended Practices.* US Department of Justice. https://www.usmarshals.gov/prisoner/suicide_prevention.htm.

Vaske, J., Galyean, K., & Cullen, F. T. (2011). Toward a biosocial theory of offender rehabilitation: Why does cognitive-behavioral therapy work? *Journal of Criminal Justice*, *39*(1), 90–102.

Wilson, D., Bouffard, L., & Mackenzie, D. (2005). A quantitative review of structured, grouporiented, cognitive-behavioral programs for offenders. *Criminal Justice and Behavior, 32* (2), 172–204.

Young, S., Hopkin, G., Perkins, D., Farr, C., Doidge, A., & Gudjonsson, G. (2012). A controlled trial of a cognitive skills program for personality-disordered offenders. *Journal of attention disorders, 7,* 598–607.

Chapter Nine

Substance Abuse Treatment in Prisons and Jails

David Olson

Although the provision of substance abuse treatment in prisons and jails in the United States has a long history, there has been a renewed focus and emphasis on the provision of this type of rehabilitative programming to incarcerated individuals since the early 1990s. This increased focus has been fueled by two primary factors. First, as a result of the increased emphasis on drug enforcement during the mid- to late-1980s, there has been a dramatic increase in the number of individuals incarcerated for drug-law violations in the United States and, as a result, a greater recognition of the link between substance abuse and crime. Second, the body of research that supports the efficacy of drug treatment to reduce recidivism among those released from correctional facilities also has grown dramatically over the past 30 years. However, despite this increased awareness and recognition of the need to provide substance abuse treatment services to those who are incarcerated, for a variety of reasons, effectively meeting the treatment needs of those in prison and jail has been limited.

Some of the reasons for this are due to the different functions that prisons and jails serve, but others are more universal and get to the heart of the challenges of providing rehabilitative programming within secure correctional facilities. Regardless, the fact is that the majority of those released from prison recidivate, with two-thirds rearrested and one-half returned to prison within 3 years (Durose, Cooper, & Snyder, 2014). Thus, it is critical to understand the degree to which rehabilitation is being provided, and the impact this can have on recidivism. This chapter will explore in greater detail the extent and nature of substance abuse treatment within prisons and jails, trends over time, the state of the current research on the topic, as well as the implications and challenges from the standpoint of policy and practice in meeting the substance abuse treatment needs of those incarcerated in the United States.

THE NATURE OF THE ISSUE

Over the past 40 years, research has reached four consistent conclusions when it comes to substance abuse, crime, and substance abuse treatment in prisons and jails: (1) individuals who have substance abuse disorders—which includes both alcohol and illegal drugs—are more likely to be involved in crime and to continue their involvement in crime; (2) a high proportion of those under the custody of the correctional components of the justice system are in need of substance abuse treatment; (3) when substance abuse treatment is delivered and incorporates the risk, needs, and responsivity principles, it reduces the odds of continued involvement in crime (i.e., recidivism); and (4) there is a substantial gap between the need for substance abuse treatment and access to that treatment among correctional populations. When considering the degree to which those in prisons and jails are provided with substance abuse treatment services, it is important to distinguish between the functions of prisons and jails and how this may impact the degree to which substance abuse treatment services can be provided, and also to be clear on what is meant by substance abuse treatment.

First, while both prisons and jails are secure correctional facilities, two of the major differences that have implications for the provision of substance abuse treatment are the certainty of length of stay and the size/economies of scale present in the two types of facilities. In terms of length of stay, given that the majority (63% in 2014) of individuals in local jails are pretrial detainees (i.e., not yet convicted or sentenced), how long they will stay in jail is unknown (Minton & Zhen, 2015). On the other hand, among those sentenced to prison, their projected length of stay is relatively easy to determine. Generally it is viewed that to be effective, jail-based treatment programs should last at least 3 months while prison programs should last between 6 and 12 months (Stayee, 2014).

The other issues that need to be considered when examining substance abuse treatment within prisons and jails are the sizes of the facilities and the degree to which they have the resources to operate specialized treatment programs in a cost-efficient manner. Given that almost 60% of jails house fewer than 100 detainees, according to Stephan and Walsh (2011), while the average rated capacity of prisons in the United States is 900 detainees (author's analysis of 2005 prison census data), often there is not sufficient need for services in most of the individual jails because the number of inmates is too small to make provision of services efficient. Since jails are operated and funded independently by individual counties, most small jails cannot take advantage of scales of economy to fund treatment programs.

It also is important to be clear about what is meant by substance abuse treatment within the context of this discussion. Along the continuum of services that can be provided to those who are identified as substance abusers or substance dependent are detoxification (managing the withdrawal from drugs), drug education/awareness classes (often to prepare people for treatment and motivate them for treatment), clinical/therapeutic counseling that ranges from outpatient to residential settings ("treatment"), followed by post-treatment social support groups through programs like Alcoholics Anonymous (AA), Narcotics Anonymous (NA), etc. Thus, the provision of drug education or drug awareness programming alone does not constitute treatment, but it could prepare people for participating in treatment in the future. Similarly, self-help and support groups are intended to support sobriety and a drug-free lifestyle following the completion of clinical treatment. One of the most successful substance abuse treatment approaches with individuals who have significant substance abuse issues are therapeutic communities (TCs), "residential [programs] that use a hierarchical model with treatment strategies that reflect increased levels of personal and social responsibility. Peer influence, mediated through a variety of group processes, is used to help individuals learn and assimilate social norms and develop more effective social skills" (National Institute on Drug Abuse [NIDA], 2002, p. 1). TCs are also one of the most common and widely studied drug-treatment modalities for prison inmates (Lurigio, 2000; Prendergast, Hall, Wexler, Melnick, & Cao, 2004). The effectiveness of these approaches are described later in this chapter.

To understand the nature of substance abuse treatment for those in prison and jail in the United States, it is first necessary to get some understanding of the degree to which correctional populations have substance abuse or dependence issues. Based on a variety of sources, the prevalence of the need for substance abuse treatment among correctional populations is anywhere from one-half to three-quarters of those on probation, in jails, or in prison. Although dated, in one of the only nationally representative samples of probationers in the United States, it was estimated that nearly two-thirds of adults on probation in 1995 had "at least one type of involvement with alcohol or drug abuse in the time leading up to their current offense" (Mumola & Bonczar, 1998, p. 7). Similarly, it was estimated that 68% abusers during the year leading up to their incarceration (Karberg & James, 2005). Finally, when examining the prevalence of substance abuse among prison populations, estimates have ranged between 50 and 70%, depending on the data source and methods of measuring drug dependence or abuse.

Using a nationally representative sample of prison inmates incarcerated in 1997, Belenko and Peugh (2005) estimated that approximately 70% of state

prison inmates were substance abusers or dependent during the period leading up to their incarceration and were in need of some type of substance
abuse treatment. Using a more recent sample of prison inmates in the United
States, and data that more explicitly allowed for a determination of a clinical
diagnosis of drug dependence and abuse, Mumola and Karberg (2006) estimated that in 2004, more than one-half (53%) of all state prison inmates met
DSM-IV criteria for drug dependence or abuse.

Importantly, the prevalence of drug dependence or abuse among correctional populations is not as strongly tied to the crime for which the individual
has been charged or convicted as is often assumed. For example, while a
larger proportion of those in state prison for a drug-law violation were identified as meeting the criteria for drug dependence or abuse (63%), the same
proportion (63%) of those in prison for a property crime were identified as
being drug dependent or a drug abuser, as were nearly one-half (46%) of
those in prison for a violent crime (Mumola & Karberg, 2006). Similarly,
more than 70% of those in jail for a drug-law violation or a property crime
were identified as substance dependent or abusers, as were 63% of those in
jail for violent crimes (Karberg & James, 2005).

However, despite the significant level of substance abuse and dependence
among correctional populations, there is also a substantial gap between treatment need and the receipt of these services. As described above, it is important to distinguish what types of "services" are provided to those who have
substance abuse or dependence needs. Although the types of programs available to prison and jail inmates will be described in more detail below, the two
primary groups of programs are those that are clinical/therapeutic in nature—
longer term, more intensive, and provided by trained clinical staff—versus
those that provide individuals with drug education/awareness or self-help
support groups.

Among jail and prison populations, it is estimated that only 7 to 20% of
those in need of clinical treatment services actually received those services
during their incarceration. For example, among those in jail who were identified as substance abusers or dependent in 2002 and were serving a sentence
in jail (i.e., they were convicted inmates), only 7% had participated in substance abuse treatment while in jail (Karberg & James, 2005). Further, of
those identified as substance abusers or dependent in jail, less than one-half
(44%) had ever received any type of substance abuse treatment at any point
in their lives. Among prison inmates, a similarly low-level of access to substance abuse treatment while incarcerated is evident. Considering state prison
inmates that met DSM-IV criteria for drug dependence or abuse, only 15% of
these inmates had received any type of formal substance abuse treatment
while incarcerated (Mumola & Karberg, 2006). Indeed, among those prison
inmates identified as having the most severe substance abuse/dependence
disorder, and in need of the most intensive treatment intervention, only about

20% had received any clinical treatment while incarcerated (Belenko & Peugh, 2005). By comparison, it appears that those sentenced to probation tend to have greater access to substance abuse treatment services. Among a 1995 nationally representative sample of probationers in the United States, it is estimated that roughly one-half of those identified as alcohol or drug-involved received some type of sentence condition to participate in substance abuse treatment (Mumola & Bonczar, 1998).

TRENDS

The provision of substance abuse treatment within prisons in the United States is not necessarily a new concept. Substance-abuse treatment for incarcerated offenders in the United States dates back to the early 1930s, following the passage of federal drug laws and the period of prohibition, when the US Public Health Service Hospital in Lexington, Kentucky began treating federal prison inmates addicted to drugs (White, 1998). This focus on the provision of treatment as a means to rehabilitate those in prison was part of the increasingly popular view during the period from the late 1800s through the early 1900s—that those who commit crime did so not because of free will (i.e., the classical school of criminology), but as a result of factors beyond their control, such as socialization, psychology or biological factors (i.e., the positivist school of criminology). Indeed, the reflection of rehabilitation as one of the primary goals of prison during this period was evident in the indeterminate sentencing structure used in every state, which based release from prison on the degree to which inmates had taken advantage of programming to rehabilitate and change themselves. During most of the period from 1920 through the early 1970s, the prison population and incarceration rate in the United States was relatively stable, but began to increase beginning in the mid-1970s (Blumstein, 2011).

A number of factors during the late 1960s and early 1970s resulted in less of an emphasis on treatment and rehabilitation within the justice system, and a greater focus on punishment, deterrence, and incapacitation as the primary goals of prisons. One significant factor was the increased politicization of crime, which caused elected officials to offer responses to crime that were quickly implemented, so as to appease the electorate, such as mandatory prison sentences and a switch to determinate sentencing, which emphasized certainty and severity of punishment over rehabilitation (Simon, 2007).

This period of time also saw an increase in both drug use and crime, and as a result, the desire to identify the most effective strategies that could address these two threats to public safety and security. Finally, during the mid-1970s, a review of research regarding the effectiveness of treatment for offenders in prison was published that called into question the efficacy and effectiveness of this approach to reducing crime. Martinson's 1974 "nothing works" review of the research was initially presented as reaching the conclusion that there were no treatment programs that could effectively reduce involvement in crime or substance abuse (Martinson, 1974).

Although these conclusions regarding treatment's effectiveness were later recast to suggest the more subtle conclusion there were no programs that appeared to be universally effective for all offender populations (Martinson, 1979), the narrative that treatment was ineffective as a crime control mechanism had already taken hold. The convergence of all of these factors led to a dramatic shift in criminal justice practice and policy in the United States away from treatment and rehabilitation to one that emphasized personal responsibility and deterrence (i.e., the neo-classical school of criminology), punishment and incapacitation.

During the 1970s and 1980s, there were also dramatic shifts in the criminal justice system's response to drug-law violations—the so called "War on Drugs" launched by President Nixon in the early 1970s and President Reagan in the 1980s. Although the increased focus during the early 1970s led to dramatic increases in arrests for drug-law violations—with drug arrest rates nearly doubling between 1969 and 1974, there was not a subsequent increase in the US prison population for offenses involving drug-law violations as a result of this (Justice Research and Statistics Association, 2000). It was not until the 1980s that the increased emphasis on drug enforcement caused a dramatic shift in the types of drugs targeted by police—away from marijuana and toward the "hard" drugs of cocaine/crack, heroin, and methamphetamine—and a subsequent increase in prison admissions for drug-law violations. Between 1982 and 1992, overall arrest rates for drug-law violations increased 58%, but arrests involving cannabis fell by 30%, while arrests for all other drugs (primarily cocaine) increased 280% (Federal Bureau of Investigation, n.d.). During the 1980s and early 1990s, there were also increases in the number of crimes occurring in the United States, and as a result, an increase in the number of people being arrested for non-drug-law violations as well.

As a result of this dramatic shift in drug enforcement, increase in crime overall, and increase in the number of people arrested and charged with a felony-level drug-law violation as well as other crimes, the number of people under the custody of the justice system—including those on probation, and in prisons and jails—more than doubled between 1982 and 1992. For example, the number of adults on probation in the United States increased 110 percent between 1982 and 1992, reaching 2.8 million in at the end of 1992, and by 2014, it topped 3.8 million (Bureau of Justice Statistics, 2016). Of those on probation in 2014, one-quarter had been convicted of a drug-law violation (Kaeble, Maruschak, &, Bonczar, 2015). Similarly, the number of people confined in jails across the United States jumped 112% between 1982 and

1992, and reached 744,000 by 2014 (Bureau of Justice Statistics, 2016). In 2002, roughly one-quarter of jail inmates had a drug-law violation as their most serious current charge/offense (Karberg & James, 2005). Finally, the United States prison population more than doubled, increasing almost 110% between 1982 and 1992 with the most substantial increase—a 560% increase—seen in the number of people in prison for drug-law violations (Bureau of Justice Statistics, 2016). In the early 1980s, drug-law violators accounted for less than 10% of all state prison inmates, but throughout the 1990s and into the 2000s, more than one-in-five state prison inmates had been convicted of a drug-law violation (Carson & Golinelli, 2013). By 2014, more than 1.3 million people were incarcerated in state prisons in the United States, and roughly 15% of those in prison were serving a sentence for a drug-law violation (Carson, 2015).

A significant proportion of those under the custody of the justice system are charged/convicted of drug-law violations, and the disparate increase in the number of these individuals under the custody of the corrections system during the 1980s and 1990s fueled an increased focus on substance abuse, crime and correctional populations. However, as mentioned earlier, the degree to which those under the custody of the justice system (probation, prisons, and jails) have substance abuse or dependence needs is, to a large degree, independent of the nature of their current offense: regardless of whether the offense is a drug-law violation, a property crime or a crime of violence, most of those under the custody of the justice system are in need of substance abuse treatment.

Another trend seen over the last three decades has been the dramatic increase in the amount of empirical evidence that has identified a wide array of rehabilitative approaches that could be used to address the relationship between substance abuse and criminal activity, both within institutional settings, such as prisons and jails, as well as through community-based interventions, such as drug treatment courts. Further, subsequent examinations of the research conducted by Martinson (1974) using more sophisticated methods of meta-analysis, and including more programs that had fidelity to treatment interventions and approaches, reached a different conclusion than reached in the 1970s: treatment was effective if it was targeted at the right individuals and had fidelity to the therapeutic design.

It was also during the 1990s that both the methods of assessment of criminal populations to identify their risks and needs, and the substance abuse treatment approaches being utilized, became more evidence-based and sophisticated. Research, and reviews of research, conducted by Andrews and Bonta (2015) identified and articulated the idea behind what is referred to as static versus dynamic risk factors. Static risk factors are those that are fixed or have occurred in the past, and therefore cannot be changed, such as the number of prior arrests, age at first arrest, or age at which drug use was initiated. On the other hand, dynamic risk factors could be changed or altered through the provision of therapeutic interventions, such as criminal thinking patterns and anti-social attitudes, association with pro-criminal peers, and substance abuse patterns (Andrews & Bonta, 2015). Importantly, Andrews and Bonta point out that substance abuse is not necessarily the risk factor most strongly associated with criminal behavior, but it is among those malleable through treatment and among the "central eight" factors that explain criminal behavior (p. 64).

Spurred by the increase in correctional populations, and the increased visibility of substance abuse being related to criminality due to the influx of those charged with drug-law violations, the degree to which both prisons and jails sought to address these needs also changed. As pointed out earlier, however, there is a substantive difference between providing substance abuse education classes and self-help groups to inmates versus clinical treatment and counseling. Thus, there is a need to distinguish between the existence of these different types of services, and also the degree to which these services meet the needs of the populations in the nation's prisons and jails. Further, recognizing the gap between the need for, and provision of substance abuse treatment services to both jail and prison populations, the federal government provided significant increases in funding to support the expansion of prison- and jail-based treatment through the federal Residential Substance Abuse Treatment (RSAT) grant program. From the initiation of RSAT in 1996, through 2003, more than $400 million was provided to states to support substance abuse treatment for incarcerated populations (Bureau of Justice Assistance, 2007).

In terms of the existence of substance abuse programming, the majority of prisons in the United States appear to have some type of services, whereas the majority of county jails do not. For example, based on a 2005 census of state prisons in the United States, 73% of all prisons had a drug or alcohol program (Stephan, 2008), however, the availability of these programs varied considerably from state to state. For example, in five states, 90% or more of the prisons offered some type of drug or alcohol program, whereas in other states fewer than 20% of their prisons had programs (author's analysis of prison census data in Stephan 2008). By comparison, in 2006, roughly 40% of jails reported that they had alcohol or drug "dependency/counseling/ awareness" programs. Further, those jails that housed more inmates—larger jails, which tend to be in more metropolitan areas—tended to be more likely to report the existence of these "dependency/counseling/awareness" programs than smaller jails. For example, in jails housing fewer than 50 inmates, less than 30% reported having any of these alcohol or drug programs, whereas almost 70% of jails housing 1,000 or more inmates had programs (author's analysis of jail census data in Stephan & Walsh, 2011).

While this may appear to suggest that there is substantial availability of substance abuse treatment programming, it is important to point out that most of the services, and the majority of services accessed by inmates in jails and prisons, "can be more clearly characterized as educational or awareness building" and not the more needed, and intensive, therapeutic or clinical interventions (Taxman et al., 2007, p. 251). Further, while a substantial portion of prisons have substance abuse counseling programs and even operate therapeutic community (TC) programs that are segregated from the general inmate population, the capacity in these programs tend to be low and result in only a fraction of those in need of those services being able to access them (Taxman et al., 2007).

However, over time there appears to have been changes in how jails and prisons saw their role in the provision of substance abuse treatment as reflected in the degree to which these institutions viewed substance abuse treatment as one of their functions. For example, in a 1999 census of local jails in the United States, 156 reported that the provision of alcohol or drug treatment was a function of the jail (Stephan, 2001), and by 2006, when a similar jail census was completed, 314 jails indicated that this was one of their functions (Stephan & Walsh, 2011). Thus, while the number of jails indicating that the provision of substance abuse treatment was one of their functions has increased over time, it is important to place this into the larger context of how many jails there are: less than 10% of the 3,271 local jail facilities in the United States identified "alcohol/drug treatment confinement" as one of the functions of their facility, and this also varied across the states (Stephan & Walsh, 2011).

A similar trend was evident across prisons in the United States in what they saw as one of their functions. In 1990, 117 prisons in the United States identified themselves as having an "alcohol/drug treatment confinement" function (Stephan, 1992). By the year 2000, this number had doubled to 249, according to Stephan and Karberg (2003), and by 2005, 352 prisons in the United States viewed themselves as having this function (author's analysis of prison census data in Stephan, 2008). However, while 352 (19%) of the 1,821 adult correctional facilities operating under state or federal authority in 2005 saw themselves as having a alcohol/drug treatment confinement function, only 61 of these 352 indicated that the largest percent of inmates at their facility were being served by this function (author's analysis of prison census data in Stephan, 2008). Furthermore, a national survey in 2003 found that there were only 22 state operated prisons in the United States where all inmates in the facility were participating in substance abuse treatment (i.e., a dedicated treatment facility for inmates), and only 16 of those facilities provided services to a general inmate population, as opposed to a restricted population of probation or parole violators (Olson, Juergens, & Karr, 2004).

Thus, while the degree to which both jails and prisons have increased their view that one of their functions is the provision of substance abuse treatment services is a clear trend, the majority of both prisons and jails do not recognize this as one of their functions. Further, despite the increase in federal support to provide substance abuse treatment services through RSAT, and an increased recognition and view that drug and alcohol treatment was one of the functions of prisons and jails, it appears that the *proportion* of inmates receiving prison-based substance abuse treatment services decreased during the 1990s due to the dramatic increases in the number of offenders admitted to prison (Mears, Winterfield, Hunsaker, Moore, & White, 2003; Mumola, 1999).

It also appears that in an effort to provide at least some type of substance abuse services to a growing number of inmates, the form of the services provided to inmates shifted during the 1990s and into the early 2000s. For example, in 1991, it was estimated that more than one-third (36%) of state prison inmates who had used drugs in the month prior to their current offense participated in what would be considered substantive treatment while in prison, such as counseling or being housed in a residential drug treatment unit within prison, and 24% participated in other substance abuse programming, such as drug education or self-help groups (Mumola, 1999). However, as the prison population increased dramatically in the United States during the 1990s and into the early 2000s, the proportion of inmates receiving substantive treatment services fell, while the proportion receiving the non-treatment, and less expensive, services such as drug education and self-help groups increased. By 1997, only 15% of those identified as having used drugs in the month leading up to their current offense had participated in substantive treatment while in prison (Mumola, 1999), a rate that was similar to that seen 7 years later, in 2004 (Mumola & Karberg, 2006). On the other hand, the likelihood that these inmates were receiving other programming, such as drug education or self-help groups increased, from 24% in 1991 to 28% in 1997 (Mumola, 1999) to 34% in 2004 (Mumola & Karberg, 2006). Thus, despite increased federal support through RSAT, and increased attention and recognition that substance abuse treatment was one of the functions of prisons, the proportion of inmates receiving substance abuse treatment actually decreased during the 1990s and 2000s. This also was noted by Chandler, Fletcher, and Volkow (2009), who summarized the situation as few correctional facilities making use of effective, evidence-based clinical programs in favor of the less effective drug education programs.

CURRENT RESEARCH AND POLICY IMPLICATIONS

On the heels of the discredited review of the literature regarding the effectiveness of treatment programs for offender populations by Martinson (1974) came a steady stream of increasingly sophisticated and rigorous evaluations regarding effective interventions to address the substance abuse of those within the criminal justice system as a whole, but in particular, programs designed for incarcerated populations. Indeed, for those individuals identified as requiring a period of incarceration to address concerns of public safety, or to satisfy the expectation for punishment, recovery from addiction can begin to take hold in prison, where inmates have "the time and opportunity for comprehensive treatment" (Inciardi, Martin, & Surratt, 2001, p. 4). With the growing number of individuals under the custody of the justice system who are in need of substance abuse treatment, over the years the techniques used to treat addictions have also expanded greatly and have a track record of evaluations to illustrate their effectiveness.

Not only have there been evaluations of specific, large scale, and high-profile prison-based TC programs, including the Amity program operating in California (Wexler et al., 1999), those operating in Texas prisons (Knight et al., 1999, 2004), the Key-crest program in Delaware (Inciardi et al., 1997), and Illinois' Sheridan Correctional Center (Olson & Lurigio, 2014), there also have been a number of meta-analyses of prison-based drug treatment interventions (see Lipton, 1995; MacKenzie, 1997; Mitchell et al., 2012; Pearson & Lipton, 1999; Pearson et al., 2002). The Mitchell et al. (2012) review is one of the most comprehensive, rigorous, and recent meta-analyses published on the effectiveness of incarceration-based drug treatment. Mitchell and colleagues found that, across the 73 studies summarized, there was an average of a 17% reduction in the recidivism rate associated with program participation relative to a comparison group, and 84% of the studies found a reduction in recidivism that varied in magnitude depending on the specific elements of the program or population served. For example, Mitchell et al. found that corrections-based programs that served large proportions of white offenders, those serving exclusively female offenders, and those specifically for non-violent offenders produced greater reductions in recidivism than their counterparts. Further, Mitchell et al. also found that those corrections-based programs that required a longer length of participation, were voluntary, required post-release aftercare, and had been operational for a longer period of time all had larger reductions in recidivism than did their counterparts. This is not to say, however, that these other participant or program characteristics were not associated with positive outcomes—just that the magnitude of effect was lower.

Continuity of care is particularly crucial to the recovery of drug-involved offenders who leave correctional settings (National Institute on Drug Abuse,

2012; Peters, 1993). Offenders who complete structured substance abuse treatment programs in prisons and jail need to be assisted in their transitions to community-based services through prerelease planning and access to community-based services. Without aftercare services (i.e., continuity of care), the gains that offenders make in prison drug-based treatment programs are frequently diminished or lost altogether (Lipton, 1995; National Institute on Drug Abuse, 2012). As noted above, the review by Mitchell et al. (2012) found that programs that required post-release aftercare had better outcomes/ larger reductions in recidivism than did programs not requiring aftercare. This finding has been reached by others, including Inciardi et al. (2004), although some (Welsh, 2007) found reductions in recidivism associated with prison-based TCs even when aftercare was not included in the program design. Still, most agree that aftercare enhances the positive gains made through corrections-based programs and should be used to ensure long-term reductions in recidivism (Cullen & Gendreau, 2000; Gaes et al., 1999).

The recognition of the importance of post-release aftercare for prison-based substance abuse treatment programs is so widespread that the federal Residential Substance Abuse Treatment (RSAT) grant program encourages that aftercare be incorporated into the design of the jail- and prison-based programs (Bureau of Justice Assistance, 2007). However, despite this encouragement, few sites receiving RSAT funds for prison-based treatment provided post-release aftercare (Harrison & Martin, 2000), and Lipton et al. (2000) found that fewer than one-half of RSAT-funded programs placed participants in some type of aftercare. Part of this is likely due to not all of those released from jails and prison remaining under correctional supervision, coupled with limited availability for these aftercare services in many of the communities where inmates return.

Making aftercare services available, or mandatory, does not ensure that those released from prison—or jail-based substance abuse treatment programs will enter, participate in, or complete those programs. To some degree, the motivation (or coercion) to participate in aftercare would come from the conditional requirements imposed on those released from prison or jail. This becomes an issue for policy and practice from two perspectives. First, it assumes/requires that individuals released from prison or jail be subject to some type of supervision or monitoring to encourage/ensure access to and participation in aftercare. As a result of nationwide shifts in sentencing practices and prison release mechanisms, the proportion of inmates released from prison without any supervision has increased. For example, in 2014, roughly 30% of inmates released from prison in the United States were released "unconditionally," meaning that they had served their entire sentence in prison and were not subject to post-release supervision, and this proportion varied dramatically from state to state (Carson, 2015).

This state variation in the degree to which prison inmates are released with or without conditions reflects each individual states' sentencing and release policies. Indeed, even among inmates participating in prison-based treatment programs that *require* aftercare as a condition of release, many may not enter aftercare due to limited availability within certain communities, or may not complete it successfully (Olson, Rozhon, & Powers, 2009). This issue needs to be recognized by practitioners and policy makers, since the requirement of aftercare as a condition of release could result in an increased risk for technical violations of supervision (i.e., not participating in aftercare) and subsequent return to prison for those technical violations. Similarly, large portions of those released from jail are not under any immediate supervision—either because they have posted bond and are still awaiting the disposition of their case, because the charges against them have been dropped, or they have completed their sentence in the jail and are no longer under the jurisdiction of the justice system.

In addition to the implications for policy and practice associated with aftercare, another policy consideration is whether inmates who participate in prison-based substance abuse treatment programs should be given additional time off their sentence (earned time) for their participation, or, in the case of pretrial jail detainees, if their participation in treatment should be considered a mitigating factor in sentencing decisions. Because there is no way to ensure that those who are admitted to treatment are truly in need of treatment, some express concerns that inmates will "game the system" by participating in these programs, even though they do not need them, in order to be released sooner or receive a less punitive sentence. Partly because of this concern, but also as a result of truth-in-sentencing laws that limit the amount of time that can be reduced from a prison sentence, the number of states that allow earned time for participation in substance abuse treatment programs is limited.

As of 2009, only 11 states allowed for inmates to receive sentence credits for participation in rehabilitative programs, such as substance abuse or mental health treatment, although most states (31) did allow "earned time" for participation or completion of other types of programming (most often educational and vocational) (Lawrence, 2009). In recent years, some states have revisited this option, including Utah, which in 2015 passed legislation granting earned time for inmates who complete programming directly related to their criminogenic need. This renewed interest in earned time has been fueled by the recognition that it has the potential of motivating offenders to participate in treatment, it reduces length of stay in prison (and therefore prison populations), and it appears to increase the likelihood that inmates will complete treatment (Olson & Lurigio, under review).

ISSUES AND CHALLENGES

It is clear that there is a significant unmet need for substance abuse treatment services to those in prisons and jails, despite the fact that there is now a body of rigorous research and evaluations that have identified the necessary components for these programs and the impact they have on recidivism. This leads to a need to understand the practical issues and challenges facing practitioners and policy makers when it comes to providing substance abuse services to those in correctional settings. While this usually comes down to an issue of available resources, it is also important to place the goal of providing rehabilitation to those in custody with the other, more immediate goals to those working in these environments. When individuals are convicted and sentenced, there are often multiple goals sought through the imposed sanctions. Broadly speaking, the goals of sentencing generally include deterrence, retribution, incapacitation, and rehabilitation. However, which of these is the primary or most immediate goal will depend on the offense and/ or the offender, along with the prevailing views of the public, practitioners and policy makers. Further, among those who work within prisons and jails, these long-term or theoretical goals may be secondary to the more immediate goals of staff and inmate safety, and preventing escapes.

This is where correctional institutions often face challenges, since rehabilitation is but one of the multiple, and often viewed as conflicting, goals they are expected to achieve. Research indicates that those individuals identified as the highest risk for recidivism should be the focus of treatment efforts, as it is this population that can be helped the most through treatment. However, often individuals considered high risk for recidivism are also considered high risk from the standpoint of prison and jail security classification. As a result, often the highest risk inmates, and those with the greatest need for treatment, are housed in facilities that are less likely to offer substance abuse treatment programming. That said, it is important to understand how treatment may actually advance the more immediate needs of those working in correctional settings to ensure safety and security. Specifically, prison-based drug-treatment programs are often some of the safest and least-crowded units in correctional institutions, which not only incentivizes inmates to stay in treatment but also makes for a better working and living environment for both staff and inmates (Lipton, 1995).

Even if sufficient treatment services are available within prisons, the ability to provide effective substance abuse treatment to correctional populations is still a challenge. Not only do those in need of treatment need to be effectively identified, but they also have to be motivated to want treatment, be able to access and matriculate successfully through treatment while incarcerated, and have access to and complete aftercare services following their release from secure confinement. Even among those admitted to RSAT programs in state prisons and local jails, roughly one-quarter of those admitted to these programs in the first half of 2013 did not successfully complete the institution-based programs, and only about one-half that were released to aftercare successfully completed (Stayee, 2014).

Finally, a challenge to rehabilitating those in prisons and jails is that they often enter with multiple criminogenic needs, one of which may be substance abuse. Those entering prisons and jails often have extensive criminal histories, which limit employment and other opportunities, and most have limited educational achievement and vocational skills. Further, a significant portion of those in prisons and jails also have mental health issues that may need to be addressed prior to their ability to effectively participate in substance abuse treatment and other rehabilitative programming. Correctional facilities need to be able to effectively identify all of these criminogenic risks and needs, and prioritize which will be addressed during the period of incarceration to ensure staff and inmate safety while incarcerated, but also reduce post-release recidivism. Given the complexity of these cases and limited resources specifically for rehabilitative programming, unfortunately most inmates leave jail and prison without having had all (or even most) of their needs met, including substance abuse treatment. It is this gap between rehabilitative needs and services that contributes to the high rates of recidivism.

FUTURE PROSPECTS

Despite all of the doom and gloom that may appear to be facing prisons and jails when it comes to providing quality substance abuse treatment, there is some reason to be optimistic about the future. First, over the past few years, the number of people incarcerated in the nation's prisons and jails has decreased. Reversing the dramatic increase experienced in the number of people in the United States under correctional supervision during the 1980s through the mid-2000s, correctional populations have actually decreased since 2010, with state prison populations falling by 3% between 2010 and 2014 (Bureau of Justice Statistics, 2016). Although not dramatic, this does reflect a shift in sentencing practices over the past few years, as well as a renewed focus on the need for rehabilitation for those who are under the custody of the justice system. Further, numerous states have begun to modify their drug laws and the penalties associated with drug offenses in an effort to not only reduce prison populations, but also reverse what many saw as overly punitive changes that had been made in the late 1980s and early 1990s.

There has been a substantial drop in the number of drug-law violators serving sentences in state prisons since the mid- to late-2000s, which contributed to much of the decrease in the overall prison population seen during that period. For example, 65% of the decrease in prison admissions in the United

States between 2006 and 2011 was attributed to admissions for drug-law violations (Carson & Golinelli, 2013), and just between 2011 and 2013, the number of drug-law violators serving sentences in state prisons in the United States fell from an estimated 223,000 (Carson & Golinelli, 2013) to 208,000 (Carson, 2015). It is important to keep in mind, however, that whether or not individuals are in prison or jail for a drug-law violation does not necessarily reduce the need for treatment services: regardless of the current offense, the majority of those in prisons and jails are substance abusers and in need of treatment. The "ramping down" of the war on drugs that appears to be occurring should not be viewed as justification to place less emphasis on meeting the substance abuse treatment needs of those incarcerated in the United States.

There also has been a substantial increase in the degree to which correctional agencies—from community to institutional corrections—have adopted and begun to use risk and needs assessments that are more sophisticated than ever, and provide much clearer direction as to which individuals are most in need of specific rehabilitative programming. While there is a significant need for substance abuse treatment among those under the custody of the justice system, ensuring that those who will benefit from that treatment most are a priority, coupled with appropriate matching of needs to the type of treatment intervention used, will hopefully improve the effectiveness and efficiency of substance abuse treatment programming. Finally, advances in the identification of substance abuse treatment needs and improved quality and availability of evidence-based programs at the point of probation (or even before a case reaches that point) will also reduce recidivism and continued involvement in crime, thereby further reducing the number of individuals that continue to engage in substance abuse, and ideally that leads to less involvement in the justice system, and in particular jails and prisons, in the future.

DISCUSSION QUESTIONS

1. If we know that treatment can reduce recidivism when done using evidence-based principles, that the recidivism rate of people released from prisons is high, and that very few of those who need substance abuse treatment get the needed services, why is it that we cannot provide more capacity to provide substance abuse treatment within prisons and jails?
2. Many view the high recidivism rate of those released from prison as evidence that treatment does not work to reduce crime. Given what you have read, what would be your response to that view?
3. Prisons and jails are very effective at incapacitation (few escapes) and punishment, but not very effective at meeting the treatment needs of

those incarcerated. Do you think we can effectively accomplish all three goals: incapacitation, punishment, and rehabilitation at the same time? Could resources be reallocated within prisons to increase the capacity to provide treatment?

4. Why do you think there was a switch from providing substantive, clinical programming for those in need of substance abuse treatment to less substantive services, like drug education or self-help groups?

5. What do you see as some of the most significant challenges to ensuring continuity of care as someone moves from probation to jail to prison (assuming that most of those who end up in prison are involved with these two other components of the correctional system at some time before they end up in prison)?

6. Research has found that, in the long-run, the investment in substance abuse treatment today will save substantial resources down to road. Given this, why do you think we do not invest enough resources into serving a larger proportion of those in jails and prisons who need substance abuse treatment?

REFERENCES

Andrews, D. A., & Bonta, J. (2015). *The psychology of criminal conduct, 5th edition.* New Providence, NJ: LexisNexis Group.

Belenko, S., & Peugh, J. (2005). Estimating drug treatment needs among state prison inmates. *Drug and Alcohol Dependence, 77,* 269–281.

Blumstein, A. (2011). Bringing down the U.S. prison population. *The Prison Journal, 91,* 12s–26s.

Bureau of Justice Assistance. (2007). *Residential substance abuse treatment (RSAT) for state prisoners program FY 2008 formula grant announcement.* Washington, DC: Bureau of Justice Statistics. Retrieved from https://www.bja.gov/Funding/07RSATsol.pdf.

Bureau of Justice Statistics. (2016). *Estimated number of persons supervised by U.S. adult correctional systems, by correctional status, 1980–2014.* Retrieved from http://www.bjs.gov/index.cfm?ty=kfdetail&iid=487.

Carson, E. A. (2015). *Prisoners in 2014.* NCJ 248955, Washington, DC: US Department of Justice, Office of Justice Programs, Bureau of Justice Statistics.

Carson, E. A., & Golinelli, D. (2013). *Prisoners in 2012: Trends in admissions and releases, 1991–2012.* NCJ243920, Washington, DC: US Department of Justice, Office of Justice programs, Bureau of Justice Statistics.

Chandler, R. K., Fletcher, B. W., & Volkow, N. D. (2009). Treating drug abuse and addiction in the criminal justice system: Improving public health and safety. *Journal of the American Medical Association, 301,* 183–190.

Cullen, F. T., & Gendreau, P. (2000). Assessing correctional rehabilitation: Policy, practice, and prospects. In *Criminal Justice 2000: Policies, Processes, and Decisions of the Criminal Justice System* (pp. 109–176). Washington, DC: US Department of Justice.

Durose, M. R., Cooper, A. D., & Snyder, H. N. (2014). *Recidivism of prisoners released in 30 states in 2005: Patterns from 2005 to 2010.* NCJ244205, Washington, DC: U.S. Department of Justice, Office of Justice Programs, Bureau of Justice Statistics.

Federal Bureau of Investigation (n.d.). Crime in the United States. Retrieved from https://ucr.fbi.gov/crime-in-the-u.s U.S. Department of Justice.

Gaes, G. G., Flanagan, T. J., Motiuk, L. K., & Stewart, L. (1999). Adult correctional treatment. In M. H. Tonry & J. Petersilia (Eds.), *Prisons* (pp. 361–426). Chicago, IL: University of Chicago Press.

Harrison, L. L., & Martin, S. S. (2000). Residential substance abuse treatment (RSAT) for state prisoners formula grant: Compendium of program implementation and accomplishments. Newark, DE: Center for Drug and Alcohol Studies. Retrieved from https://www.ncjrs.gov/pdffiles1/nij/grants/187099.pdf.

Illinois Criminal Justice Information Authority. (2003). *2003 annual report.* Retrieved from http://www.icjia.state.il.us/assets/pdf/AnnualReport/ar03.pdf. Chicago, IL.

Inciardi, J. A., Martin, S. S., & Surratt, H. L. (2001). Therapeutic communities in prisons and work release: Effective modalities for drug involved offenders. In B. Rawlings and R. Yates (Eds.), *Therapeutic communities for the treatment of drug users* (pp. 241–256). London, UK: Jessica Kingsley Publishers.

Inciardi, J. A., Martin, S. S., Butzin, C. A., Hooper, R. M., & Harrison, L. D. (1997). An effective model of prison-based treatment for drug-involved offenders. *Journal of Drug Issues, 27,* 261–278.

Inciardi, J. A., Martin, S. S., & Butzin, C. A. (2004). Five year outcomes of therapeutic community treatment of drug involved offenders released from prison. *Crime and Delinquency, 50,* 88–107.

Justice Research and Statistics Association. (2000). *Crime and justice atlas 2000.* Washington, DC: US Department of Justice. Retrieved from http://www.jrsa.org/projects/Crime_Atlas_2000.pdf.

Kaeble, D., Maruschak, L. M., & Bonczar, T. P. (2015). *Probation and parole in the United States, 2014.* NCJ249057, Washington, DC: US Department of Justice, Office of Justice Programs, Bureau of Justice Statistics.

Karberg, J. C., & James, D. J. (2005). *Substance dependence, abuse, and treatment of jail inmates, 2002.* NCJ209588, Washington, DC: US Department of Justice, Office of Justice Programs, Bureau of Justice Statistics.

Knight, K., Dwayne, S. D., Chatham, L. R., & Camacho, L. M. (1997). An assessment of prison-based drug treatment: Texas' in-prison therapeutic community program. *Journal of Offender Rehabilitation, 24,* 75–100.

Knight, K., Simpson, D. D., & Hiller, M. L. (1999). Three-year reincarceration outcomes for in-prison therapeutic community treatment in Texas. *The Prison Journal, 79,* 337–351.

Lawrence, A. (2009): Cutting corrections costs: Earned time policies for state prisoners. Denver, CO: National Conference of State Legislatures. Retrieved from http://www.ncsl.org/documents/cj/earned_time_report.pdf.

Lipton, D. S. (1995). *The effectiveness of treatment for drug abusers under criminal justice supervision.* NCJ 157642, Washington, DC: National Institute of Justice.

Lipton, D. S., Pearson, F. S., & Wexler, H. K. (2000). *Final report: national evaluation of the residential substance abuse treatment for state prisoners program from onset to midpoint.* (Document no. 182218), Washington, DC: US Department of Justice, National Institute of Justice. Retrieved from https://www.ncjrs.gov/pdffiles1/nij/grants/182218.pdf.

Lurigio, A. J. (2000). Drug treatment availability and effectiveness studies of the general and criminal justice populations. *Criminal Justice and Behavior, 27,* 495–528.

MacKenzie, D. L. (1997). Criminal justice and crime prevention. In L. W. Sherman, D. Gottfredson, D. MacKenzie, J. Eck, P. Reuter, and S. Bushway (Eds.). *Preventing crime: What works, what doesn't and what's promising.* Washington, DC: National Institute of Justice.

Martinson, R. (1974). What works? Questions and answers about prison reform. *The Public Interest, 35,* 22–54.

Martinson, R. (1979). New findings, new views: A note of caution regarding prison reform. *Hofstra Law Review, 7,* 243–258.

Minton, T. D., & Zhen, Z. (2015). *Jail inmates at mid-year 2014.* NCJ 248629, Washington, DC: US Department of Justice, Office of Justice Programs, Bureau of Justice Statistics.

Mitchell, O., Wilson D. B., & MacKenzie, D. L. (2012). *The effectiveness of incarceration-based drug treatment on criminal behavior.* Oslo, Norway: The Campbell Collaboration.

Mears, D. P., Winterfield, L., Hunsaker, J., Moore, G. E., & White, R. M. (2003). *Drug treatment in the criminal justice system: The current state of knowledge.* Washington, DC: Urban Institute. Retrieved from http://www.urban.org/research/publication/drug-treatment-criminal-justice-system.

Mumola, C. J., & Bonczar, T. P. (1998). *Substance abuse and treatment of adults on probation, 1995.* NCJ166611, Washington, DC: US Department of Justice, Office of Justice Programs, Bureau of Justice Statistics.

Mumola, C. J. (1999). *Substance abuse and treatment, state and federal prisoners, 1997.* NCJ 172871, Washington, DC: US Department of Justice, office of Justice Programs, Department of Justice.

Mumola, C. J., & Karberg, J. C. (2006). *Drug use and dependence, state and federal prisoners, 2004.* NCJ 213530, Washington, DC: US Department of Justice, Office of Justice Programs, Bureau of Justice Statistics.

National Institute on Drug Abuse (2002). *Therapeutic community–research report series.* Washington, DC: Department of Health and Human Services. Retrieved from http://archives.drugabuse.gov/pdf/RRTherapeutic.pdf.

National Institute on Drug Abuse. (2012). *Principles of drug addiction treatment: A research-based guide.* Washington, DC: Department of Health and Human Services. Retrieved from https://www.drugabuse.gov/publications/principles-drug-addiction-treatment-research-based-guide-third-edition/acknowledgments.

Olson, D. E., Juergens, R., & Karr, S. P. (2004). *Program evaluation summary: The impetus and implementation of the Sheridan Correctional Center Therapeutic Community.* Chicago, IL: Illinois Criminal Justice Information Authority.

Olson, D. E., & Lurigio, A. J. (2014). The long-term effects of prison-based drug treatment and aftercare services on recidivism. *Journal of Offender Rehabilitation, 53*, 600–619.

Olson, D. E., Rozhon, J., & Powers, M. (2009). Enhancing prisoner reentry through access to prison-based and post-prison aftercare treatment: Experiences from the Illinois Sheridan Correctional Center Therapeutic Community. *Journal of Experimental Criminology, 5*, 299–321.

Pearson, F., & Lipton, D. (1999). A meta-analytic review of the effectiveness of corrections-based treatment for drug abuse. *The Prison Journal, 79*, 384–410.

Pearson, F. S., Lipton, D. S., Cleland, C. M., & Yee, D. S. (2002). Effects of behavioral/cognitive behavioral programs on recidivism. *Crime and Delinquency, 48*, 476–496.

Peters, R. H. (1993). Drug treatment in jails and detention settings. In J. A. Inciardi (Ed.), *Drug treatment and criminal justice* (pp. 44–80). Newbury Park, CA: Sage.

Prendergast, M. L., Hall, E. A., Wexler, H. K., Melnick, G., & Cao, Y. (2004). Amity prison-based therapeutic community: 5-year outcomes. *The Prison Journal, 84*, 36–60.

Simon, J. (2007). *Governing through crime.* New York: Oxford University Press.

Stayee, J. (2014). *Program performance report: Residential Substance Abuse Treatment (RSAT) Program, January–June 2013.* Washington, DC: US Department of Justice, Bureau of Justice Assistance. Retrieved from https://www.bja.gov/Publications/RSAT_PPR_Jan-Jun13.pdf.

Stephan, J. J. (2008). *Census of state and federal correctional facilities, 2005.* NCJ 222182, Washington, DC: US Department of Justice, Office of Justice Programs, Bureau of Justice Statistics.

Stephan, J. J. (2001). *Census of jails, 1999.* NCJ 186633, Washington, DC: US Department of Justice, Office of Justice Programs, Bureau of Justice Statistics.

Stephan, J. J. (1992). *Census of state and federal correctional facilities, 1990.* NCJ 137003, Washington, DC: US Department of Justice, National Institute of Justice, Bureau of Justice Statistics.

Stephan, J. J., & Walsh, G. (2011). *Census of jail facilities, 2006.* NCJ 230188, Washington, DC: U.S. Department of Justice, Office of Justice Programs, Bureau of Justice Statistics.

Stephan, J. J., & Karberg, J. C. (2003). *Census of state and federal correctional facilities, 2000.* NCJ 198272, Washington, DC: US Department of Justice, Office of Justice Programs, Bureau of Justice Statistics.

Taxman, F. S., Perdoni, M. L., & Harrison, L. D. (2007). Drug treatment services for adult offenders: The state of the state. *Journal of Substance Abuse Treatment, 32*, 239–254.

Wexler, H. K., De Leon, G., Thoms, G., Kressler, D., & Peters, J. (1999). The Amity Prison TC evaluation. *Criminal Justice and Behavior, 26*, 147–167.

Welsh, W. N. (2007). A multisite evaluation of prison-based therapeutic community drug treatment. *Criminal Justice and Behavior, 34*, 1481–1498.

White, W. L. (1998). *Slaying the dragon: The history of addiction treatment and recovery in America*. Bloomington, IL: Chestnut Health Systems/Lighthouse Institute.

Chapter Ten

Correctional Education and Social Reintegration

Daniel R. Lee

It has been reported widely that inmate populations in the United States have increased considerably over the past 40 years, and for the past decade, incarcerated populations have remained somewhat stable at about 2.2 million inmates (Kaeble, Glaze, Tsoutis, & Minton, 2015). In 2014, over 600,000 offenders were admitted into US prisons, and a nearly identical number of inmates were released (Carson, 2015); a pattern of near equal admissions and releases ensures that the incarcerated population remains stable. The reliance on incarceration as a means of punishment is related to public and political sentiments, but in recent years, it is difficult to determine if public sentiment drives political action or if political action has driven public sentiments about crime and punishment. Regardless, existing policies and practices have been described by many as a strategy of mass incarceration. While retributive and punitive sentiments toward offenders remain popular, attitudes about punishment philosophy include the need to focus on preparing offenders for their release from incarceration.

This chapter is focused on correctional education programming and how it has been incorporated into punishment strategies. The chapter begins with a description of the history of correctional education and the variation within correctional education programming. Trends related to correctional education programming are presented, and this is followed by a review of research related to the effectiveness of correctional education programs on subsequent offending, employment, and other important outcomes. This research evidence is presented in relationship to criminal justice policies, programming and evaluation issues, and future prospects of correctional education programs.

NATURE OF THE ISSUES

Among inmates, rates of educational attainment are low, with over 40% of inmates having less than a high school education (Harlow, 2003). This is contrasted with the proportion of the general population reported as having less than a high school degree being at approximately 18% (Harlow, 2003). Rates are lower when considering postsecondary education, and collectively, attainment rates vary by gender, age, race, and ethnicity with younger, male, and minority inmates having the lowest rates and levels of educational attainment (Harlow, 2003). This suggests that risk factors related to criminal participation are matched with lower education, and it is possible that lower educational attainment exacerbates the effect of other risk factors to criminal participation. Functional literacy is evident among undereducated inmates, and the likelihood of a successful reintegration into society upon release from incarceration will be low if the inmate lacks the skills that can lead to employment, economic stability, and self-sufficiency.

Among the wide array of contemporary rehabilitation strategies, correctional education programs can help remove or mitigate many risks, but other expectations are important to consider. Most directly, correctional education programs are expected to increase an inmate's level of education (e.g., GED or vocational certification) and academic skills (e.g., literacy), but indirectly, education earned while incarcerated can improve an inmate's self-esteem, employability, social integration, and lifetime earnings. It is these attributes that can be expected to have a relationship with reductions in criminal behaviors.

Criminological theory helps us understand the importance of correctional education and the effect that it might have on subsequent behavior. In Hirschi's (1969) version of control theory, offending behavior was related to lower levels of prosocial attachment, commitment, and involvement. Education can provide individuals with access to consistent employment and higher earnings (i.e., involvement) and a reason to remain free of criminal behavior (i.e., commitment). Likewise, active employment could increase the ability of the former inmate to interact with other prosocial individuals, some of whom might establish themselves as appropriate role models or mentors, and these mentors might provide opportunities to establish prosocial attachment.

If education does lead to employability, differential association (Sutherland, 1947) and social learning theories (Akers, 1973) could explain potential social benefits. Tests of these theories have identified that associations with other criminals is related to criminal participation. Sustained employment might increase the likelihood of exposure to and relationships with prosocial individuals, and these relationships might provide the grounding for a new crime-free social identity.

Employment is likely to benefit economic self-sufficiency, and this might be related to criminal behavior through the principles of strain theory. Merton (1938) wrote about how the failure to achieve goals, including economic success, could lead to antisocial responses that include criminal participation. Education and employment might facilitate the ability to achieve economic goals and limit criminal behavior.

Another important theoretical concept to consider is the dynamic nature of criminal risks and social bonds. In their age-graded theory of social control, Sampson and Laub (1994) described the possibility of prosocial turning points throughout a person's life course. In this sense, criminals who have accumulated and acted in accordance with the risk factors that increase the likelihood of criminality might have the ability to alter their criminal trajectories. That is, offenders who appear to be on a track for continued criminal participation might get married, become a parent, or become employed, and this new life event could be the impetus for developing the social capital that inhibits further criminal behavior.

If correctional education programs can be linked to reductions in criminal behavior, an issue that remains is the expense of programming and if the programs have a benefit relative to their cost. While the cost to incarcerate inmates varies across states, the average cost is reported as being more than $20,000 per year per inmate (Stephan, 2004). Costs for correctional education programs will add to this total, but the issue is if the costs are warranted. That is, if the cost to educate a prisoner reduces the likelihood of continued criminal behavior upon release and subsequent reincarceration, the costs are justified if a former inmate remains out of prison for a length of time that equates to an overall savings in total incarceration expenses. Recent assessments have considered the costs of prison administration, providing correctional education programs, and rates of recidivism among participants and have argued that the costs are, in fact, justified (see Davis, Bozick, Steele, Saunders, & Miles, 2013)

Collectively, these issues keep the debate about correctional education programs focused on the needs of the offenders, the connections between offender needs and risks for criminal behavior, and the economic benefits that might be provided through improved social reintegration and reduced recidivism. This is best accomplished by matching the inmates with a wide variety of educational programs, and today, most correctional facilities do include some type of educational programming. While juvenile facilities are mandated by compulsory education laws to provide education programming, most local, federal, and private prisons also have some type of educational program available to inmates (Harlow, 2003). Programs include Adult Basic Education (ABE), Adult Secondary Education (ASE), Post-Secondary Education (PSE) (to include college-level instruction and vocational certification), special education, and life skills instruction (see Inmate Education

Programs, 2008; Harlow, 2003; MacKenzie, 2008). What needs to be identified is the effect that each of these specific types of instruction might have on improving the lives of the inmates who participate and if this participation might be related to reductions in recidivism.

TRENDS

The history of correctional education programming dates back to the earliest uses of prisons as a form of punishment, but support for correctional education programs has fluctuated over time. Clergymen provided educational instruction at the Walnut Street Jail in 1787 and other early institutions (Gehring & Eggleston, 2006; Hanneken & Dannerbeck, 2007). This early practice of correctional instruction was focused on the importance of literacy, as this literacy allowed inmates the ability to study the Bible, seek redemption for their misbehavior, and develop a greater moral sense of being. Later, Zebulon Brockway included educational instruction as part of his plans for rehabilitating inmates at the Elmira Reformatory (Brockway, 1912), but Brockway's focus on education included expectations for behavior that were more secular than religious.

As the use of prisons increased as a form of punishment in the United States throughout the early 20th century, the focus on rehabilitative programming developed and included many aspects of educational instruction. Correctional education seemed to become more formal with the research of MacCormick (1931) and the founding of the Correctional Education Association (Correctional Education Association, n.d.). Education programs became more specific to include basic education, literacy, and vocational training with the expectation of changing the inmate's behavior, but the sentiments on punishment and rehabilitative programming changed in the 1970s. Martinson's (1974) report on the limited ability of correctional programs to be evaluated with appropriate methodology and to document their success at reducing recidivism led to criticism of rehabilitation programs and philosophies, and while other types of programming might have ended more dramatically, the availability of some type of correctional education in most prisons remained (see Harlow, 2003).

As the successful reentry and reintegration of formerly incarcerated individuals has become more prominent, prison education programs are facing strict scrutiny (see Petersilia, 2003; Travis, 2005). Programs are being designed with greater concern for identifying offenders' risks, needs, and responsivity to treatment, and evaluations are becoming more methodologically rigorous. The call to identify what works in correctional programming has included the identification of how and why correctional education programs reduce recidivism and for which types of offenders they seem to work the best (see Sherman, Farrington, Welsh, & MacKenzie, 2002).

CURRENT RESEARCH

Empirical evaluations of correctional education programs can identify if the intended consequences are being achieved. The challenge with identifying the success of correctional education programs is that there is little agreement for what the intended outcome of a correctional education program should be (e.g., recidivism, educational achievement, or sustained employment), and if the outcome of importance is reduced criminal involvement, how that involvement should be measured (e.g., rearrest, reconviction, or reincarceration).

Gehring (2000) has questioned the reliance on recidivism as a measure for establishing correctional education success and outlined several related problems. To begin, Gehring argued that no one really knows what recidivism means. More specifically, there are varying jurisdictional definitions for criminal behavior, so what qualifies as recidivism in one study might not apply to other contexts or situations. Likewise, while recidivism might refer to continued criminal behavior, different identifications of criminal behavior exist to include self-reported offending, offending identified officially through arrest, reconviction, or being punished with reincarceration. Concerns about using official measure of criminal offending include the possibility for bias due to offender characteristics (e.g., race) that could inflate the measured rates of recidivism.

In addition to the definition and identification of recidivism, Gehring (2000) noted that the period of observation for the measurement is inconsistent across studies. Some studies observe recidivism after treatment for a short duration of 12 months, but others might observe recidivism for 36 months (or more). The variation across studies biases results from shorter periods of observation toward being more successful (i.e., less recidivism) than those with longer periods of observation, because the longer periods of observation increase the possibility of any criminal involvement being identified as evidence of recidivism.

While many researchers stress the methodological concerns with using recidivism, Gehring (2000) suggested a different concern is that recidivism might be counter to the philosophy of most rehabilitation programs. That is, if correctional education programs are intended to produce positive changes within offenders, measures less focused on the attributes of the criminal justice system (e.g., those associated with aptitude, vocational skill, and employment) might be more appropriate morally and in line with the philosophy of producing changes in the quality of the human participants. Outcome measures different from criminal justice action might focus on the positive attributes of well-being and social inclusion.

While the argument presenting concerns related to recidivism as an outcome measure of success for correctional education programs is interesting, the fact remains that most evaluators of rehabilitation programs rely on criminal justice actions to identify what works. While altruistic concern for the participants of correctional education programs is compelling, it is important to identify success in some manner that compares to other evaluations. In this regard, successful correctional education programs are likely to be identified in terms of some measure of reduced criminal offending. A separate measure of success is related to participants' ability to gain and/or maintain employment, because as outlined above, employment is expected theoretically to be related to reductions in criminal offending. Finally, correctional education programs can be identified as successful if it can be established that they reduce recidivism to such an extent that fewer offenders return to prison, and the cost of educational programming is offset by the savings incurred from lowered inmate populations. A comprehensive review of correctional education evaluations might not be necessary for this essay, but a summary review of selected evaluations can highlight most of the relevant issues.

Zgoba, Haugebrook, and Jenkins (2008) examined the effect of earning a GED on recidivism among offenders in New Jersey. In this study, recidivism was measured with the identification of rearrests, reconvictions, and reincarceration with attention paid to the degree of the offense and level of violence. Additionally, the date of the rearrest was collected to determine the elapsed time between release and subsequent offending. The authors examined an extended period of time (7 years) and considered offenses within the local jurisdiction (i.e., New Jersey) and other jurisdictions. They found that obtaining a GED while incarcerated reduced the likelihood of recidivating but did not have a significant effect on the amount of time it took for former inmates to recidivate when released.

Nuttall, Hollmen, and Staley (2003) evaluated the effect of a GED program administered to incarcerated offenders in New York. They measured recidivism as being reincarcerated into the New York Department of Corrections within 36 months of release. The results indicated a small effect on the recidivism rates with slightly fewer GED earners being returned when compared to those who did not earn a GED, and the rate among GED earners was similar to those inmates who had a GED or higher level of education prior to being incarcerated. This suggests that low levels of education might present a risk for recidivism, but basic education programs such as GED training can mitigate that risk.

Gordon and Weldon (2003) examined the effect of participating in GED and vocational programming while incarcerated in West Virginia. In this analysis, recidivism was measured as parole revocation providing a broader coverage of post-release behaviors. In comparing the rates of recidivism among program participants and those who did not participate, lower rates of recidivism were identified among those who participated in the educational programs.

Fabelo (2002) studied the relationship between educational achievement, recidivism, and employment among inmates from Texas. Educational achievement was measured by improved scores in the Test for Adult Basic Education (TABE), and results indicated that inmates who participated had improved scores in reading, literacy, and high school equivalency. Gains in educational achievements were then compared to recidivism, and those with higher levels of education had the lowest rate of recidivism. The relationship between education and recidivism varied by age, offender type, and type of educational attainment. For instance, the greatest reductions in recidivism were among older property offenders who moved from nonreader status to reader. Among groups of offenders who were beyond the level of basic education when they started correctional education programming, little or no recidivism reduction was recognized suggesting that a greater impact from correctional education might be found among those who have the most basic needs. Further analyses indicated that those with the highest levels of education were the ones most likely to gain employment after release from prison, and this gives credence to the importance of many levels of instruction being available to inmate populations.

Batiuk, Moke, and Rountree (1997) evaluated the success of a postsecondary education program in Ohio by examining post-release employment and recidivism. Offenders released from prison and placed on parole were evaluated in regards to whether they had been returned to prison for any reason (including parole violations and convictions due to new criminal charges) within ten years of release. A separate measure of success was employment status at the time parole expired or at the time an offender was rearrested. Education was measured as being able to complete the requirements for an associate's degree while incarcerated. They found that college education while incarcerated decreased recidivism, and this recidivism was due to the effect that college education had on increasing post-release employment.

Duwe and Clark (2014) examined the effect of earning secondary and postsecondary degrees while incarcerated in Minnesota. Recidivism was measured separately as rearrest, reconviction, reincarceration, and as revocation due to a technical violation. Results varied across the correctional education participants in that obtaining a secondary degree did not affect rearrest but those who obtained a postsecondary degree were rearrested at a lower rate than those offenders who did not earn a postsecondary degree. Reconviction and reincarceration rates were lower for education program participants regardless of the degree earned, but considering revocation, only the postsecondary degree earners showed reduced rates. When considering the relationship between education and employment, those who earned degrees (both secondary and postsecondary) had higher rates of employment, worked more hours, and earned more total wages during the evaluation period.

Lockwood, Nally, Ho, and Knutson (2012) examined post-release recidivism among correctional education participants from Indiana. The study provides an interesting understanding of risk factors associated with criminal behavior and how correctional education might mitigate their effects on recidivism. In Indiana during the evaluation period, Department of Corrections administrators and officials were reported to have made good use of state and federal funds to develop and provide correctional education programming, and over 57% of those who were incarcerated participated in education programs at some level. This was expected to improve the likelihood that released inmates would have the necessary skills to become employed, and their employment would reduce their rate of recidivism. Recidivism was measured through reincarceration within five years of being released from prison. Overall, 62.4% of the released offenders maintained some employment during the five-year study period, and almost 38% had never been unemployed. During this period of study, 48% were reincarcerated within the first year of release and nearly all of them were reincarcerated within three years of release. Multivariate results indicated that education led to employment, and employment mitigated the effects of risk factors such as age, race, and preincarceration levels of education.

Hull, Forrester, Brown, Jobe, and McCullen (2000) studied the inmate population in Virginia that was released during the period of 1979–1994 to examine the effect that being involved in education programs while incarcerated had on post-release employment. Educational participation was distinguished as those who had participated, those who enrolled but did not complete the program, and those who completed educational programming. Results indicated that those who completed the educational programming had the lowest rate of recidivism, but some participation, even without completing the program, was better than not having participated. A similar effect was found when examining effects on employment in that some participation increased rates of post-release employment, but the greatest employment rates were found among those who completed educational programming.

Collectively, these studies indicate that evaluations of state-level educational programs provide evidence of the ability to lower recidivism. Additionally, these investigations indicated that employment opportunities are enhanced among those inmates who improve their level of education while incarcerated. These studies have established that there is a connection between employment and education, and that framing these issues as interactive can improve our understanding of the dynamic risk of criminal offending and the need for providing post-release reentry and reintegration support in finding employment. Similarly, it might be important for correctional administrators to provide educational programming that addresses the educational needs of varying types of inmates and the changing demands of local and regional job markets.

While these analyses have the ability to inform our knowledge about what has happened within one type of program, within one time period, or within one jurisdiction, our ability to generalize the results to other situations or contexts can be limited. Generalizability, or applying the results across populations, situations, and strategies, demands a closer examination or control of the subtle variations that exist. Variations in program effectiveness could be due to the unique nature of correctional education programming. That is, one program might be deemed effective when analyzed initially, but the same program could be administered differently, at a different time or in a different setting or to a different type of offender population, and any unobserved differences could alter the results. If the differences are not accounted for or considered in the program evaluation, varying results could suggest that the program is ineffective. To be certain of the effectiveness of correctional education programming, researchers have turned to systematic reviews and meta-analyses. Systematic reviews and meta-analyses examine results from multiple studies concurrently to determine if there is consistency in effects. If these reviews and meta-analyses establish that correctional education programs lead to reductions in recidivism and increased rates of employment, greater confidence can be assigned to the programs as being warranted and necessary components of contemporary reentry and reintegration strategies.

Gerber and Fritsch (1995) provided a summary assessment of correctional education programs. In their review, they identified the shifts in correctional education programming from the early forms of religious instruction to the more modern attempts at providing rehabilitation. Their summary suggests that the mid-20th century expectations of rehabilitative programs not being effective was a premature conclusion, and they emphasized that academic and vocational programs administered in prison reduce disciplinary problems while incarcerated, reduce recidivism post-release, increase employment opportunities, and increase continued educational participation outside of incarceration.

In more recent years, summary assessments have become more focused on being as comprehensive as possible and quantifying the size of effects related to correctional education programs. Wilson, Gallegher, and MacKenzie (2000) attempted to identify all evaluations of correctional education programs with a focus on measuring recidivism and having treatment and comparison groups identified appropriately. They identified 33 programs that met their expectations for inclusion in the meta-analysis, and with allowances for multiple treatment and control groups, they assessed the impact across 53 program comparisons. They distinguished programs by level and type of instruction and found that all types of correctional education pro-

gramming were associated with lower rates of recidivism among participants. Further analysis confirmed that, across studies, program participation
increases employment and that employment accounts for a large proportion
of the recidivism effects.

Cecil, Drapkin, MacKenzie, and Hickman (2000) conducted a systematic
review on a more specific selection of ABE and life skills programs. Across
12 ABE program evaluations, most presented methodological concerns to the
reviewers, and only five were determined to be methodologically rigorous in
that they controlled for group differences among participants and nonpartici-
pants. Among those analyses with statistical tests, program participation was
determined to have moderate to low effects on recidivism. The methodological rigor of the life skills program evaluations were inconsistent and only
marginally strong; these analyses showed support for life skills training reducing recidivism, but most analyses did not include statistical tests for sig-
nificance. Overall, this summary evaluation of ABE and life skills training
emphasizes the importance of methodological consideration when evaluating
correctional education strategies.

Chappell (2004) focused exclusively on post-secondary correctional education evaluations from 1990–1999; program variation included any type of
instruction that was beyond high school to include vocational, academic, and
college level courses and a measure of recidivism was the assessed outcome
of all studies included. Fifteen studies were included in the analysis. The
studies were analyzed collectively and across categorical subsets (i.e., complete postsecondary education program, recidivism as reincarceration, recidivism measured at three-years or less, and studies with control groups) and
results indicated significant reductions in recidivism. While this analysis
provided strong summary support, Chappell (2004) suggested that future
analyses need to consider the types of correctional education programming
that seem to have the greatest benefit.

Reed (2015) conducted a meta-analysis of correctional education programs, and instead of focusing attention on the long-term outcomes of employment and recidivism, she focused on the more immediate academic
achievement of participants. She focused on assessments of General Educational Development (GED) programming, and narrowed the analysis to include evaluations of programs addressing a distinct version of GED instruction (i.e., between revisions to the curriculum and limited to the years 2002
and 2014). The programs that were evaluated focused on improving academic and vocational skills. She identified six studies that met these criteria and
concluded that participants across studies improved their academic and vocational abilities. While most studies included representative samples, she
noted that they included low representations of Hispanic inmates and suggested that correctional education evaluations should attempt to identify the
effect that ethnicity might have on program effectiveness. She noted con-

cerns that most evaluations had not considered or measured completely the delivery of the instruction and instructor capabilities; while motivation of the participants is something to be considered, the quality and type of instruction or program delivery also should be assessed.

Hall (2015) examined ten evaluations of correctional education programs published from 1995 to 2010 and focused her attention on the relationship that risk factors (e.g., age, race, and marital status) had with educational programming and recidivism. Her review was more focused on summarizing the research systematically than analyzing the collective data quantitatively, but her findings are consistent with other meta-analyses. She concluded that across the identified studies, correctional education programs have the ability to reduce recidivism, and it is apparent that the recidivism reduction is operating through the increased employability that is provided to the participating offenders.

Davis et al. (2013), operating with funds set aside from the reauthorization of the Second Chance Act, began conducting a comprehensive assessment of correctional education programming in 2010. The research team prepared to assess all evaluations related to correctional education from 1980 through 2011 by searching for published research and less accessible research they described as grey literature. These less accessible reports might be unpublished documents, conference presentations, government reports, or other evaluation materials that might not have been included in peer-reviewed academic journals. Then, they conducted a meta-analysis that took into consideration the methodological rigor of the research designs and the impact that correctional education had on important outcomes like recidivism and employment. Within the analysis, they assessed the importance of program characteristics that might influence participation and learning, such as if the curriculum had been presented via computer-assisted instruction. They concluded that correctional education programming reduced the risk of recidivism by 13%, and all types of correctional education programs (i.e., ABE, postsecondary, and vocational) were associated with significant reductions in recidivism. Also, they concluded that participation in correctional education programs increased the likelihood that released offenders would obtain employment; the highest increases in employment likelihood were associated with dedicated vocational training programs.

Collectively, these individual and meta-analyses provide consistent results that correctional education programs are associated with reductions in recidivism and increases in employment among participating offenders. The challenge that remains with these analyses is that many evaluations have not considered issues that might affect the results in ways that make the programs appear to be successful. For example, these evaluations rarely considered the method of delivery, and it is possible that different learning styles or learning environments might provide different results. Also, many states al-

low inmates to self-select into educational programming. If inmates are motivated to attend correctional education programming because they want to
improve their level of knowledge or skills, they might have the motivation
that is necessary to cease criminal participation regardless of educational
attainment. What is necessary is for program administrators and program
evaluators to work together to isolate the remaining mysteries regarding how
and why correctional programs seem to work.

Another issue related to correctional education evaluations is the need to
have departments of corrections and program evaluators agree on common
terms, concepts, and data definitions related to correctional education programming and participants. Tracy and Steuer (1995) addressed this concern
and recommended a Model Evaluation Instrument. Their expectation was
that improved communication of results across reported evaluations could
drive the science of correctional education programming forward and advance the quality of programming. Researchers need to be aware of how
recidivism is measured, how offenders are tracked upon release, and how
programming objectives are measured and observed. By increasing consistency across studies, better information could be developed, and improvements to programs could be made.

Advances in correctional education data collection instruments have been
made. Lee, Giever, Tolbert, and Rasmussen (2012) implemented a pilot data
collection project built off of the Correctional Education Data Guidebook
established under the direction of the US Department of Education. The Data
Guidebook and subsequent Correctional Education Data Network established
that state departments of corrections can use their own data collection strategies related correctional education programming and offender monitoring
and align them within a common data definition guide. By allowing data to
be aligned along common definitions for programming and subsequent offender behavior, cross-state and perhaps national data analyses can be conducted. Such an analytical strategy could identify results that are generaliz-
able to the national population of offenders and correctional education participants, and if proper data definitions are included, programmatic variations
might allow for analyses that identify which strategies work best for different
types of offenders in different types of environments.

POLICIES

There are several policies that are relevant to the discussion of correctional
education programming, and most of these policies address the importance of
implementing and establishing correctional education programs. Some policies relate to the structural elements of instructional programs, and other
policies have been put in place to limit public concerns. What the policies

presented here suggest is that correctional education programs remain controversial, but time will dictate if modern sentiments about punishment and rehabilitation change and lead to new political discussions and changes in policy.

Relevant to the development of correctional education programming is the Office of Correctional Education. This office was created in 1991 as a part of the Carl D. Perkins Vocational and Applied Technology Education Act (US Department of Education, 2016). This office was established to coordinate and support correctional education programs, and currently, these duties are being met by the Office of Career, Technical and Adult Education (OCTAE) Division of Adult Education and Literacy (DAEL). Establishing a federal office to oversee the operation of correctional education programs showed a stark contrast to some of the public and political sentiments that developed in the 1990s as crime rates continued to increase and reach historic high levels.

As a response to rising crime rates, President Clinton signed the Violent Crime Control and Law Enforcement Act (VCCLEA) of 1994. This Act, while including provisions for many different types of crime control initiatives, addressed public concern about being soft on crime, and it included directions that prohibited inmates from applying for Pell Grants that paid for many inmates to pursue post-secondary education programs administered in correctional settings.

Tewksbury, Erickson, and Taylor (2000) have reported on the impact of the elimination of Pell grants for inmates. Prior to the VCCLEA, postsecondary programs were available in 92% of correctional systems, but after the passage of the act, availability and participation in postsecondary programs diminished quickly and significantly. Within three years of the act, postsecondary programs were available in only 55% of surveyed correctional systems (Tewksbury, Erickson, & Taylor, 2000). Coincidentally, the authors reported that the percentage of participating inmates decreased. More recently, states' correctional systems have been able to identify newer streams of funding to support inmates interested in postsecondary education, and postsecondary correctional education programs still exist despite changes in the availability of funding. In some states (e.g., Texas), postsecondary education student inmates must pay for classes on their own or agree to reimburse the state as part of their parole (see, Armstrong, Giever, & Lee, 2012). For a complete review of the effect that Pell Grant elimination has had on postsecondary correctional education programs, see Ubah (2004).

According to Koo (2016), there are three policies that are relevant to correctional education participants with documented learning disabilities. Section 504 of the Rehabilitation Act directs that individuals with disabilities cannot be excluded from programs and activities, and this includes education programs administered in federal jails and prisons. In a related manner, the

Americans with Disabilities Act (ADA) expanded the extent of this coverage by prohibiting discrimination by any public entity regardless of federal funding status. The Individuals with Disabilities Education Act (IDEA) ensures free public education to all children with disabilities. These acts demand that education be accessible to a wide reach of citizens, and inmates may seek litigation to ensure their continued participation in educational programming.

Over the past few decades, criminal justice policies have responded to public sentiment about being punitive, but recently, shifts in politics have occurred. In 2015, the United States Departments of Education and Justice announced plans to initiate a temporary, experimental relaxation of the ban on Pell grant funding available to inmates. Under this program, a limited number of inmates within five years of their release from prison will be included in a pilot program allowing for the granting of Pell funding (McIntire, 2015). Initiatives like this suggest that the political climate might be responding to both the needs of the inmates and the evidence of correctional education program success.

ISSUES AND CHALLENGES

The greatest challenge to correctional education programming might be the public and political sentiments that surround discussions of and responses to crime. Punishment philosophy changes slowly, and while attitudes about successful rehabilitation and reentry are becoming more prominent, politicians and members of the public still fear being soft on crime. As successes of rehabilitation programming become more prominent, these attitudes might change.

An opportunity to direct these attitudes about crime and punishment is related to the advances being made in establishing methodological rigor in program evaluations. In the 1990s, Congress commissioned a review of existing literature related to crime control activities with an emphasis on identifying what works and how effective programs can be replicated (see Sherman et al., 2002). What came out of that report was not only a greater concern for establishing program effectiveness through consistent methods but an interest in establishing, distributing, and replicating successful program. Evidence of this can be seen with the free exchange of information provided by the Model Programs Guide (http://www.ojjdp.gov/mpg) and Crime Solutions (http://www.crimesolutions.gov). These websites, sponsored by federal funding, provide reviews and assessments of crime prevention programs. Among the programs evaluations that are summarized on these sites, many include educational components. As correctional education programs are evaluated with more rigor, it is likely that their inclusion on sites like these will be evident and the administration of correctional education programs more available.

Considering methodological rigor of program evaluations, a continued challenge will be the identification of common measures of success. As has been addressed above, recidivism is a common measure of success in crime prevention programming. Since correctional education programs are expected to limit criminal behaviors, consistent measures of recidivism will need to be developed. Given the advice of Gehring (2000), it might be better to invest effort into developing additional measures of success that reflect the true nature and purpose of educational programming.

Educational programs are designed to educate the participants, and this suggests that measuring educational attainment is a worthy measure of success. Coincidental to meeting curricular objectives, students often experience other changes, and these could be explored as reasonable measures of success. For instance, different levels of cognition or awareness about the individual participant's place in a social structure could be indicative of positive change or success. Outside of the effect that education might have on employment, additional measures of success could be developed to reflect how embedded the participants become in their communities. For instance, a socially embedded person would become employed, buy a house, pay taxes, and volunteer in civic associations. Such behaviors could be measureable outcomes that establish a broader measure of success for correctional education programs.

FUTURE PROSPECTS

Today, the future of correctional education programming looks bright. Reentry and reintegration services for former inmates are improving and are becoming more established. Rehabilitative programming is following the sentiment that success is driven by matching the offenders' needs, risk, and responsivity to treatment, and this is likely to include the development and administration of correctional education programs.

Carver and Harrison (2016) have called for a more holistic approach for correctional programs, including correctional education. They describe this holistic approach as embracing a shift toward system thinking or identifying how separate aspects of the criminal justice system relate to each other and to the identification and control of criminal behavior. This systems thinking is poised to embrace correctional education, because it can identify the needs of the offenders and provide a gateway for a successful reentry. With a focus on correctional education, inmates will see themselves differently and as having a place in society, and members of the public might see returning inmates as being more deserving of reintegration. In this sense, correctional education might improve the lives of individual offenders and facilitate the development of better communities.

DISCUSSION QUESTIONS

1. Inmates, in general, are undereducated compared to the general population. How can deficits in education be related to criminal behavior?
2. How has the availability of education for inmates changed over time? To what extent do you think changes in the philosophy of punishment have affected the availability and type of education for inmates?
3. Based on the research evaluating correctional education, what is the relationship between education, employment, and recidivism? In your opinion, what is the best way to identify the success of correctional education programs?
4. What aspects of public policy have encouraged or discouraged the availability of educational programs for inmates?
5. Both prison administration and educational programming for inmates are expensive; which cost is easier to justify as an appropriate use of public funds?

REFERENCES

Akers, R. (1973). *Deviant behavior: A social learning approach.* Belmont, CA: Wadsworth.

Armstrong, G., Giever, D., & Lee, D. (2012). Outcomes evaluation of the Windham School District correctional education programming. Huntsville, TX: Sam Houston State University.

Batiuk, M., Moke, P., & Rountree, P. (1997). Crime and rehabilitation: Correctional education as an agent of change-A research note. *Justice Quarterly, 14,* 167–180.

Brockway, Z. (1912). *Fifty years of prison service: An autobiography.* New York. Charities Publication Committee.

Carson, E. A. (2015). *Prisoners in 2014.* NCJ #248955. Washington, DC: US Department of Justice.

Carver, L., & Harrison, L. (2016). Democracy and the challenges of correctional education. *Journal of Correctional Education, 67,* 2–16.

Cecil, D., Drapkin, D., MacKenzie, D., & Hickman, L. (2000). The effectiveness of adult basic education and life-skills programs in reducing recidivism: A review and assessment of the research. *Journal of Correctional Education, 51,* 207–226.

Chappell, C. (2004). Post-secondary correctional education and recidivism: a meta-analysis of research conducted 1990–1999. *Journal of Correctional Education, 55,* 148–169.

Correctional Education Association, n.d. Retrieved from http://www.ceanational.com/history.htm, June 20, 2012.

Corrections Compendium (2008). Inmate Education Programs. *Corrections Compendium, 33,* 9–25.

Davis, L., Bozick, R., Steele, J., Saunders, J., & Miles, J., (2013). *Evaluating the effectiveness of correctional education: A meta-analysis of programs that provide education to incarcerated adults.* Santa Monica, CA: RAND.

Duwe, G., & Clark, V. (2014). The effects of prison-based educational programming on recidivism and employment. *The Prison Journal, 94,* 454–478.

Fabelo, T. (2002). The impact of prison education on community reintegration of inmates: The Texas case. *Journal of Correctional Education, 53,* 106–110.

Gehring, T. (2000). Recidivism as a measure of correctional education program success. *Journal of Correctional Education, 51,* 197–205.

Gehring, T., & Eggleston, C. (2006). *Correctional education chronology.* San Bernardino, CA: California State University San Bernardino.

Gerber, J., & Fritsch, E. J. (1995). Adult academic and vocational correctional education programs: A review of recent research. *Journal of Offender Rehabilitation, 22,* 119–142.

Gordon, H., & Weldon, B. (2003). The impact of career and technical education programs on adult offenders: Learning behind bars. *Journal of Correctional Education, 54,* 200–209.

Hanneken, D., & Dannerbeck, A. (2007). Addressing offenders' educational opportunities and challenges. *Corrections Compendium, 32,* 1–4, 37.

Hall, L. (2015). Correctional education and recidivism: Toward a tool for reduction. *Journal of Correctional Education, 66,* 4–29.

Harlow, C. W. (2003). *Education and correctional populations.* NCJ # 195670. Washington, DC: US Department of Justice.

Hirschi, T. (1969). *The causes of delinquency.* Berkely, CA: University of California Press.

Hull, K., Forrester, S., Brown, J., Jobe, D., & McCullen, C. (2000). Analysis of recidivism rates for participants of the academic/vocational/transition education programs offered by the Virginia Department of Correctional Education. *Journal of Correctional Education, 51,* 256–261.

Kaeble, D., Glaze, L., Tsoutis, A., & Minton, T. (2015). *Correctional Populations in the United States, 2014.* NCJ # 249513. Washington, DC: US Department of Justice.

Koo, A. (2016). Correctional education can make a greater impact on recidivism by supporting adult inmates with learning disabilities. *Journal of Criminal Law and Criminology, 105,* 233–269.

Lee, D., Giever, D., Tolbert, M., & Rasmussen, L. (2012). *Bridging the correctional education information gap: Lessons learned from piloting a voluntary correctional education data collection system.* Berkley, CA: MPR Associates, Inc.

Lockwood, S., Nally, J., Ho, T., & Knutson, K. (2012). The effect of correctional education on postrelease employment and recidivism: A 5-year follow-up study in the state of Indiana. *Crime & Delinquency, 58,* 380–396.

MacCormick, A. (1931). *The education of adult prisoners: A survey and a program.* New York: AMS Press.

MacKenzie, D. (2008). Structure and components of successful educational programs. Paper presented at the Reentry Roundtable on Education at John Jay College of Criminal Justice, New York.

Martinson, R. (1974). What works? Questions and answers about prison reform. *The Public Interest, 35,* 22–54.

McIntire, M. (2015, August 3). What the experts say about offering Pell Grants to prisoners. *Chronicle of Higher Education.* Retrieved from http://chronicle.com/.

Merton, R. (1938). Social structure and anomie. *American Sociological Review, 3,* 672–682.

Nuttall, J., Hollmen, L., & Staley, M. (2003). The effect of earning a GED on recidivism rates. *Journal of Correctional Education, 54,* 90–94.

Petersilia, J. (2003). *When prisoners come home: Parole and prisoner reentry.* New York, NY: Oxford University Press.

Reed, D. (2015). A synthesis of the effects of correction education on the academic outcomes of incarcerated adults. *Educational Psychology Review, 27,* 537–558.

Sampson, R., & Laub, J. (1994). *Crime in the making: Pathways and turning points through life.* Cambridge, MA: Harvard University Press.

Sherman, L., Farrington, D., Welsh, B., & MacKenzie, D. (2002). *Evidence-based crime prevention.* New York: Routledge.

Stephan, J. (2004). *State prison expenditures, 2001.* NCJ # 202949. Washington, DC: US Department of Justice.

Sutherland, E. (1947). *Principles of criminology.* 4th ed. Philadelphia, PA: Lippincott.

Tewksbury, R., Erickson, D., & Taylor, J. (2000). Opportunity lost: The consequences of eliminating Pell Grants eligibility for correctional education students. *Journal of Offender Rehabilitation, 31,* 43–56.

Tracy, A. & Steurer, S. (1995). Correctional education programming: The development of a model evaluation instrument. *Journal of Correctional Education, 46,* 156–166.

Travis, J. (2005). *But they all come back: Facing the challenges of prisoner reentry.* Washington, DC: Urban Institute Press.

Ubah, C. (2004). Abolition of Pell Grants for higher education prisoners: Examining antecedents and consequences. *Journal of Offender Rehabilitation, 39,* 73–85.

US Department of Education. (2016). About ED. Retrieved from http://www2.ed.gov/about/offices/list/ovae/pi/AdultEd/correctional-education.html.

Wilson, D., Gallagher, C., & MacKenzie, D. 2000. A meta-analysis of corrections-based education, vocation, and work programs for adult offenders. *Journal of Research in Crime and Delinquency, 37,* 347–368.

Zgoba, K., Haugebrook, S., & Jenkins, K. (2008). The influence of GED obtainment on inmate release outcome. *Criminal Justice and Behavior, 35,* 375–387.

Chapter Eleven

Conclusion

Corrections Tomorrow

John P. Walsh and Carly M. Hilinski-Rosick

As we conclude this volume, it is important to assess where we are in regard to incarceration in prisons and jails in the United States. Many who have been affected by incarceration, including those who are incarcerated and their families, significant others, and communities have suffered immensely from this national experiment rooted in retribution and incapacitation. Many reformers, activists, lawyers, criminal justice practitioners, academics, and researchers have worked toward ameliorating what seems to be the ever increasing prison-industrial complex. Many citizens have only recently become aware of the size and scope of the US correctional industry and many more are not aware or have ignored the exponential growth of our incarcerated population over the past 40 years. Overall, the complexity of the problem of who we punish, how we punish, and why we punish citizens with the sanction of incarceration is enormous. Prior to summarizing the work of the scholars within this volume, we offer some polemic views of the state of incarceration and corrections in general. We ask not that you adopt one of these views in favor of the other but instead to reflect upon where you find yourself along the continuum of pessimism and measured optimism that we present. It is somewhere along this continuum that the informed and critical thinking citizen must place themselves as they return to the rationales of punishment (i.e., retribution, incapacitation, deterrence, rehabilitation, and restoration) and choose a path forward.

THE POLEMIC OF PESSIMISM

The future of prisons and jails within the United States is not in doubt. As we return to the timeline of corrections, we place our current location within a realm of pessimism. The number of inmates held in US prisons and jails has quadrupled to an excess of 2 million people over the past four decades (Carson, 2015). The crime control era and its subsequent policies have imbued our underclass urban neighborhoods with a sense of hopelessness where young men of color assume incarceration as a normative process in their lives. Nearly one-third of all African American men are under some form of correctional control (Western, 2006). Five percent of the world's female population lives in the United States, but the United States accounts for almost 30% of the world's incarcerated women (Kajstura & Immarigeon, 2016).

The expanded correctional institution and its daily administration are shaped and embedded by ever larger bureaucratic control, civil service systems, and collective bargaining. The loosely-coupled subsystems of policing and the courts control the inflow of citizens into local, state, and federal incarcerated settings. Finite public funds are spent on prisons and prisoners as opposed to classrooms and students. The containment of citizens suffering from pre-existing mental health problems, as well as incarceration-initiated mental health issues is routine as the criminal justice system masquerades as a public health system. Private prisons expanded through the earlier 2000s holding nearly 9% of the prison population in 2012 (Carson, 2015; Selman & Leighton, 2010). America did not invent the prison but it has refined it over the past 40 years into a prison-industrial complex that warehouses more citizens than anywhere else in the world. Incarceration is big business.

THE POLEMIC OF MEASURED OPTIMISM

The future of prisons and jails within the United States is not in doubt. As we return to the timeline of corrections our current location is within a realm of measured optimism. Crime rates, specifically violent crime rates, have been in decline since the late 1990s. The disproportionate confinement of minority citizens as a policy issue has entered the active public policy agenda with bipartisan discussion of sentencing reform at the federal and state level. Prison populations in some states have decreased by as much as 26% between 2006 and 2012 (Mauer & Gandnoosh, 2014). Alternatives to incarceration such as fines, probation, and short jail stays for non-violent, non-serious crimes, even at the felony level are considered plausible options for punishment across a multitude of offenses that had been resulting in long prison sentences just two or three decades ago.

The federal judiciary has ruled in favor of "dignity" as a constitutional value across landmark cases revolving around state use of punishment (Simon, 2014). Specifically, the culminating case *Brown v. Plata* (2011) thrusts the issue of "dignity as a human rights issue" squarely within the realm of the Eighth Amendment of the US Constitution and suggests mass incarceration as form of cruel and unusual punishment. The resulting California Public Safety Realignment has forced the California state legislature to reimagine the role of state and local criminal justice and incarceration across the board. Treatment of mental illness is seen as a necessity amongst correctional system professionals even as they struggle to fund these initiatives in the incarcerated setting and within community corrections. Investment in reentry initiatives, strength-based reentry courts, and the importance of reentry support networks are viewed as integral to addressing high recidivism rates (Maruna & LeBel, 2003).

Justice Reinvestment Initiatives (JRI) have moved from a theoretical perspective to a funded initiative by the US Department of Justice, albeit with a need for further focus and refinement. MacArthur Justice Foundation funding along with justice reform research organizations such as the Center for Court Innovation, the Vera Institute, and the Pretrial Justice Institute are initiating technical assistance programming across twenty core and partner jail sites to improve and reduce local incarceration capacity (MacArthur Foundation, 2016). These initiatives demonstrate that while we have a long way to go, recent years have seen strides in policies and programs aimed at reducing our prison population and addressing the underlying causes of crime.

WHERE ARE WE GOING?

In essence, while it is early, the aforementioned initiatives within the polemic of measured optimism provide us with a sense, as well as some supporting objective data points, that we are moving away from the "nothing works" perspective of rehabilitation programming as a concept that is untenable (Martinson, 1974). In other words, it appears quite possible that we are beginning to move away from the overtly heavy influences of retribution and incapacitation that define the crime control era. On the other hand, the polemic of pessimism clarifies just how entrenched we are within retribution and incapacitation practices within our justice system and makes us wonder if and how we will possibly turn that ship around to encompass alternative sanctions that are not as reliant on retributive incarceration. This is the continuum we must all reflect upon as we move forward.

SUMMARIZING THE CONTRIBUTIONS

Purposely, this volume focuses upon the incarcerated setting as opposed to areas of community corrections and reentry. Section I sought to place the reader within the magnitude of current US jail and prison systems. The identification of not only the vast number of individuals incarcerated but also the demographic nature of those incarcerated, including the disproportionate number of poor and minority citizens who are challenged daily by the loss of liberty that incarceration produces individually, as well as the loss and obstacles incarceration places upon their families and communities. Chapter 2 draws specific attention to the jail as a local, politically-controlled institution serving an amalgam of differing types of defendants and offenders in pretrial and posttrial circumstances. In addition, they draw attention toward the consistent tension between the federal judiciary and local governments in attempting to achieve constitutionally acceptable public institutions across local jurisdictions with differing perceptions of the role of federal government.

Walsh and Light (Chapter 2), Hilinski-Rosick (Chapter 3), and Buist and Lenning (Chapter 4) all point toward the specific challenges of special populations within the incarcerated setting. In particular, Hilinski-Rosick identifies the special challenges posed by elderly inmates and how as a result of enhanced sentencing policies during the crime control era larger subpopulations of inmates are "aging in place" within institutions originally built for young, healthy, and physically mobile inmates. Further, institutional challenges and shortcomings related to inmate mental illness, in the case of veteran inmates suffering from PTSD (see Chapter 3), as well as comorbidity issues related to substance abuse, mental illness and prior victimization of a rapidly growing female inmate population within jails (see Chapter 2) and within prisons (see Chapter 4) focuses on one of the most challenging issues within incarceration.

Chapter 3 provides an analysis of prison misconduct including violence and sexual misconduct and attempts to address inmate contraband. Chapter 4 also focuses on sexual misconduct in the analysis of gender and incarceration placing the challenges associated with cisgender and transgender inmates squarely within the framework of patriarchy. Buist and Lenning point out that while transgender inmates are an understudied population within the incarcerated setting the literature that is available shows this particular population experiencing disproportionate rates of victimization prior to and during periods of incarceration.

Section II of this volume is not mutually exclusive of the discussion of subpopulations and misconduct within institutions. Where this section differs is that it provides an analysis of the literature produced as a result of administrative approaches to control inmates for safety, security, and programming needs of institutions. Yet, within the crime control era it is important to recognize that institutional safety and security needs preempt individual inmates programming needs. Pierce (Chapter 5) outlines the processes of classification for inmates and the difficulty with creating predictive models of classification, the problem of misclassification, and the need for re-classification of inmates on a regular basis. In addition, this chapter draws attention toward administrative discretionary decisions to place higher or lower levels of security on particular inmates than their assigned classification scores. The role of security threat groups (STG) or gangs as discussed at length by Crank and Marcum (Chapter 6) is highly correlated with classification, inmate misconduct, inmate victimization, as well as racial animus within prisons. In addition, Chapter 6 points toward the administrative challenges associated with the growth of STGs within institutions, the relation to high recidivism rates for STG members, renunciation programming, and the need to root future research regarding gang involvement within the life-course importation model and desistance theory.

As noted by Marcum and Crank in Chapter 6, one of the most common strategies for controlling gangs within incarcerated settings is the use of administrative segregation. As Sundt (Chapter 7) points out, the use of solitary confinement, disciplinary segregation, and protective custody as an administrative tool has increased exponentially in recent decades. Chapter 7 analyzes the literature associated with the more recent decline in the use of solitary confinement as a result of judicial intervention and legislative activity to limit its use. In addition, Chapter 7 draws attention toward the reliance of restrictive housing by correctional administrators even as correctional research consistently finds that restrictive housing areas are more dangerous for inmates and employees than non-restrictive housing. In addition to institutional safety issues, the role of isolation in relation to the degrading mental health of those confined in restrictive housing is analyzed.

Section III approaches inmate subpopulations from the perspective of rehabilitative programming. As noted earlier in the chapter, the crime control era has focused much more on retribution and incapacitation than on rehabilitation of inmates. Further, as noted in the previous paragraph, safety and security continue to preempt rehabilitative programming today. Yet, rehabilitative programming does continue to exist and psychological treatment programs, substance dependency programming, and educational and vocational programs serve inmates who will inevitably be released. All three chapters in this section (like the introduction and earlier chapters) discuss the impact of the 1975 Martinson "nothing works" report on correctional rehabilitation and programming.

As Lasko and Posick (Chapter 8) note, the result of the Martinson report was the creation of the "what works" movement in corrections; a major focus of that movement was the creation of the Risk-Needs-Responsivity model in 1990 and the idea that effective correctional treatment needs to focus on these three things in order to reduce criminal activity. Olson (Chapter 9) discusses the impact of Martinson's findings on substance abuse treatment, which was all but abandoned in the mid-1970s. As the war on drugs took hold in the 1980s, and prison populations, particularly drug offenders, increased dramatically, the number of inmates in need of substance abuse treatment also grew exponentially. Despite this need, and despite the availability of numerous studies that have illustrated effective principles for substance abuse treatment in both the institutional and community setting, substance abuse treatment for correctional populations remains inadequate in many jurisdictions. Finally, Lee brings this section to a close with his chapter on educational programming within the prison. His chapter incorporates criminological theory and illustrates the ability of various theories to explain the importance of education in reducing recidivism. He also notes the impact of the Martinson report on educational programs, noting that the focus on what works in corrections has resulted in more scrutiny on correctional programs, particularly educational programs, and the call for more methodological rigor when assessing the effectiveness of these programs.

SOCIAL SCIENTIFIC METHOD AND A RETURN TO THEORY

As you reflect upon the differing authors' perspectives and analysis, a final and prominent theme to consider, one that runs through each of the authors' chapters, is the need for more research within correctional settings, particularly within the oftentimes closed setting of incarceration. Truly understanding what works, what is promising, and what does not work in correctional programming and administration is reliant on social science research and access to incarcerated settings and populations by external researchers and evaluators. Through quantitative and qualitative methods of social scientific inquiry and through a return to criminological theory, theory building, and theory testing, we can begin to have a better understanding of the social world of incarceration. From a positivist perspective, researchers can apply the premise of falsification whereby, even after consistent corroboration as to a program's value and strength, the outcome is only a theory that has yet to be disconfirmed (Popper, 1959). This is the underlying basis of the Maryland Scientific Method Scale which not only provides an indication of what works, what is promising, and what does not work, but also places those findings within a scale to assess the methodological quality of differing program evaluations and research (Sherman, Farrington, Welsh, & MacKenzie, 2002). In addition, qualitative research designs rooted in "grounded theory" offer opportunities to develop new lines of questioning and research premises that compete and challenge existing frameworks (Geertz, 1983; Rubin & Rubin, 1995). Finally, from a post-positivist perspective, which values the positivist tradition but also recognizes the effects of biases brought from our own knowledge and values, we must remain aware of the power we hold over those we choose to punish.

Corrections, punishment, and incarceration are ever changing. As active citizens within a democracy we must remain cognizant as to how we punish our fellow citizens. As we observe these incremental changes within years, and shifts in broader eras across years, we need to continually question why we are doing what we are doing in the field of corrections. While the policy pendulum will continue to swing, the need for further professionalism, education, and training for those who work within incarcerated settings is integral to creating more humane approaches to dealing with individuals we deem as worthy for punishment. Physically, mentally, and socially incarcerated settings are unhealthy environments. Removing individuals who are not dangerous and will become further disadvantaged by the carceral setting is crucial in creating a just correctional system. Community justice measures which move us away from the tethers of retribution and incapacitation as a first response to individuals who violate our normative order are a good start.

REFERENCES

Carson, E. A. (2015). *Prisoners in 2014.* Washington, DC: Bureau of Justice Statistics.

Geertz, C. (1983). *Local knowledge.* New York: Basic Books.

Kajstura, A., & Immarigeon, R. (2016). *States of women's incarceration: The global context.* Retrieved from: http://www.prisonpolicy.org/global/women/.

MacArthur Foundation. (2016). *Safety and justice challenge.* Retrieved from: http://www.safetyandjusticechallenge.org/about-the-challenge/.

Martinson, R. (1974). What works? Questions and answers about prison reform. *The Public Interest, 35,* 22–54.

Maruna, S., & Lebel, T. (2003). Welcome home? Examining the "reentry court" concept from a strengths-based perspective. *Western Criminological Review, 4,* 91–107.

Mauer, M., & Gandnoosh, N. (2014). *Fewer prisoners, less crime: A tale of three states.* Washington, DC: The Sentencing Project. Retrieved from http://sentencingproject.org/wpcontent/uploads/2015/11/Fewer-Prisoners-LessCrime-A-Tale-of-Three-States.pdf.

Popper, K. R. (1959). *The logic of scientific discovery.* New York: Basic Books.

Rubin, H., & Rubin, I. (1995). *Qualitative interviewing: The art of hearing data.* Thousand Oaks, CA: Sage.

Selman, D., & Leighton, P. (2010). *Punishment for sale: Private prisons, big business, and the incarceration binge.* Lanham, MD: Rowman & Littlefield Publishing.

Sherman, L., Farrington, D., Welsh, B., & Mackenzie, D. L. (2002). *Evidence-based crime prevention: Revised addition.* New York: Routledge.

Simon, J. (2014). *Mass incarceration on trial: A remarkable court decision and the future of prisons in America.* New York, NY: The New Press.

Western, B. (2006). *Punishment and inequality in America.* New York: Russell Sage.

Index

About the Contributors

Carrie L. Buist is an Assistant Professor of Criminal Justice at Grand Valley State University. She has publications in *Critical Criminology: An International Journal*, the *Journal of Culture, Health & Sexuality*, and the *Journal of Crime and Justice*. Dr. Buist has also published book chapters on topics from white collar crime to the social construction of gender, and LGBTQ issues. Most recently, her book *Queer Criminology*, coauthored with Dr. Emily Lenning, calls for a more inclusive criminology exploring the experiences of the LGBTQ population as victims, offenders, and criminal legal personnel. Dr. Buist has been recognized by the American Society of Criminology Division on Women and Crime as New Scholar of the Year in November of 2015.

Beverly R. Crank, PhD, is an Assistant Professor of Criminal Justice at Kennesaw State University. She received her doctorate in Criminal Justice & Criminology from Georgia State University. Her research interests include corrections, crime and the life course, and juvenile delinquency and juvenile justice. Her recent publications have appeared in *Deviant Behavior, Criminal Justice Review,* and *Criminal Justice Studies.*

Carly M. Hilinski-Rosick is an Assistant Professor of Criminology and Criminal Justice at the University of Tampa. She received her doctorate in criminology from Indiana University of Pennsylvania. She has taught corrections at the graduate and undergraduate level for over 10 years, has taught inside prisons, and has conducted research on prisons and prison life, particularly inmate misconduct. Her research agenda centers on corrections and inmates and she also teaches research methods, victimology, and criminological theory courses.

Emily Lasko is a Graduate Research Assistant and Master's student in the Psychology Department at Georgia Southern University. She is currently conducting research in the Psychology and Law Lab of the department. She has a Bachelor's degree in Psychology from the University of North Carolina Wilmington.

Daniel R. Lee, PhD, is a Professor of Criminology at Indiana University of Pennsylvania (IUP). He earned his PhD from the University of Maryland Department of Criminology and Criminal Justice in 2001. His research and scholarship has focused on correctional education, tests of criminological theories, and evaluations of criminal justice policies with specific topics including, crime prevention strategies, fear of crime, juvenile delinquency, neighborhood crime, sentencing policy, and victimization.

Emily Lenning is an Associate Professor of Criminal Justice at Fayetteville State University. Her publications cover a diverse range of topics, from state-sanctioned violence against women to creative advances in pedagogy. Her most recent publication, co-authored with Dr. Carrie L. Buist, was the book *Queer Criminology*, which is part of Routledge's New Directions in Critical Criminology series. Her accomplishments in and out of the classroom have been recognized by several awards, including the Fayetteville State University Teacher of the Year Award and the American Society of Criminology Division on Women and Crime's New Scholar Award.

Sarah Light is a Graduate Research Assistant and Master's student in the School of Criminal Justice at Grand Valley State University She is currently conducting research on incarcerated populations. She has a Bachelor's degree in Psychology from Grand Valley State University.

Catherine D. Marcum, PhD, is an associate professor of Government and Justice Studies at Appalachian State University. She received her doctorate in Criminology from Indiana University of Pennsylvania. Her areas of teaching and research focus on corrections, cybercrime, and victimization issues. Her recent publications have appeared in *Crime & Delinquency, American Journal of Criminal Justice,* and *International Journal of Criminal Justice.*

David Olson is the Co-Director of Loyola's interdisciplinary Center for Criminal Justice Research, Policy and Practice (with Diane Geraghty of Loyola's Law School), and is also a Professor and Graduate Program Director in the Department of Criminal Justice and Criminology. Throughout his 30 year career, Dr. Olson has worked with a variety of federal, state, and local agencies to develop and evaluate programs and policies, and has conducted and published research on a wide range of justice topics. Dr. Olson received his BS in Criminal Justice from Loyola University Chicago, his MA in Criminal Justice from the University of Illinois at Chicago, and his PhD in Political Science/Public Policy Analysis from the University of Illinois at Chicago, where he was the recipient of the Assistant United States Attorney General's Graduate Research Fellowship. Dr. Olson is currently the chairperson of the advisory boards for both the Illinois Department of Corrections and the Illinois Department of Juvenile Justice, and as an appointed member to the Illinois State Commission on Criminal Justice and Sentencing Reform. In 2015, Dr. Olson received the John Howard Association Outstanding Research Contributions Award.

Mari B. Pierce is an Associate Professor in the Administration of Justice department at The Pennsylvania State University, Beaver campus. She received her PhD in Criminology from Indiana University of Pennsylvania in 2009. Dr. Pierce's research focuses on three related areas: the sentencing of adult offenders, the perceptions of offenses against children, and the impacts of incarceration. She has recent publications in *Applied Psychology in Criminal Justice, The Prison Journal,* and *Journal of Aggression, Maltreatment and Trauma.*

Chad Posick is an Assistant Professor of Criminal Justice and Criminology at Georgia Southern University. He received his doctorate in criminal justice and criminology from Northeastern University in 2012 and his Master's degree in Public Policy from the Rochester Institute of Technology in 2009. His major research interests include violence prevention, restorative justice, and police-community relations. He teaches in the areas of victimology, criminal behavior, and statistics. He is a board member of the Ogeechee Court-Appointed Special Advocates (CASA) program for abused and neglected children.

Jody Sundt is Associate Dean and Associate Professor at the School of Public and Environmental Affairs at Indiana University, Indianapolis. Professor Sundt holds a PhD in Criminal Justice from the University of Cincinnati. She is interested in social responses to crime, particularly the use of punishment. Her research focuses on the effectiveness of correctional policy, the work experiences of correctional employees, and public attitudes about crime and punishment. She has published more than 30 articles and book chapters, which have appeared in journals such as *Criminology, Justice Quarterly, Crime and Delinquency, Criminal Justice and Behavior, Journal of Criminal Justice,* and *The Prison Journal.* Her current research focuses on training transfer and program implementation, the effect of administrative segregation on prison management, and prison downsizing. In 2006, professor Sundt was named a Distinguished New Scholar by the American Society of Criminology's Division of Corrections and Sentencing. Her research on prison chaplaincy was recognized in 1999 by the Academy of Criminal Justice Sciences, which awarded the work the Anderson Outstanding Paper Award. She is past chair of the American Society of Criminology's Division on Corrections and Sentencing and a former member of the executive board of the Academy of Criminal Justice Sciences.

John P. Walsh is an Associate Professor of Criminal Justice at Grand Valley State University in Grand Rapids, Michigan. He received his doctorate in criminal justice from Indiana University and his Master's degree in Criminal Justice from Southern Illinois University. His major research interests include urban jail systems, the culture and politics of incarceration policy, restorative justice, and communities. He teaches in the areas of corrections, policing, race crime, and culture.